INTRODUCTION TO MUSIC APPRECIATION

INTRODUCTION TO MUSIC APPRECIATION

An Objective Approach to Listening

REVISED EDITION

WILLIAM HUGH MILLER

CHILTON BOOK COMPANY
Philadelphia New York London

Also published in a trade edition under the title
"Everybody's Guide to Music"

Published in Philadelphia by Chilton Book Company

SBN: 8019 5539 4

Library of Congress Catalog Card Number 78–103617

Designed by William E. Lickfield

Manufactured in the United States of America
by Quinn & Boden Company, Inc., Rahway, N. J.

To "DOT"

"patience" is surely her middle name

Preface

The writer has long felt the need for a course of study in which *active* rather than *passive* listening occurs. Our aim is to encourage critical listening by coming into direct contact with great music throughout the several periods of music history. The Units which follow become, through study and listening to music, an aesthetic and psychological approach to understanding and enjoyment.

Philosophy

The philosophy behind the Units is based on modern psychology which believes that (1) everyone is capable of some degree of music appreciation, (2) that aesthetic enjoyment is both a mental and an affective process, and (3) that musical taste can be developed (and changed) through training. This, then, becomes a positive rather than a negative approach to the study of music literature. Its purpose is to bring the untrained listener to the threshold of aesthetic enjoyment.

Scope

The music literature covered by the Units is concentrated in the Baroque, the Classic, the Romantic, and the Modern periods of music history. While the Units have been prepared with some consideration for the chronology of music history, the main purpose has been to pyramid the elements of music—rhythm, melody, harmony, and tone color—by studying and analyzing the aspects of each, their juxtaposition, and, finally, their effect on musical form and style. While the Units may be used independently of each other, and in any sequence, the end result is better if the continuity of the Units remains as shown so that the student becomes aware of music as a unified whole made up of its parts.

The Units are a compendium of relevant thinking and knowledge pertaining to philosophy, aesthetics, and psychology as applied to the field of music. Each in its own way explains what music is, what it does or what it cannot do. In contrast to prevalent practice, this text amply discusses the basic fundamentals of music and their workings, thereby insuring a complete and well-integrated concept of the art of music. To this end, the Units have been tested many years in the classroom.

One of the distinct advantages of this course is the flexibility of the material. By making use of the complete record lists and the bibliography, a class may be led into major musicological research of considerable interest, especially in groups where independent work is encouraged.

Record Lists

Appendix V includes an extensive record list for the several Units. The following suggestions are given for the use of the records:

1. Compositions should be selected from the lists which meet the needs of the listeners and the purpose of the instructor.
2. Allow the listeners to hear the composition or the movement as a whole as many times as possible before study—psychological evidence supports the belief that through repetition and familiarity there is an increase in comprehension—then proceed to a study of its parts. Deal with the music abstractly. Avoid explanations while the music is being played. The essence of the Units is listening to music—experiencing—rather than talking about it. We are interested in aesthetic experience rather than popularizing the music by taking the music out of music by the use of program notes, etc., to set the stage.
3. It is suggested that the Spot-Quiz Chart (p. ix) be used for ease in recording and checking of student answers. The quiz is administered by placing the phonograph needle at any spot on the record previously studied for recognition as shown by the items across the heading of the sample Spot-Quiz Chart. Scores are derived by adding up the number of possible answers and subtracting one point for each mistake. The instructor may also count off for misspelled names and titles. For the spot quizzes, the records are cumulative for the semester. Records for each Unit should be included in each quiz so that the student is always held responsible for those records previously studied. The final exam comes from the entire list.
4. It will be necessary for the instructor to seek out the respective spot on the record which illustrates the material being studied. Obviously with 78 rpm., 45 rpm., and 33 rpm. records, it would be an endless task to explain where each spot is located. It should be mentioned that, while the record list is quite complete, it is not all-inclusive.

Sample Spot-Quiz Chart (may be mimeographed or multigraphed)

Composer	Title	Movement	Period	Analysis	Illustration of
1. Debussy	La Cathédrale engloutie		Modern	—	Program music
2. Leoncavallo	Pagliacci	Prologue	Romantic	—	Melody–Homophonic
3. Ravel	Introduction and Allegro		Modern	—	Color–Harp
4. Mozart	Symphony No. 41—Jupiter	3	Classic	Compound ABA form	Deviation and Return
5. Beethoven	Symphony No. 5	1	Romantic (Classicist)	—	Motive
6. Handel	Xerxes	Largo or Ombra mai fu	Baroque	—	Harmony–Vertical
7. Ravel	Bolero	—	Modern	—	Rhythm–Bolero
8.					
9.					
10.					

As the instructor finds other examples, he should add them to the list.

5. Almost every composition listed is available on phonograph records. See Irving Kolodin's *The New Guide to Recorded Music* and David Hall's *Records*. Another excellent record source is Schwann's "Long Playing" *Record Catalogue* which is issued monthly and is obtainable at nominal cost.
6. While it is intended that the records will be presented and discussed in class, outside listening is intended for each student if at all possible.

Quotations

The documentation for the several Units is to be found in Appendix I.

Specific Bibliography

The references found in Appendix II are intended to give the listener a broad overview of the material presented, and also to help the listener orient himself in each Unit. The listener should familiarize himself with the abbreviations shown earlier, for they will be used in subsequent Units. The references are confined to a rather small selective list to minimize the necessity for an extensive library of books. Since the essential material is contained in the text, the listener and/or the instructor may exercise his freedom of choice in the selection of references for required reading. The references cited in Appendix II constitute the bibliography for the several Units.

If desired, periodic quizzes may be given over the reference material in the list.

General Bibliography

The bibliography listed in Appendix III is of a general nature and is intended to serve three purposes: (1) general reading, (2) reference, and (3) as source material, to help the listener with the program notes which he may be asked to write for each composition. It is suggested that the program notes include four to eight measures of the pertinent thematic material of each composition. Whether or not the program notes are documented with sources listed as footnotes is left to the instructor.

The books having to do with specific composers and their works are listed only once and are correlated with the first appearance of the respective composer in the record lists of Appendix V.

Supplementary Material

Certain technical information having to do with Unit VII is to be found in Appendix IV. If there is a need for additional information on acoustics, this material may be used.

William Hugh Miller

Acknowledgments

The author is deeply indebted to Professor Glenn D. McGeoch of the School of Music of the University of Michigan for the original inspiration for this manuscript; to Dr. Ruth Watanabe, Librarian of the Sibley Music Library of the Eastman School of Music, for the many constructive criticisms in reading the manuscript and for making available certain source material; and to the writer's students who had *experienced* the preparation of this text.

The author also expresses herewith his thanks to the following, who have kindly granted permission to reprint copyrighted material.* Specific credits for musical and pictorial illustrations are shown with the respective material.

American Psychological Association for a quotation from an article in the *Psychological Review* by K. Hevner.

Appleton-Century-Crofts, Inc., for extracts from the *Evolution of the Art of Music* by Charles Hubert Parry; and *The Principles of Aesthetics* by DeWitt H. Parker.

Bureau of Publications of Columbia University for quotations from *A Study of Chord Frequencies* by Helen Budge.

Criterion Music Corporation for extracts from *The Shaping Forces in Music* by Ernst Toch.

Esquire, Inc., for an excerpt from a pictorial feature in *Coronet* on Frank Lloyd Wright.

Victor Alexander Fields (Columbia University Press) for a quotation from *Training the Singing Voice.*

Harper & Brothers for selections from *The Understanding of Music* by Max Schoen.

* See full credit lines, Appendix II.

Harvard University Press for extracts from *A Composer's World* by Paul Hindemith; *The Harvard Dictionary of Music* by Willi Apel; and from three volumes of *The Loeb Classical Library.*

McGraw-Hill Book Company, Inc., for selections from *Psychology of Music* by Carl E. Seashore; and *What to Listen for in Music* by Aaron Copland.

Music Educators Journal to quote descriptive material from an article *The Making of Four Miniatures* by Vladimir Ussachevsky.

Music Publications, Ltd., for a news item in *Musical America.*

Musical Periodicals Corporation for an article by Bennet Ludden in *Musical Courier.*

W. W. Norton & Company, Inc., for selections from: *The History of Musical Instruments* by Curt Sachs; *Music in Western Civilization* by Paul Henry Lang; *The Rise of Music in the Ancient World, East and West* by Curt Sachs; and *Source Readings in Music History* by Oliver Strunk.

Dika Newlin (Columbia University Press) for an extract from *Bruckner-Mahler-Schoenberg.*

The New York Times for an excerpt from an article by Aaron Copland.

Novello & Company, Ltd. (H. W. Gray Company, Inc.) for quotations from *On the Beautiful in Music* by Eduard Hanslick.

Oxford University Press for an excerpt from *Style in Musical Art* by Charles Hubert Parry.

Prentice-Hall, Inc., for a quotation from *Acoustics of Music* by Wilmer T. Bartholomew.

Ronald Press Company for selections from: *In Search of Beauty in Music* by Carl E. Seashore; *An Objective Psychology of Music* by Robert William Lundin; and *The Psychology of Music* by Max Schoen.

Saturday Review for permission to reprint the caption from a pictorial feature on Walter Carlos and the Moog Synthesizer.

Contents

PART II—Musical Elements

PART III—Synthesis of Musical Elements

Prologue

Man, Music, and Society. In the course of man's progress from the primitive to the present, music has been a needful part of his existence. In the cycle from birth to death, primitive man's experiences in the art of living ranged through five basic types of *utilitarian* music—music that is used to satisfy basic needs, namely, (1) work songs, (2) war dances, (3) ballads, (4) ritual dances, and (5) chants. Through the enlightenment and refinement of taste acquired by intellectual and aesthetic training resulting from education and discipline, this utilitarian music has evolved into the following: (1) art songs, (2) marches and march songs, (3) art ballads, (4) social dances—folk, court, and ballroom, and (5) liturgical music.

It is not our purpose to trace these five basic types through another history of music but, rather, to enhance man's contemporary living by providing a guide to understanding and the enjoyment of music by: (1) building a diversified listening repertory, (2) probing the psychological and aesthetic aspects of music and its elements, (3) presenting essential historical background, (4) showing the relationship of music to the allied arts, and (5) providing a description of voices and instruments, styles, and musical textures.

So, as Tonio sings in the "Prologue" to the opera *I Pagliacci* by Leoncavallo,

"Andiam, Incominciate!"
("Come on! [Let us] begin!")

PART I

General Principles

UNIT I

Aesthetic Principles of Music and the Allied Arts: A Comparison of Media

THE EVOLUTION OF MUSIC

For many centuries people have speculated as to how music began. Speculation has been necessary because the music of the most primitive peoples has been obliterated by time. Actually, all we have for reference today is the crude music of the present-day primitives which is still extant.

From Primitive to Aesthetic Art

No one has yet proved beyond the shadow of a doubt how music began because no one has been able to get close enough to its origin. But many theories have been advanced by philosophers, scientists, and musicologists. One theory has it that music came into existence through the primitive's imitation of bird songs; another speculates that music may be traced to the act of mating and wooing (Darwin). Primitive songs which required rhythmic co-ordination of the movements of the singers as they worked were adjudged to be the source of music (Bücher). Still another theory is that man's first musical impulse was a purely rhythmic one—hence, music had its roots in the dance (Wallascheck); then there is the theory which still persists that music had its origin in emotional speech (Rousseau, Spencer). However, the same fallacy exists in all these theories, namely, that music had a common source. If we do not accept the theory of a common root, then music had to begin of and by itself, but how? A plausible answer is that it had its beginning in song (however primitive) and arose at the same time, separate and apart from impassioned speech (Sachs,[1] Parker[2]).*

The requirements of primitive life undoubtedly gave rise to a variety

* The sources of these and subsequent references are to be found in Appendix I.

of sounds which were used for communication. When associated with recurring events, these sounds probably gave forth various voice inflections created by the mood of the occasion, such as shouts of joy, anger, sorrow, or pain—impassioned speech. But the primitive singer often used devices to "mask" his voice so that the singing would have a characteristic sound different from that of speech.[3] As primitive singing reached emotional heights, the singer changed the quality of the sound, by such means as falsetto, or nasal placement, to render it unlike the speaking voice.[4]

We may further theorize that man later discovered that sounds could be made apart from him and such percussion instruments as gongs, drums, and cymbals came into existence. These had the utilitarian purpose of providing rhythmic accompaniment for the dance and other communal activities. It may have taken centuries for the primitive peoples to begin creating pleasurable tones and rhythmical sounds apart from their tribal ceremonies. As long as music remained in a natural and practical state, it could not be a free art form. At the time when tribal instruments and song were *made for their own sake,* music became a free art and took its place with the *purely aesthetic—art music*—which is its ultimate stage of development.

PHILOSOPHY OF ART (AESTHETICS)

Definition of Aesthetics

Though the science of aesthetics contributes to the field of the natural and social sciences and philosophy, we shall be concerned here with aesthetics as applied to the arts. We need to know the meaning and scope of the word if we are to use it effectively. Coming from the Greek word *aisthesis,* meaning feeling—sensation, aesthetics is that branch of philosophy and psychology which attempts to systematize a body of ideas and principles that deal with the beautiful, sensation, and emotion, as related to works of art.[5] Therefore, aesthetics explains what art is by adapting scientific method to works of art, thus raising them to the level of intelligence and understanding.

Definition of Art

If you were observing a clump of trees, what would be your reaction? Actually, it would depend on whether you are a practical individual looking for firewood, a botanist investigating the trees, or an artist who sees them as something beautiful. Here are three people looking at the same thing but obviously not seeing the same thing—one is practical, one scientific, and one artistic. What we see depends on our purpose. To some extent each of us is practical, scientific, and artistic, but a predominance of any one of these inclinations causes different end results. Transferred to canvas, the clump of trees becomes, in the hands of a master craftsman, a thing of beauty and a work of art.

This brings us to the question of what is art? Simply and briefly stated, art is free expression in which the artist vividly communicates to others, perhaps less gifted, what he sees in his mind's eye. The observer calls the clump of trees a work of art when he sees them not as trees but as a form which so interests him that he becomes absorbed and steeped in it. For the philosopher, this is the true aesthetic experience and one which has intrinsic value for the observer. To do this the artist must rise above mere skill and present a perfect subject in an inimitable way. The true lover of art is susceptible and responsive to this perfection.

THE AESTHETICS OF MUSIC

Definition of Musical Aesthetics

What is the meaning and scope of the aesthetics of music? In the words of Apel, "Musical aesthetics is the study of the relationship of music to the human senses and intellect."[6] This, of course, implies that the aesthetics of music deals with the beautiful in music. What is beautiful depends on whether the philosopher, the psychologist, or the critic makes the evaluation. The key words for each of these are: philosopher —*value,* psychologist—*behavior,* and critic—*standards.* Not only does each one of the fields just named contribute to the other and to musical aesthetics, but musical aesthetics contributes to each in its own way. Philosophers who are untrained in music tend to deal with musical aesthetics in a very theoretical—abstract—manner. But we are to be primarily concerned with those philosophers—critics, performers, composers —and psychologists who are versed in the field of music and who, on the basis of values, standards, and behavior, tend to supply musical aesthetics with practical criteria.

Let us examine the aesthetics of the several periods of music history. We shall be concerned not only with those philosophers who hold a preeminent place in music history, but with the respective theories which influenced the musical aesthetics of a given period. It will be apparent that each of these periods was dominated by the philosophies of men who were long since dead. It should be remembered also that both utilitarian and art music existed in varying degrees during these periods.

In Antiquity (A.D. 350–600)

Though music in various forms had been in existence in southwest Asia and Egypt prior to this time, it remained for the Greeks to establish what has been termed the science of music. The musical aesthetics of Pythagoras (c. 550 B.C.), the mathematician and philosopher, related the mathematical theory of harmony to the harmony of the universe.[7] Musical philosophy of the period was preoccupied with the relationship of numbers to music, and it was Pythagoras who established the acoustical principles on which the laws of proportion—the relation of the length of a vibrating body to pitch—in our music are based (see p. 95 ff.).

Plato's (427–347 B.C.) philosophy, based on education, related good and useful music to moral conduct. His philosophy had psychological implications in that he taught that music developed and fortified one's personality, and had therapeutic value in that it soothed one's emotions. For him, culture could be fulfilled only through education which would foster a love of the beautiful and result in man's own beauty and goodness.[8] For Plato, music was the foremost of the arts and, as such, was not to be used merely for amusement.

This period saw the rise of Christian chant (Gregorian) (see p. 76 ff.).

In the Middle Ages (600–1300)

This era was dominated by the writings of the philosopher-psychologist Aristotle (384–322 B.C.), a pupil of Plato, who based his aesthetics on a realistic view of music, believing that a knowledge of music comes through actual experience with it. He advocated the study of music for its educational value, therapeutic value, amusement, and its appeal to the intellect. In Aristotle, the parallelism of scientific investigation and the principle of purification of the emotions by music is in evidence.[9]

The Middle Ages saw the development of Gregorian chant to its highest point (see p. 76 ff.), the beginning of polyphony (see p. 79 ff.), and the rise of secular music. Architecture stood at the head of the other arts. The people to be reckoned with in music were Leoninus, Perotinus, Franco of Cologne, Petrus de Cruce, and the Troubadours, Trouvères, Minnesingers, and Meistersingers.

In the Gothic Period (1200–1450)

Pointing toward Boethian (Boethius) philosophy was a work by St. Augustine (A.D. 354–430)—one of the early Christian Fathers. In the sixth book of his *De Musica,* St. Augustine based his principles on mathematical law, thus establishing music as a science. In addition, the sixth book is an erudite psychological analysis, unique at this stage of music history, of musical perception and understanding of (1) sound, (2) hearing, (3) imagination, (4) memory, and (5) mental activity. Moral strength was to be derived from the ability of the mind to assimilate music.

Boethius (A.D. 480–524) in his *De institutione musica,* written about one hundred years after the *De musica* of St. Augustine, developed a philosophy of music which possessed a broader base than any which had

Plate I—Gothic. *The Salisbury Cathedral* from the Bishop's Garden. Constable, John—1776–1837. (Courtesy, The Metropolitan Museum of Art. Bequest of Mary Stillman Harkness, 1950.)

been advocated heretofore, and it served to influence musical thought for about a thousand years. While he believed that music not only possessed the attributes akin to the universal harmony of the planets as professed by Pythagoras, he insisted that music also possessed qualities which benefited the body and the mind. His aesthetics placed the emphasis, however, on music as a mathematical science and music as sound—acoustics. He states explicitly in *De institutione* that "[music] is founded in reason and speculation."[10] This conception meant that the moral power of music acts on the mind.

Boethius classified those concerned with the art of music as performer —especially for the purpose of earning a livelihood—poet, and critic. Always the scientist, he favors the critic.

Cassiodorus (c. A.D. 490–580), a contemporary of Boethius, merely summarized what was previously known. He supported the Pythagorean theory of the music of the universe, the close association of music and religion, and music as the science of sounds. In addition, Cassiodorus divided music into three parts: *harmonics*—high and low sounds, *rhythmics*—the combination of words with music, and *metrics*—analysis of the various meters.

In this period architecture eclipsed the other arts. Music moved from sacred to secular. The leading musical figures were Guillaume de Machaut, Francesco Landini, John Dunstable, Guillaume Dufay, and Gilles Binchois.

In the Renaissance Period (1450–1600)

The aesthetic point of view of this period may best be expressed by one word—*humanism*—the rebirth, spiritually and intellectually, of man, and characterized by man's desire for personal expression uncontrolled by the Church. Beauty was cultivated for its own sake. Secular music benefited the most from this new aesthetic principle. In all, this movement resulted in a development of artistic taste and the elevation of musical standards. Heretofore, books and music had been available only in manuscript, but the year 1450 saw the printing of the first book, and in 1501 the first printed music made its appearance. These two inventions proved to be great socializing forces, for they made literature and music available not only to the elite but to large segments of the middle class as well. Learning was cultivated for its own sake. Harmony became the essence of musical-aesthetic doctrine represented first by the perfection of the horizontal—contrapuntal—texture and later by the advent of vertical—chordal—texture. Diatonic harmony was superseded by a new chromatic (see p. 110 f.)—enharmonic style (*musica ficta*) (see p. 91 ff.). Since harmony played such an important part in the aesthetic doctrine of this period it is appropriate to mention the great contribu-

Plate II—Renaissance. *Madonna and Child* enthroned with Saints Catherine, Peter, Cecilia, Paul, and the Infant Saint John the Baptist. Raphael—1483–1520. (Courtesy, The Metropolitan Museum of Art. Gift of J. Pierpont Morgan, 1916.)

tion of Zarlino (1517–1590) to the theoretical aspects of the new aesthetic. By means of three invaluable works—*Istitutioni harmoniche, Dimostrationi harmoniche,* and *Sopplimenti musicali*—he reshaped the whole structure of harmony. Among other contributions he gave legitimate status to the troublesome third (see p. 81), established the triad (see p. 97 ff.) as the cornerstone of harmonic construction, and advocated the division of the octave (see p. 98 ff.) into twelve equal half steps (see p. 91).[11]

The Renaissance brought a renewed emphasis on sacred music and also marks the starting point of instrumental music. In this period painting reigned supreme. In music, the names of Jacob Obrecht, Jan van Ockeghem, Giovanni Pierluigi da Palestrina, Orlando di Lasso, William Byrd, Tomás Luis de Victoria (Vittoria), and Giovanni Gabrieli dominated the period.

In the Baroque Period (1580–1730)

This period may well be called one of musical extravagance. In this respect music followed in the paths of painting, sculpture, architecture, and literature. The emergence of form as an aesthetic precept was of paramount importance to the artist, so much so that form was often cultivated for its own sake. The Baroque was a period of creative virtuosity. Music and the other arts combined in a fanciful display for about 150 years. All of this served to develop in all forms of art an elaborate, and sometimes outlandish and grotesque, style. Although the Baroque represents rich color and splendor, the overtheatrical and the sentimental, the importance of all this should not be underestimated. Here, forms and styles were created which have come down to us today. Chordal harmony—thorough bass (realizing an accompanying part or parts to a given bass by a system of numbers)—was the dominant method in music. Of all the arts in this period, music reigned supreme. In the Baroque period we find the beginning of monody—accompanied solo song (see p. 85)—opera (see p. 85 f.) with its offshoots of oratorio and cantata, and the recitative—intoned speech used to emphasize a text of more or less narrative character; the rise of instruments and such instrumental forms as the variation (see p. 201 ff.), fugue (see p. 205 ff.), suite (see p. 57 ff.), sonata—a three- or four-movement work for solo instrument or solo instrument with accompaniment, concerto—usually a three-movement work for solo player and orchestra, and symphony—a sonata for orchestra in four extended movements. These are the heritage of the music of our time.[12]

The dominant musical figures in the Baroque period were Claudio Monteverdi, Jacopo Peri, Jean Baptiste Lully, Henry Purcell, Johann Sebastian Bach, and Georg Friedrich Handel.

Plate III—Baroque. *Flora.* Rembrandt Harmensz. van Ryn—1606–1669. (Courtesy, The Metropolitan Museum of Art. Gift of Archer M. Huntington, in memory of his father, Collis Potter Huntington, 1926.)

In the Rococo Period (1715–1750)

There were two styles which developed after the Baroque period: (1) the Rococo which was courtly and aristocratic, and (2) the *style bourgeois*—middle class—which led to so-called classical music. The Rococo period represented a distinct change from the philosophical doctrine of effect—from Baroque seriousness and heaviness to Rococo lightness and elegance (*gallant style*). The cultural center shifted from the church to

Plate IV—Rococo. *The Toilet of Venus*. Boucher, Francois—1703–1770. (Courtesy, The Metropolitan Museum of Art. Bequest of William K. Vanderbilt, 1920.)

the rarefied atmosphere of the "salon," with the emphasis being placed on secular music in which melody—profusely decorated—was the dominant element. The Rococo was doomed because it was geared to the wrong segment of society—aristocracy.

The leading musical figures were François Couperin, Georg Philipp Telemann, Domenico Scarlatti, and Jean Philippe Rameau.

In the Classic Period (1750–1825)

Although the Rococo (*gallant style*) added elegance and ornamentation, it was the *style bourgeois* which spawned the classic period. Here was a style which embodied simplicity, warmth, soul, and sentiment. While the aesthetics of the classic period leaned heavily on the psychological with sensuousness being the essence of the style, the cultural center moved from the rarefied atmosphere of the salon to the warmer climate of the middle class. Thus was developed a somewhat "popular" style in which melody was the dominant element, though somewhat less decorative than the pure Rococo. As evidence we may cite the great number of accompanied solo songs, the accepted topic being love. In this period there also arose a newly educated middle class which accounts for the fact that this period is called the Age of Enlightenment. The music represents simplicity of chordal structure—tonic (see p. 96), dominant (see p. 99 f.), subdominant (see p. 100 f.)—augmented by a simple melodic line embroidered with filigree.[13] Foreshadowing what actually happened to German music toward the end of the century, Quantz advocates a mixture of the Italian, French, and German taste to create a new aesthetic called sensitive style (*Empfindsamer Stil*). This new aesthetic principle insisted on greater expressiveness in music. The use of contrasting dynamic effects, from triple piano (ppp) to triple forte (fff), and tone color (see p. 134 ff.), became the handmaidens of this new sensitive style foreshadowing Classical and Romantic music.[14]

This greater expressiveness is evident in the development of the sonata form (see p. 10) by such classicists as Joseph Haydn, Wolfgang Amadeus Mozart, Ludwig van Beethoven, and Franz Schubert. While the Rococo spirit is still evident in the music of these composers, the latter part of the eighteenth century may be more correctly called the Classic period, due to the emphasis on the classic idea of beauty of form and style; the arts had turned toward the strictest classicism by 1789. The trend was toward absolute music (see p. 28) with the symphony (see p. 10) being considered the highest form of instrumental music.

In America the works of Handel and other Baroque composers were reflected in the music of Francis Hopkinson (1737–1791) and William Billings (1746–1800).

Plate V—Classicism. *Mrs. Richard Brinsley Sheridan*(?) (Elizabeth Ann Linley, 1754–1792). Reynolds, Joshua—1723–1792. (Courtesy, The Metropolitan Museum of Art. Bequest of Mary Stillman Harkness, 1950.)

In the Romantic Period (1825–1900)

In this era we find a revolt against the aesthetics of the classic period which we should remember were based on order, form, discipline, and logical use of materials. Music became exceedingly personal, and freedom became the essence of the Romantic period—freedom of style and form—freedom of thought and imagination. The essence of music was to be found in feeling—the emotions. Jean Paul, one of the literary giants of the period, gave a definition of the new-found freedom of expression: "Romanticism is beauty without bounds—the beautiful infinite, just as there is an exalted infinite."[15] In discussing the music of Beethoven, E. T. A. Hoffmann, a champion of romanticism, describes the new aesthetic: "Beethoven's music sets in motion the lever of fear, of awe, of horror, of suffering, and awakens just that infinite longing which is the essence of romanticism."[16]

All the arts moved within the orbit of romanticism to such an extent that one complemented the other. Particularly was this true of music, poetry, and drama. Through this union of the arts the way was opened for romantic opera. On this subject E. T. A. Hoffmann has this to say:

> . . . I regard the romantic opera as the only genuine one, for only in the land of romance is music at home. . . . A genuinely romantic opera is written only by a gifted and inspired poet, for only such a one can bring to life the wondrous phenomena of the spirit world; on his wings we are lifted over the chasm which otherwise divides us from it; and, grown accustomed to the strange country, we believe in the marvels which, as inevitable effects of the action of higher natures on our being, take place visibly and bring about all the strong, powerfully affecting situations which fill us, now with awe and horror, now with the highest bliss. . . . In an opera the action of higher natures on our being takes place visibly, thus opening up before our eyes a romantic existence in which language, too, is raised to a higher power, or rather, is borrowed from that faraway country—from music, that is, from song—where action and situation themselves, . . . take hold of us and transport us the more forcefully.[17]

Into this philosophy Richard Wagner was born. After Beethoven the romantic period stressed an aesthetic called descriptive—program—music in which the essence of music was believed to lie in its extramusical qualities. The Romantic period served to give new life to a centuries-old aesthetic. *Realism* and *naturalism* were offshoots of descriptive music. The former had its foundation in description (Berlioz, Wagner, Liszt). The latter was a reaction to realism and its essence lay in the true-to-life situations (Bizet and the French School).

The critic Eduard Hanslick was in vigorous opposition to the fusion of the arts as advocated by Wagner and his followers. Believing that the new romanticism was a dangerous path for music to follow, he wrote

Plate VI—Romanticism. *Christ on Lake Gennesaret*. Delacroix, Eugène—1796–1863. (Courtesy, The Metropolitan Museum of Art. Bequest of Mrs. H. O. Havemeyer, 1929. The H. O. Havemeyer Collection.)

a pamphlet, *On the Beautiful in Music,* in which he declared that music is an autonomous art—an abstract study through its elements—being absolute and without extramusical qualities and incapable of representation.

> *Its nature is specifically musical.* By this we mean that the beautiful is not contingent upon, or in need of any subject introduced from without, but that it consists wholly of sounds artistically combined. The ingenious coordination of intrinsically pleasing sounds, their consonance and contrast, their flight and re-approach, their increasing and diminishing strength—that it is, which in free and unimpeded forms, presents itself to our mental vision.[18]

From the foregoing we are able to see that the Romantic period is a study in aesthetic contrasts.

Representative composers besides those already named are Franz Schubert, Robert Schumann, Johannes Brahms, Hugo Wolf, Giuseppe Verdi, Peter Ilyich Tschaikowsky, Nicholas Rimsky-Korsakov, Camille Saint-Saëns, and César Franck. In the twilight of romanticism are Paul Dukas, Ernst von Dohnányi, Sergei Rachmaninoff, Anton Bruckner, Gustav Mahler, Alexandre Scriabin, Erik Satie, and Richard Strauss. In America we find such men as John Knowles Paine, George W. Chadwick, and Edward MacDowell continuing in the Romantic spirit.

Chromatic harmony (see p. 91 f., p. 110 f.) was one of the chief devices in this new aesthetic, resulting in free use of chromatic alterations and modulation to remote keys.

In the Modern Period (1900–)

At the turn of the century romanticism was experiencing a breakdown because of the desire of composers for a new aesthetic. *Impressionism* became the answer to this desire for revolt against the romanticism of Beethoven and Brahms and the realism of Wagner and Liszt. This "ism" had its origin in such impressionist poets and painters as Verlaine and Mallarmé, Monet and Renoir, respectively. Impressionism may be described as impressions which are alluded to rather than stated—as "seeing through a glass darkly"—vagueness—the play of tonal colors to create a sensuous quality indicative of the elusiveness of life. In other words, to substitute the impression of an image which is left on the mind's eye for photographic clarity, reality, and naturalness. Claude Debussy was the founder of the new aesthetic and to implement it in music he developed the whole-tone scale (see p. 92 f.); a harmonic structure composed of chords with added seconds, fourths, sixths, and sevenths (see p. 87); chords moving in parallel motion which avoids a system of key-relationships of major and minor tonality (see p. 88 ff.); and a fragmentary melodic line (see p. 71 f.), all of which served to weaken the cadences (see p. 184 f.). With these new materials and devices Debussy created new

Plate VII—Impressionism. *Rouen Cathedral*. Monet, Claude—1840–1926. (Courtesy, The Metropolitan Museum of Art. The Theodore M. Davis Collection. Bequest of Theodore M. Davis, 1915.)

sounds and a new style. Although he denies it in the Rice Institute (Texas) Lectures of 1928 (see LangMWC, DorianHMP, ApelHD, FinneyHM), Maurice Ravel was also an exponent of this style, albeit his approach was somewhat more classical with regard to structure and line. The modernism of Isaac Albéniz, Béla Bartók, Frederick Delius, Paul Dukas, Manuel de Falla, Paul Hindemith, Arthur Honegger, Darius Milhaud, Francis Poulenc, Ottorino Respighi, Albert Roussel, Arnold Schoenberg, Jean Sibelius, Igor Stravinsky, Ralph Vaughan Williams, and in America that of Charles Griffes and Charles Martin Loeffler, was greatly influenced by the methods employed by Debussy.

Another reaction to the clichés of a waning romanticism was that of *nationalism.* This *ism* promoted national and racial traits of a given country by the use of its folk tunes and dance rhythms. Representative composers of this movement are: Michael Glinka, Bedřich Smetana, Alexander Borodin, Modeste Moussorgsky, Antonin Dvořák, Emmanuel Chabrier, Albéniz, Gabriel Fauré, Edward Elgar, Bartók, de Falla, Sibelius, Carlos Chávez, Zoltán Kodály, Ernest Bloch, Vaughan Williams, and Benjamin Britten. In America Henry Burleigh, Nathaniel Dett, Arthur Farwell, Harvey Loomis, Charles S. Skilton, Charles Wakefield Cadman, John Rosamond Johnson, Henry F. Gilbert, Frederick Converse, Charles Ives, Roy Harris, Aaron Copland, Douglas Moore, Ernst Bacon, Randall Thompson, Elie Siegmeister, and Morton Gould are exponents of this movement. (See Plate VIII.)

As in other countries, music in Russia has been influenced by the classicism and romanticism of Western Europe. It remained, however, for the aesthetic principle of nationalism to offer the greatest potential because of the rich source of folk music in Russia. Here was an aesthetic which made possible the development of a Russian national school of composition founded on work done by Glinka—father of Russian music.

The Communist Party, through the Soviet hierarchy, has imposed on its modern composers an aesthetic principle called *socialist realism.* Music, like all art, must be a socially significant communication which must, through emotional imagery, come to grips with the realities of life—dictatorially manipulated by government—for the perpetuation of Communism. In essence, the Soviet composer arranges for the benefit of the people, thus depriving him of his individual freedom of style and subject. Socialist realism rejects the bourgeois formalism of neoclassicism and the twelve-tone system as abstract and unrelated to life. Based on folk, popular, and exotic ingredients, the music retains the Russian flair for colorful orchestration and rhythms, employing repetition and sequence rather than thematic development.

Such modern composers as Serge Prokofieff, Dimitri Shostakovich, and Aram Khatchaturian in 1948 felt the long arm of the totalitarian state

Plate VIII—Nationalism. *General George Washington* before the Battle of Trenton. Trumbull, John—1756–1843. (Courtesy, The Metropolitan Museum of Art. Bequest of Grace Wilkes, 1922.)

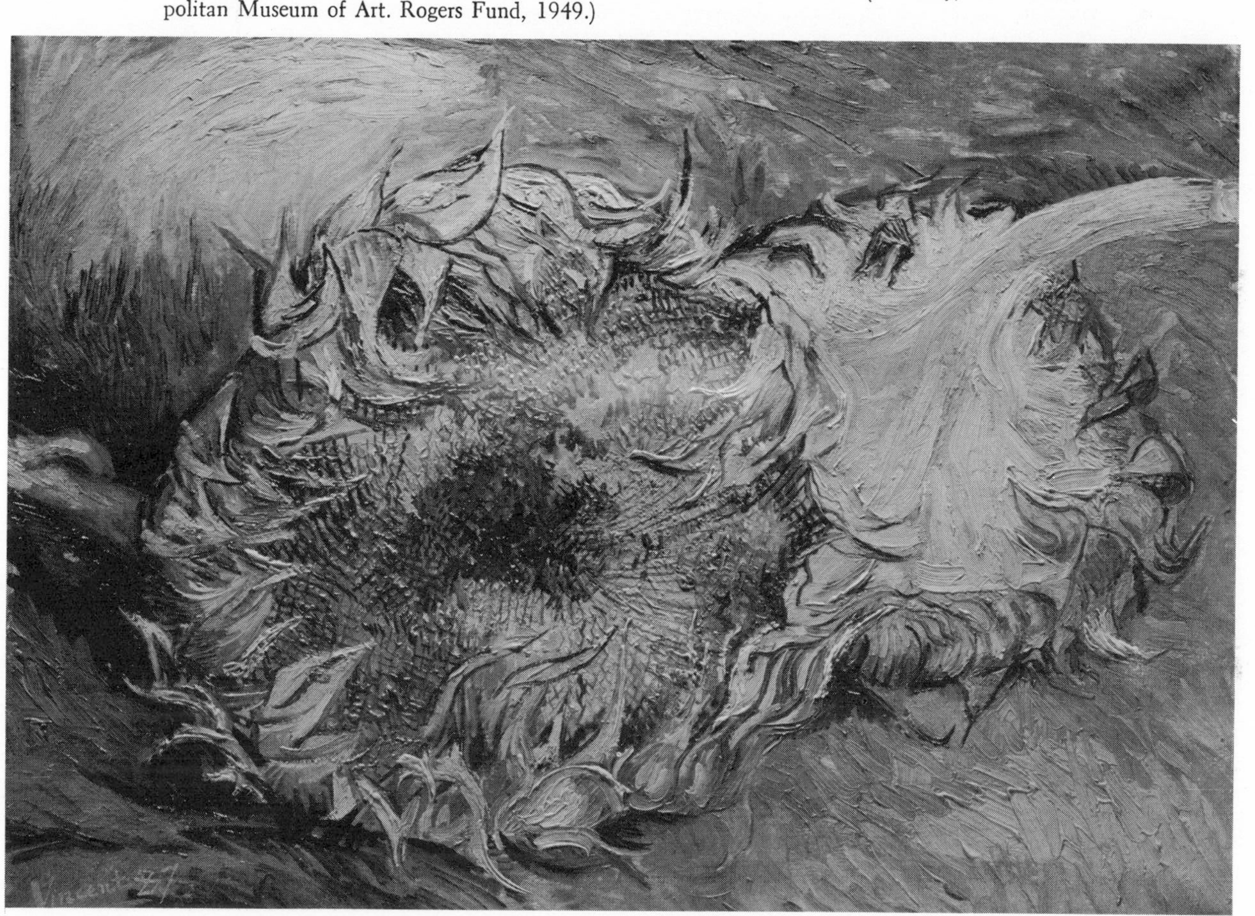

Plate IX—Expressionism. *Sunflowers.* Gogh, Vincent van—1853–1890. (Courtesy, The Metropolitan Museum of Art. Rogers Fund, 1949.)

Plate X—Modernism. "*Falling Water*," Bear Run, Pa. Wright, Frank Lloyd—1869–1960, architect. An example of functional architecture, and "a fine illustration of his now famed cantilever construction." (*Coronet*, August, 1957.) Photo courtesy of Bill Hedrich, Hedrich-Blessing.

Plate XI—American Folk Art. *Victorian Interior*. Pippin, Horace—1888–1946. (Courtesy, The Metropolitan Museum of Art. A. H. Hearn Fund, 1958.)

when it reached out and officially condemned their works in a critical manifesto. As early as 1936, Shostakovich was castigated by the government paper *Pravda* for his "leftist" and modern leanings in his Fourth Symphony. In his Fifth Symphony he returned to the romantic style of his First, which brought him once again into the good graces of the Party. *Pravda* quoted Shostakovich, having just completed his Fourteenth Symphony,* as saying that "I wish my new symphony would prompt the listener to think it is his duty to live life honestly, fruitfully."

Other modern Russian composers who have gained international recognition are Dimitri Kabalevsky and Tikhon Khrennikov.

However, since 1958 the Stalinist subjective viewpoint of art has been rejected in favor of a more liberal attitude toward art, literature, and music. Freedom of the individual to create has been on the ascendancy, and the new composers, led by Rodion Shchedrin, are the beneficiaries. The aesthetics of art change with Russian ideology, thus making it the political, social, and cultural enigma that it is.

In the 1920's, music and the other arts began to move in a number of divergent directions and, in so doing, established a new set of *isms*, all directed toward *objectivism* as opposed to the subjective, overexposed, emotion-packed, sensuous beauty of the romantic period. Instead of concern with subjects related to religion, love, nature, and the heroic, there was a growing interest in formalized structure—pure form—devoid of any personal feelings of the artist. In the resulting *abstractionism*, the artist was preoccupied with the nature of his materials—the linearity, shape, and surface aspects of structure. Music reflected this directness as did the painting and sculpture of the constructivists and cubists with their straight lines and flat planes.

As an escape from the highly refined sweetness and light of Debussy and Ravel, a new aesthetic called *primitivism*—once called barbarism—emerged. This was inspired by the discovery of the drive of African rhythms and abstract African sculpture. Its chief proponents were Bartók and Stravinsky.

This era also saw the beginnings of an industrialized society in which rhythm and motion symbolized man and machine. Composers glorified urban life and the power, energy, and motion of the machine. Honegger, John Alden Carpenter, George Antheil, Prokofieff, Alexander Mossolov, and Chávez are representative of this movement. Man and *urbanism* were further symbolized in rhythm and motion by sports and ballet. As evidence of the bitterness engendered by the romantic period, composers resorted to humor, irony, and satire, aided and abetted by a harmonic structure replete with dissonance. Though this aesthetic was short-lived, it did

* To be premièred in Moscow, fall of 1969.

provide an opportunity for the following composers to give vent to their feelings: Hindemith, Milhaud, Prokofieff, Satie, Shostakovich, Stravinsky, William Walton, and Kurt Weill.

But Schoenberg stands as the pivotal point for modern music. This music is also a reaction against the ultraromanticism of Wagner but partakes of the essence of impressionism—namely, vagueness and the desire for a new idiom. *Expressionism* became the opposite of impressionism—there was a shift from "outer" to "inner" impressions which had their source in the subconscious mind as exemplified in the work of the expressionist painters, notably Wassily Kandinsky, Paul Klee, Oscar Kokoschka and Franz Marc, as well as the poetry of Stefan George and Richard Dehmel, and the writings of Franz Kafka. Expressionism represented the complete disregard—in the conventional sense—for beauty of form arising from the harmony of balanced proportions. Schoenberg's music has been described as eye music rather than ear music because of its extreme complexity for the ear to grasp. Though his principal disciples are Alban Berg and Anton Webern, the following composers are also representative of the expressionist movement and the Schoenberg method—twelve-tone: Luigi Dallapiccola, Frank Martin, Goffredo Petrassi, Rolf Liebermann, Hans Werner Henze, and Stravinsky in his later works. In America the composers who have espoused Schoenberg's principles are Erich Kahn, Ernst Křenek, Mel Powell, and Wallingford Riegger, as have Carl Ruggles, Roger Sessions, Elliott Carter, Hugo Weisgall, Leon Kirchner, and Gunther Schuller with a more personal kind of expressionism. (See Plate IX.)

Neoclassicism is a movement based on the philosophy and the aesthetics of the early and late eighteenth-century styles. It represents a strong reaction against the romanticism of the nineteenth and early twentieth centuries. Emphasis was again placed on counterpoint and some of the early forms. Descriptive music, as such, became passé. Two groups emerged within the neoclassic movement: (1) those who turned for inspiration to such composers of the late Baroque as Bach and Handel, and (2) those who might be termed classicists because they embraced the classical era of Haydn and Mozart. The former group includes such men as Stravinsky, Hindemith, and Bartók, while the latter is represented by Ferruccio Busoni, Roussel, Bohuslav Martinu, Alfredo Casella, Gian Francesco Malipiero, and Vittorio Rieti; representing the second group in America are Walter Piston, Quincy Porter, William Schuman, Lukas Foss, Peter Mennin, Arthur Berger, Gardner Read, Gail Kubik, David Diamond, Robert Palmer, and Ellis Kohs.

Following the 1920's, *neoromanticism* loomed on the musical horizon as a counter to neoclassicism. This movement restored the programmatic concept and re-established melody and emotion as dominant forces in music but influenced by modern devices. Representing the new romanticism are Olivier Messiaen, Carl Orff, Ernst Toch, Mario Castelnuovo-Tedesco and, in their later works, Bartók, Hindemith, and Prokofieff. In America such men as Howard Hanson, Virgil Thomson, Samuel Barber, Alan Hovhaness, Norman Dello Joio, Robert Ward, William Bergsma, and Ned Rorem are proponents of the new romanticism.

Following World War I, a phenomenon called American jazz began to influence Europe. A few European composers of serious music were quick to make use of the jazz idioms. American composers were slower to realize its possibilities in art music. Based on primitivism, jazz has an ancestry dating back to African drums and Negro rhythms, which, when coupled with the American temperament of the twenties, made considerable impact on the serious composer as well as the general public. Having its origin in ragtime and blues, jazz relies on intricate rhythms—polyrhythms (see p. 172), counterpoint (see p. 81), novel and colorful harmonic devices and instrumentation, improvisation, and freedom from the confinements of intonation. The appeal of jazz is psychological—sensuous, primitive, and erotic.

> Occasional claims to the contrary notwithstanding, Jazz shows no signs of becoming the American music of the future, perhaps because, despite the interest and stimulation it affords, its appeal is too primitive and immediate. Nevertheless—quite apart from the essays in the traditional forms by Jazz composers themselves (Gershwin's "Concerto in F" for piano and orchestra, 1925; Morton Gould's "Chorale and Fugue in Jazz," 1936)—Jazz has contributed at least a variety of rhythmic and instrumental effects to music in general, and direct imitations as well as more subtle influences from this type of music are found in the work of more serious composers from the time of Debussy ("Golliwog's Cake Walk" from his *Children's Corner*, 1908).[1]

The jazz influence is also reflected in some of the works of Satie, Stravinsky, Milhaud, and Hindemith. The modern musical theater—opera and musical comedy—has also felt the impact of jazz in works by Gershwin, Weill, Křenek, Marc Blitzstein, and Leonard Bernstein.

After 1950 a new aesthetic called *scientism* made its appearance as the result of technological advances in the fields of electronics and acoustics. This aesthetic principle has given the composer a new medium of musical expression which is objective, purely abstract—unemotional and uncommunicative—and esoteric: understood by the specially initiated. The composer is primarily interested in new sounds and mixtures of sounds to produce new sonorities—colors—the manipulation of pitch and time as related to duration. The "new" cannot be equated with the old.

The following composers are representative of this movement: Pierre

Boulez, Pierre Henry, Messiaen, and Karlheinz Stockhausen; and in America it is represented by Milton Babbitt, John Cage, Lejaren Hiller, Otto Luening, Vladimir Ussachevsky, Edgard Varèse, and Iannis Xenakis.

THE ALLIED ARTS

The Main Fields of Aesthetic Inquiry

It is common practice to divide the arts into the following classifications which show their relationship and serve to emphasize their aesthetic qualities: (1) the *Temporal Arts*—music, dance, poetry (literature). It should be pointed out that architecture, sculpture, and painting may be considered temporal in the sense that their objects exist in time and time is involved in their perception; and (2) the *Spatial Arts*—architecture, sculpture, painting, and dance. (Music and literature may be considered spatial when it is remembered that music is motion which implies space, and literature is spatial when it creates images in the mind's eye.)

Another helpful classification which emphasizes the aesthetic qualities of the arts is the following one which is used as the basis of these Units: (1) the *Nonrepresentative* (intangible) *Auditory Art*—music; (2) the *Representative* (tangible) *Visual Arts*—architecture, sculpture, painting (poetry may be considered a visual art because it tends to classify its images); and (3) the *Mixed* (auditory and visual) *Arts*—opera, drama, dance.

Music and Poetry Compared

Music is a nonrepresentative—intangible—art while poetry is representative—tangible—with sound being inherent in both. In music, sound is of paramount importance while in poetry, though very important, it never rates a foremost position because it shares leadership with word meanings; music and poetry can be, at one and the same time, intimate and public. Though they are both very similar in emotional appeal, music has sound for its medium while poetry has words (vocalized or not). Poetry classifies its images and creates ideas though music can do neither. Poetry has meaning, music is feeling. Yet these very differences make for the complete union of poetry and music. The one supplies what the other lacks.

Architecture, Sculpture, and Painting Compared

All are representative—tangible—arts and have their origin in objects or practical needs and each is deeply rooted in nature in real or inanimate objects. Architectural purposes are, basically, utilitarian. Images of nature are reflected in painting and sculpture. The use of color and form in painting and sculpture *may* create exact reproductions of the objects themselves. The media for the pictorial arts are color and line.

Music and Representation

Music is not concerned with the origin of physical sound. It depends only on *sense* material—feeling—for expression. Music expresses only the image of emotion. Music may have color and line but it creates no *real* images. When a composer attempts to "picture" something, he deliberately creates imagery by the title of the composition only. He may suggest through imitation of sounds and events, but the sounds and events thus created will be unreal and cannot be experienced by all alike. He creates only a mood. Music is not all social and does not have to be useful. Music may be beautiful but it does not have to serve practical needs. Music is based on sounds (which are auditory, not pictorial)—sounds in music are tones—tones are abstract and cannot of themselves represent. Art which is dependent on another art belies its responsibility, loses its independence and its aesthetic value. To have aesthetic value as music it must be able to stand alone.

PROGRAM VERSUS ABSOLUTE MUSIC

Definition of Descriptive Music

Descriptive music (heteronomous art) is that which has for its purpose pictorial representation, inspired or suggested by a program. The pictorial depends on sight, music depends on hearing. In descriptive music the composer carries on a dual purpose of sight and sound, hence, it impoverishes itself as music since it does not stand on its own two feet. One should bear in mind, however, that descriptive music is an important form of art music.

Definition of Absolute Music

Absolute music (autonomous art) is pure music, that which is without extramusical qualities. Absolute and descriptive music represent the opposite poles of musical aesthetics. But they can be reconciled objectively as we shall see later. Because of the influence of the text on vocal music, it is usually excluded as absolute music. Some musicians would exclude all Romantic music from absolute music. The aesthetic of absolute music is founded on a strong, solid philosophical and psychological cornerstone which has but a single purpose—music as music.

The Autonomous Approach to Understanding Music

The autonomous approach to musical understanding is an aesthetic principle which makes it possible for us to study music as music, in its pure form, that is, through an abstract study of its elements *rhythm, melody, harmony, tone color,* and *design* (form). The definition of absolute music previously given does not preclude the study of descriptive music through its elements. In fact, in this objective manner absolute and descriptive music are readily and pleasantly reconciled.

Testing the Autonomous Theory

Select some of the paired titles—one descriptive is paired with one absolute—from the list of records for this Unit in Appendix V. The titles of the compositions should not be announced before playing and the listener should not be prepared in any way for what he is to hear. The listener should try to formulate a picture from what he hears and answer the following:

Does the music suggest the title?
How would you describe what you saw?
Were the images real?
What did you get out of the music?
Do the listeners agree on each "picture"?

Now, tell the listeners, or have them read the title of the composition after each is played.

Conclusion

From the answers to the questions it should be evident to the listeners that music cannot "picture"; that the music is dependent on the descriptive title to create the picture; that after all, music is abstract and must be studied through its elements for complete understanding; that no matter what the purpose of the composer, there is but one end result, namely, he creates music as music; that the mind's eye must be kept on the object, music.

Interest—which is emotion—is heightened when the story behind the composition becomes known. However, one should listen to the music first for its aesthetic value and on subsequent hearings keep the program in the background. To understand any form of art one needs to know its vocabulary, be able to use the tools, recognize and understand the elements involved, to analyze, to know the "why" and the "how" of the art and the composition in particular. Real aesthetic enjoyment requires active attention, the aid of the intellectual process, practice, and an affective response. *There is no short cut to a real aesthetic experience through the programmatic.*

Descriptive music may have value if the music is good in spite of the program. However, a good program does not insure good music. Some of the world's best music is written with a program in mind. Once the story is known the listener must not be content to say he "knows" the music. Strauss's *Till Eulenspiegel* is a masterpiece in creative flights of imagination, but Strauss never authorized the publishing of a program for *Till.* He was concerned with the elements at his disposal, and used the legendary *Till* only as episodic material for tonal construction. To hear something in music is not to *see* it alike. What Strauss saw in his mind's eye is abstract so far as we are concerned until we go to the music itself for the explanation. As a romanticist, Strauss was concerned with color and chromatic harmony—in themselves definite limitations. Strauss and other romanticists and moderns cannot describe definite objects, although they can create a mood. But this does not deny their genius as composers. Romanticists and moderns differ from the classicists only in the wide variety of coloring, harmonic, and rhythmic devices used. Music is still the same as it was originally—music for music's sake. In a period rich in the development of the tangible arts, Bach, Haydn, Mozart, *et al.*, gave compositions abstract titles. Beethoven straddled the fence between classicism and romanticism, but his greatest works are those which he treated abstractly as pure music.*

* The recordings to be used with this Unit are found in Appendix V, together with notes on how to listen.

UNIT II

The Art of Listening

"CLASSICAL" VERSUS POPULAR MUSIC

Have you ever wondered why the best in serious music is great while some music is not so great, or what the difference is between great music and popular music? Or whether you as an individual can ever learn to understand and enjoy great music? These and many other questions will be answered for you in the pages that follow. But first, let us agree on certain basic terminology.

Definition of "Classical" Music

To the average person, any music which is not popular or sacred is classical. The term "classical" here is a misnomer. In music history, the term classical denotes a period from about 1750 to 1825, dominated largely by Haydn and Mozart. The term "classical music," then, identifies these two men and their contemporaries together with their style of composition. This is the connotation to be used throughout these Units.

Problem of Terminology

Although neither the terms classical, nor serious, nor concert thoroughly describe the music we are about to study, for our purpose the term *serious* music seems to be the most satisfactory. Because both serious and popular music make use of the same materials and media—means by which anything is accomplished—the average person finds differentiation between serious and popular music difficult.

Suggested Solution of the Problem

Serious music—art music—is subtle music, while *popular music*—a form of utilitarian music—is obvious music. Serious music is subjective imagination, whereas popular music is merely objective feeling. Webster defines the word "subtle" as "given to or characterized by refinements of thought, insight, perception, therefore, something which is crafty and artful." The word "popular" means "suitable to the public in general; (a) easy to understand; plain. (b) Adapted to means and the generality of people, hence, cheap."

Distinctions Between Serious and Popular Music

Though serious and popular music use the same materials and media, they are not used in the same way or for the same purpose. Let us not confuse the two. Generally speaking, popular music is commercial music in which its pictorial and theatrical qualities become its stock in trade. Learning to differentiate between popular and the best in serious music is analogous to learning the difference between a cheap car and an expensive one. Learning to appreciate serious music involves sensitivity and education. Education denotes growth—a change from lack of understanding to possession of understanding through study, instruction, and contemplation. To achieve these ends one needs to listen and examine all music for itself—for what it is. "An art aims, above all, at producing something *beautiful* which affects not our feelings, but the organ of pure contemplation, our imagination."[1]

Appreciation of serious music requires *active attention, perception*—understanding—and an *affective accompaniment*—involuntary bodily movement, however small (see Appendix I, Unit II, 14). In popular music, affective accompaniment gains first place and the other two responses are relegated almost to oblivion.

Perception

Of the three requirements for the appreciation of serious music, perception is, perhaps, the most difficult to understand. As we already said, perception is understanding. How, then, can we understand understanding?

We perceive music *intellectually*. To understand this process, we must begin with the reception of musical sound by the inner ear. Once received, the musical sound is immediately transmitted to the brain in the form of a musical impression which the listener may deal with in one of two ways. Either (1) he mentally tries to build a mirrored image parallel to and simultaneous with each musical impression, or (2) he guesses the direction the musical structure will take and matches it with the image of a previous musical impression which he has cached away in his memory for future reference. By either process the aesthetic experience approaches perfection the more closely the musical impression and the mirrored image coincide.[2] Mirrored images are made up out of past musical experiences. The more primitive the past musical experience, the more primitive the mirrored image. For example, motion is common to both life and music. Thus the perception of music as motion represents a primitive but necessary judgment in the unsophisticated mind. This perception of music as motion with all it entails will be dealt with in Unit III, The Pulse of Music: Rhythm. But the perception of music as motion is a far cry from the intellectual perception of an entire composition. However, it will serve as a starting point.

We perceive music *emotionally*. We stated in Unit I (see p. 28 ff.) that music expresses the images of emotion. These are memories of feelings of previous experiences which we have stored up in memory.[3] A musical impression cannot convey grief unless the listener remembers how he personally felt when he experienced it. Musical reactions, then, like dreams and memories, are reflected images of emotion. As dreams and memories pass in review in a relatively short period of time, so musical reactions are experienced in rapid succession due to the complexity and motion of the music. Like dreams and memories, musical reactions may be either vague or clearly outlined.

The listener's reaction to music can never be the same, although it may be similar to that of the composer or the performer. Likewise, different listeners will have varying emotional reactions to the same composition. This variation is due to the fact that each listener unconsciously supplies his own image based on past experiences which are nearest and dearest to him.

Perceiving music emotionally is not in conflict with the intellectual perception of music, for each process may go on independently of the other. Music which appeals to us intellectually may be distasteful emotionally. A case in point is some of the middle and late Schoenberg *eye* pieces. Likewise, music which appeals to us emotionally may fail us intellectually, e.g., many of the *ear* pieces of Chopin.

The emotional reaction to a simple musical structure will be fairly obvious. But when we load this simple musical structure with the materials and devices which music has at its disposal, we have multiplied the number of images of emotion many times. Where there was a single image for a simple structure now there are many for a complex structure. An analogy to this would be the experience we have all had in seeing a movie more than once. On second viewing, we are made to react to more details than on the first seeing. A third viewing increases still more the number of details to which we react emotionally.

For the listener, as he hears the music unfold, the process of perceiving music intellectually and emotionally is a continuous one, and how he reacts depends on the quantity and the quality of his experiences.[4]

TYPES OF LISTENERS

Passive

This type of listener merely hears music as a pleasant auditory impression and attaches no significance to the whole composition or its parts. He responds only to a bath in sound. He is regaled by music's charms in the true Boethian sense. His response reposes in feeling and is without critical analysis. It is the passive listener who is at first attracted by popular and programme music because these types of music give him more of a feeling of security than of frustration.

Active

The active listener is one who hears musically. That is, he has a response to feeling coupled with an awareness of the whole of a composition—rhythm, melody, harmony, tone color, and form. For the active listener, indulgence in mental imagery, associated with things or objects far removed from the musical aspects of the music being heard, is minimized or excluded.

APPROACHES TO LISTENING

Typical Approach

According to Max Schoen the typical approach to listening is through *familiarity, analysis,* and *interpretation.* He warns against familiarity becoming *habituation;*[5] analysis as an end in itself;[6] and interpretation which baits the music to catch the attention of the listener.[7]

Creative Approach

Schoen's own theory is that one must have an *inborn sensitivity to tone.* The greater the sensitivity to tone in the individual the greater is the compelling force to listen to music.[8] He believes further that the listener *must exercise the inborn sensitivity to tone* in order to cultivate the individual's natural endowment for the perception of music's elements.[9] In the interests of the creative approach, Schoen makes a plea for "*experience with tone in place of talk about tone,* and the cultivation of the attitude of paying close attention to the tonal material that is being directly presented."[10]

Objective Approach

An examination of the available psychological data tends to refute the theory just stated. We, therefore, favor an objective approach which believes that "discriminatory responses are not inherent but acquired,"[11] and that "the aesthetic response is also a learned reaction."[12] Herein lies the basic philosophy of these Units.

Aesthetic Approach—The Listener's Goal

In the foregoing paragraphs we have presented theories concerning the aesthetic response—what it is, and how it may be experienced. We believe that aesthetic enjoyment is within the reach of everyone. With this end in view, the several Units have been prepared to supply the means of achieving the listener's goal—aesthetic enjoyment.

If the listener is to attain his goal, he must keep in mind certain psychological factors which bear on the aesthetic response. First, *active attention* is required—the listener must be ready and willing to listen. Active attention habits, in which muscular tension is involved, requires practice and skill.[13] Second, the aesthetic response requires *perception.* Like attention habits, this developed ability to perceive music intellectually and emotionally requires practice and skill. The beauties of music are revealed to the listener when he can, for example, recognize and understand a rhythmic pattern, a melodic progression, a harmonic structure, the tone color of an instrument or voice, or the form of a composition. Such formal aspects of music as these furnish the substance for an aesthetic response.[14] Third, one does not have an aesthetic response without an *affective accompaniment*—involuntary bodily movement though faint, such as a lift of the finger, a slight tensing of a muscle, or a lift of the eyebrows. These are feeling reactions which, though important, must remain in the background and never gain first place so as to negate the aesthetic response. Objective feeling is the result of the bodily reactions becoming so intense that attention is directed toward them. When this happens, the listener is indulging himself in an emotional spree at the expense of attention and perception. Viewed in their proper perspective, feeling reactions are subtle and must remain in the twilight of attention and perception.[15]

In the case of popular music, affective accompaniment gains first place, becomes objective feeling, and tends to obliterate active attention and perception, thus precluding the aesthetic response. This fact should be self-evident to the listener when he compares the recordings of serious, light "classic," and popular music which are shown in Appendix V, Unit II. With practice and skill in attention and perception, the listener will ultimately arrive at the following conclusions: (1) that popular music—used in its broadest sense to include jazz and so-called popular "classics" —has relatively little lasting quality because the content is shallow and, hence, it sounds trite;[16] (2) that popular music soon reaches its peak in affective value with repetition and, thereafter, suffers a rapid decline;[17] (3) that the best in serious music lives on because there is a perpetual newness every time one listens to it;[18] and (4) that popular music offers the listener only commonplace experience and ordinary pleasure, while good serious music provides the opportunity for creative experience and aesthetic enjoyment.[19]

PART II

Musical Elements

UNIT III

The Pulse of Music: Rhythm

Do you dance, sing, play an instrument, listen to music, walk, run, drive a car? If you do any of these, rhythm plays a very important part in your life. But what is rhythm and how does it affect us?

The Psychological and Aesthetic Aspects of Rhythm

Of the four media in music's construction—rhythm, melody, harmony, and color—rhythm and melody are closely allied and the most important from a psychological and aesthetic point of view. However, it is possible to have rhythm without melody but it is impossible to have melody without rhythm. One cannot be conscious of a rhythm without responding to it either subjectively or objectively. The stronger the rhythm, the greater the impulse for physical movement.[1] There is a definite relationship between the emotions and physical movement caused by rhythmic sound.[2] Hence, rhythm, the framework on which melody is hung, becomes largely a physical stimulus, while melody may be said to appeal more to the aesthetic where the term "beauty" may be applied. One speaks often of a beautiful melody but rarely of a beautiful rhythm. Rhythm provides music with forward motion, while melody provides up and down pitch-movement. Rhythm is movement in time, while melody is movement in space.

There is some psychological evidence to show that the sense of rhythm can be improved with training. It is also evident that all parts of the body respond to rhythm, though rhythm in music is not always associated with physical action. Although the listener must wait for the performer to bring the music to life, he still must first perceive and then react.

The Temporal Aspects of Rhythm

For the purpose of this Unit we must divorce ourselves from the other elements of music and concentrate as completely as possible on the one element which is the backbone of all music, namely, rhythm.

If we look about us we are consciously or subconsciously aware of rhythm in nature. If we stop to consider the universe in general, we will see that rhythm is present in many things: bodily movements, the regular recurrence of night and day, the rotation of the seasons, or the ticking of the clock, and many others. Rhythm is also present in the plastic and graphic arts, architecture, sculpture, painting, and in poetry. In all of these rhythm is systematized in some kind of a pattern.

Rhythm in music is the easiest of the elements to perceive. Rhythm means something which occurs periodically. In listening to a succession of sounds, the ear will sooner or later be consciously aware of a real or an imagined series of accents—muscular in origin, which fall into a basic scheme of strong and weak beats which we call *meter*. But rhythm is more than this. In our modern system of notation rhythm includes a system of long and short note values. When these two aspects of rhythm —accents and note values—are combined, the totality of rhythm is achieved. Rhythm, then, is a system of note values superimposed on a framework of strong and weak beats.

The basic meters in music fall into a framework of either two or three beats, or multiples of two or three. The grouping of either two or three beats is called a *measure*. In music each measure is marked off by bar lines. These specific groupings within the measure are represented by the following meters, usually referred to as *time signatures:* duple—2/2, 2/4, 2/8; triple—3/2, 3/4, 3/8; quadruple—4/2, 4/4 (also called common meter—indicated by a *C*), 4/8; compound duple—6/2, 6/4, 6/8; compound triple—9/4, 9/8; and compound quadruple—12/4, 12/8, 12/16. Quintuple meter—5/4—is either a combination of 2/4 + 3/4, or 3/4 + 2/4, depending on the location of the secondary accent. Septuple meter—7/4—is a combination of 3/4 + 4/4, or 4/4 + 3/4. Simple meters, then, are those measures which have but one accent (see p. 42), while compound meter is a combination of two or more simple measures and containing two or more accents, the first always being the strongest. The upper figure of the time signature denotes the *number* of beats to each measure; the lower figure denotes the *kind* of a note —unit—which will be given one beat. For example, a time signature of 2/4 indicates that there will be two beats to each measure with the quarter note (♩) getting one beat.

Let us see how the longer and shorter note values mentioned may be distributed within a framework of 4/4 time.

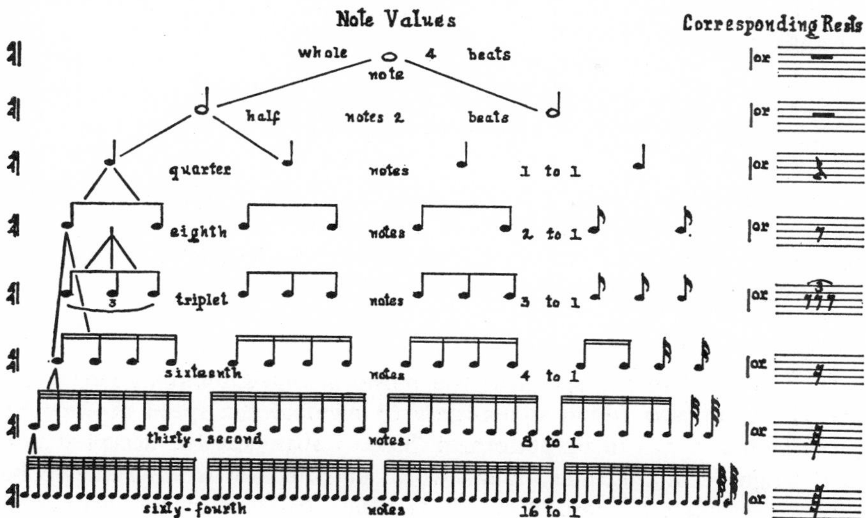

A dot beside a note adds half the value of the note, and may be used with any of the notes shown, as:

dotted half - quarter | dotted eighth - sixteenth

dotted quarter - eighth | dotted sixteenth - thirty-second

In order to lend variety to music the composer uses the different kinds of notes in a variety of rhythmic combinations. These combinations may be grouped under the general heading of regular rhythm and syncopation. A given rhythm may be used many times in the course of a composition.

Syncopation

The rhythm is said to be syncopated—irregular rhythm—when the shorter tones occupy the accents, or when longer tones are shifted to any comparatively lighter pulse of the measure as:

or

Accent

Accent, which is also a part of rhythm, may be regular or irregular, depending on where the accent is placed in the measure, as in the following:

regular accent strong beat — regular accent strong beat — irregular accent weak beat — irregular accent weak beat

In addition to greater intensity which may be applied to a specific note—dynamic accent—accent may also be achieved by the use of a higher pitch—tonic accent—or by prolonging the length of an accented note—agogic accent.

Tempo

Time related to the speed of the music is called *tempo*. Many years ago the composers found it necessary to regulate the speed at which a piece of music was to be performed. Since Italian was the accepted musical language of the time, Italian words or groups of words came to be used to designate the rate of speed. Tradition has dictated the continued use of the Italian words. A few tempo markings picked at random will suffice to emphasize the point:

PRESTISSIMO—as rapid as possible

ALLEGRO MA NON TROPPO—rapid, but not overrapid

MODERATO—at moderate speed

LARGO ASSAI—very broad, large

It should be remembered that these terms are, at best, only relative. A more exact idea of tempo may be gained if the composer or the editor indicates, in addition to the above, what is called a metronome marking, as: M.M. ♩ = 80. This indicates that the general speed should be at the rate of eighty quarter notes to the minute. Deviations from this tempo may be indicated at various places in the music for the sake of variety. Even with the exactness of tempo, it is very desirable, except in marches or dance music, that the performer be allowed a certain amount of individual freedom in tempo for adequate interpretation. This, however, does not give him license as a libertine.

Developing Structure from Basic Rhythmic Patterns

Perhaps in no other music except marches is the feeling for rhythm so strong as that found in the various dance forms; whether the dances be of the "popular"—utilitarian—or the "serious" variety as found in the idealized dance forms of art music. Here we may see the rhythmic aspect of musical structure at work through the use of basic rhythmic patterns.

It should be observed that there is always an underlying rhythmic beat of two, three, or four to the measure and superimposed on it is a characteristic rhythmic pattern which serves to identify the specific dance rhythm. Other rhythms may be added to the basic pattern by the composer to lend greater variety to the composition. The element of tempo is also important to the forward movement of the dance. Dances may have the same underlying pulse of two to the measure but because of the superimposed rhythmic pattern a certain dance may move faster or slower than another with the same beat.

Composers of serious music have, from time to time, taken the popular dances of their day and, by refining them, have lifted them into the sphere of art music. Let us see how rhythmic structure is developed by a study of some of the specific dance styles which have found their way into the art music of today. As you go from one dance to the next, notice how the rhythmic effect is changed by a different organization of note values. The placement of accent is also an important factor. The organization of notes and accent within a given meter is interesting to observe and listen to. For example, the *Tango* and the *Polka* have the same time signature—2/4—but the organization of the notes into different characteristic patterns creates an altogether different feeling and response. It is suggested that the listener contrast the two examples shown for each dance form.*

DANCES IN DUPLE METER

Habañera

A Cuban (Havana) dance probably of Spanish origin. It resembles the tango. About 1850 it was reintroduced into Spain. The tempo is slow. The basic rhythmic pattern may be one or more of the following:

2/4 ‖ or ‖ or ‖ or ‖

Compare the following earlier example of the *Habañera* with the later example by Bizet. The striking likeness was admitted by Bizet.

Ex. 1. Yradier, Sebastian: *El Areglito*†

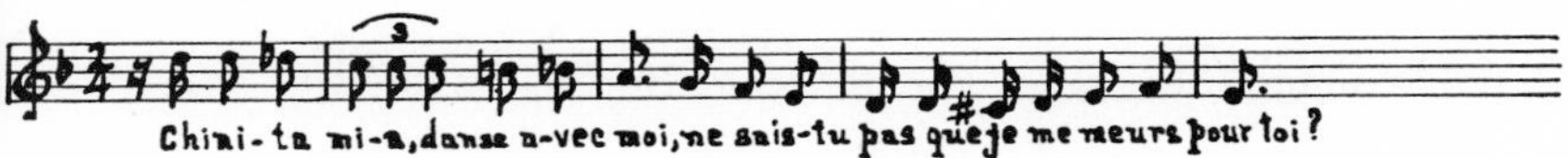

* It is suggested that the instructor exercise freedom of choice in selecting as many of the following dance forms as time and purpose will allow.

† For ease in reading, the many musical examples in this text may be found to be transposed higher or lower and/or arranged.

Ex. 2. Bizet, Georges: *Carmen,* "Habañera"

Tango

An Argentine (Buenos Aires) dance of modern origin circa 1900. Syncopation is the dominant rhythmic device in this dance. The tempo is faster than that of the habañera.

Ex. 3. Albéniz, Isaac: *Tango in D*

(*Used by permission of The Boston Music Company, Boston 16, Mass., Copyright Owner.*)

Ex. 4. Milhaud, Darius: *Le Boeuf sur le Toit,* Theme 6

(*By courtesy of Éditions Salabert, Paris, France.*)

Polka

A Bohemian round dance originating about 1830. It proved to be a very popular dance in Europe until about 1900, though it is still danced in some sections of the United States. The polka found its way into art music through the efforts of Smetana and Dvořák. The tempo is rather fast.

Ex. 5. Smetana, Bedrich: *The Bartered Bride,* "Polka"

Ex. 6. Shostakovitch, Dimitri: *The Golden Age Ballet*, Op. 22; "Polka," Theme 1

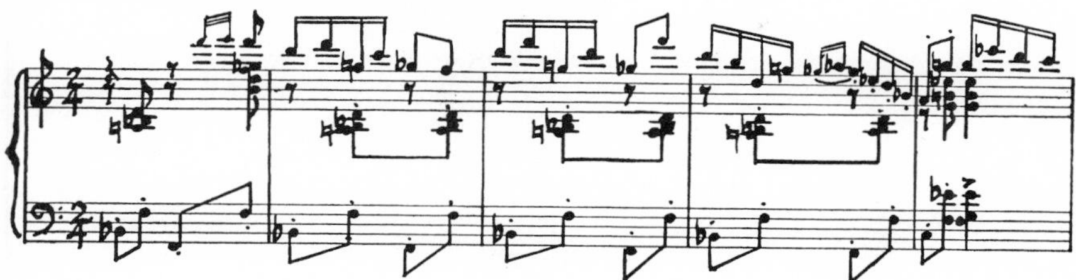

Pavane

A dance of Spanish origin which was popular in the late fifteenth century. The tempo is slow and stately. The *pavane* was used in the *suite*—a series of idealized dances in the same key—as the opening movement and was followed by the *galliard,* which was in a faster triple meter.

Ex. 7. Byrd, William: *Pavan,* "The Earl of Salisbury"

Ex. 8. Delibes, Léo: *Le Roi S'Amuse,* "Scène du Bal"

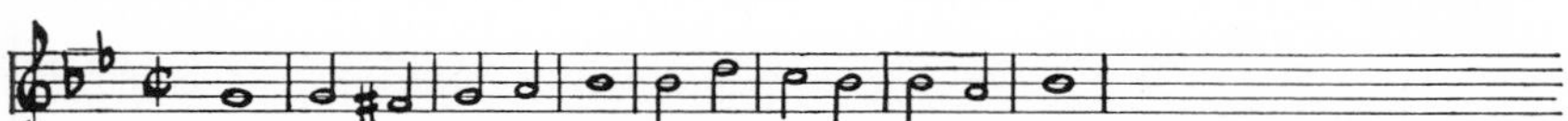

Gavotte

An old French dance form of the seventeenth century which always followed the minuet in the suite. Though much kissing and frolicking characterized the early gavotte, its subsequent progress was from formality and the majestic to stiffness and the unnatural. The distinguishing feature of the gavotte is that it starts on the upbeat of the measure (or third beat).

Ex. 9. Bach, Johann Sebastian: *French Suite No. 5,* "Gavotte"

Ex. 10. Prokofieff, Serge: *Classical Symphony,* Second Movement (Gavotte)

Galop

This dance is a polka in very fast tempo. It is a nineteenth-century peasant round dance, probably of German origin, though it was Paris which gave the galop its popularity as it did the polka and the mazurka before it.

Ex. 11. Liszt, Franz: *Grand Galop Chromatique*

Ex. 12. Khachaturian, Aram: *Masquerade Suite,* Fifth Movement (Galop)

Trepak

The trepak is a quick Russian dance having its origin in a Ukrainian folk dance. It is danced by men (Cossacks) in solo or ensemble.

Ex. 13. Tschaikowsky, Peter Ilyich: *The Nutcracker Suite*, Op. 71a; "Russian Dance" (Trepak)

Ex. 14. Khachaturian: *Gayne, Ballet*, "Dance of the Young Kurds" (Trepak)

DANCES IN TRIPLE METER

Chaconne

A dance of Mexican origin introduced into Spain circa 1600. Originally it was a wild and sensual dance, but musically the structure is a series of variations in a moderately slow tempo built on a succession of chords usually not over eight measures in length. These chords are then subjected to continuous variation.

Ex. 15. Handel, Georg Frederich: *Chaconne No. 9* (with sixty-two variations)

Ex. 16. Busoni, Ferruccio: *Toccata*, "Ciacona"

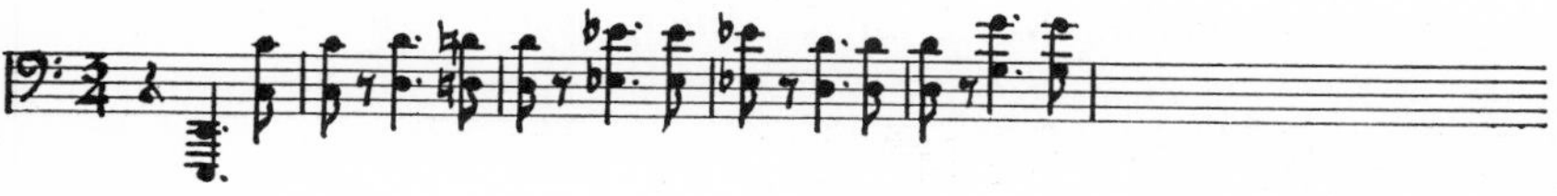

Passacaglia

This dance is closely related to the chaconne and is of probable Spanish origin. Like the chaconne, it is based on the idea of variation.

Here we have an *ostinato* or *ground bass* which is repeated throughout the composition. This melodic bass theme of up to eight measures is always in minor and, while it is introduced in the bass, it may also appear in an upper voice. The tempo is slow and stately.

Ex. 17. Bach: *Passacaglia in C Minor* (Organ)

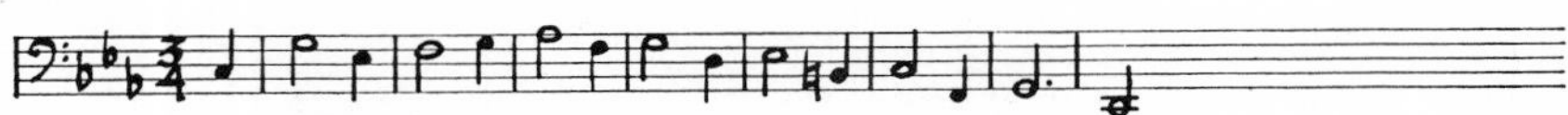

Ex. 18. Schuman, William: *Symphony* No. 3, "Passacaglia," Theme 1

Courante

Also one of the movements of the suite, the courante had its beginning in the sixteenth century. It follows the allemande in the suite. Actually, the courante was of two types, the Italian *corrente,* in 3/4 or 3/8 time containing swift passages of equal notes in rapid tempo, and the French *courante* in 3/2 or 6/4 time in a moderately rapid tempo containing many dotted notes. The rhythmic patterns are somewhat indefinite for the courante.

Ex. 19. Bach: *Partita* No. 2, *in D Minor,* Second Movement

Ex. 20. Bach: ***French Suite** No. 1, in D Minor,* First Movement

Ex. 21. Dohnányi, Ernst von: *Suite nach altem Stil,* Op. 24; "Courante"

Galliard

This dance, which appeared first in Lombardy, was popular in the sixteenth century and was danced also in Italy, France, Spain, and England. The galliard generally followed the pavane and was danced in a gay and unrestrained manner. Later, in the seventeenth century, the galliard was allowed to stand alone as a dance. The tempo is moderately fast.

Ex. 22. Byrd: *Galliard,* "The Earl of Salisbury"

Ex. 23. Respighi, Ottorino: *Antiche Danze, Suite No. 1,* Second Movement (Gagliarda)

Polonaise

The polonaise had its origin in Poland, where it was a stately processional form in the sixteenth century. Later it became a slow promenade which served to open the ballroom dancing. During the eighteenth and nineteenth centuries composers continued to perfect the polonaise to the point of its present idealized form. It is in triple meter at a moderate tempo.

Ex. 24. Beethoven, Ludwig van: *Polonaise,* Op. 89

Ex. 25. MacDowell, Edward: *Etudes,* Op. 46, No. 12; "Polonaise"

Sarabande

Having its origin in Spain in the late sixteenth century, the sarabande enjoyed its greatest popularity in the seventeenth and eighteenth centuries. It was originally a sensuous dance, and has long since passed from the ballroom. The sarabande lives on only in the theater and in music. Over the centuries composers have idealized the form of the sarabande to a point where it is now far remote from its earlier unbridled youthfulness. Its normal inclusion as the third movement in the suite with its slow triple meter made the sarabande a perfect foil for the gigue which followed. In the suites of Bach and Handel, however, the minuet was inserted between the sarabande and the gigue.

Ex. 26. Bach: *French Suite No. 1, in D Minor,* Third Movement, "Sarabande"

Sometimes instrumental forms were used in vocal music. Such an instance is shown here:

Ex. 27. Handel: *Rinaldo,* "Lascia ch'io pianga"

Ex. 28. Satie, Erik: *Three Sarabandes,* First

(By courtesy of Éditions Salabert, Paris, France.)

Fandango

Appearing in Spain in the early eighteenth century, the fandango was a sensuous courtship dance for two of different sex. The dance alternated with sung couplets and the guitar and the castanets were used for accompaniment. The tempo was lively. The castanet rhythm is shown below.

Ex. 29. Gluck, Christoph Willibald: *Don Juan Ballet,* "Fandango"

Ex. 30. Moszkowski, Moritz: *Spanish Dances,* Op. 12, No. 1

Waltz

The waltz, which is a round dance still popular today, developed from an Austrian peasant dance called the *Ländler*. Originating about 1800, the waltz made history because it was the first dance in which the partners embraced each other. The tempo is slow to moderately fast, depending on whether the waltz is the classical Viennese or the German variety. In the Viennese waltz overemphasis is placed on the first beat and less emphasis is placed on the second, with the third somewhat delayed. The tempo for the Viennese waltz is fast. The German variety is taken at a slower tempo.

Ex. 31. Schubert, Franz: *Waltz,* Op. 9, No. 1

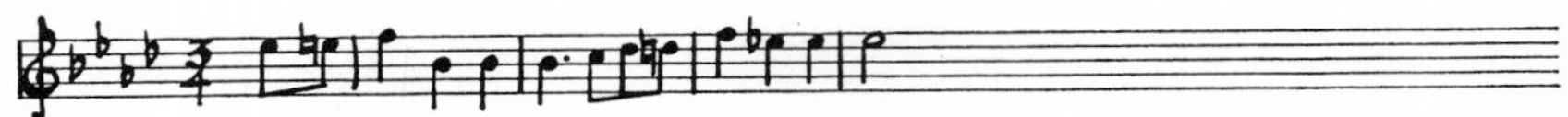

Ex. 32. Ravel, Maurice: *La Valse,* Theme 1.

(Permission for reprint granted by Durand & Cie, Paris, France, copyright owners; Elkan-Vogel Co., Inc., Philadelphia 3, Pa., agent.)

Seguidilla

This is a dance similar to the bolero except that it has song, guitar, and castanet accompaniment. The origin of the seguidilla is southern Spain. The tempo is fast.

Ex. 33. Bizet: *Carmen,* Act I, "Seguidilla"

Ex. 34. Albéniz: *Suite Español,* "Seguidilla"

Minuet

Originally a French country dance, the minuet gravitated to the court of Louis XIV about 1650 where it became a slow, dignified and stately dance in 3/4 time. It soon spread over Europe and established a new dance era. As an art form the minuet is derived from the courante and became a successor to it. In the hands of Bach and Handel the minuet was in a moderately fast tempo and was usually inserted between the sarabande and gigue for contrast. With Haydn and Mozart the minuet took on a faster and lighter character. While Beethoven wrote many *menuetten* of the Haydn-Mozart variety which are to be found in his sonatas and chamber music, his main contribution was the development of the minuet into the scherzo.

Ex. 35. Beethoven: *Minuet in G*

Ex. 36. Ravel: *Le Tombeau de Couperin,* "Minuet," Theme 1

(Permission for reprint granted by Durand & Cie, Paris, France, copyright owners; Elkan-Vogel Co., Inc., Philadelphia 3, Pa., agent.)

Bolero

The bolero is a couple dance of Moorish-Spanish derivation originating about 1780. Contrasted with the fandango it is a much more subtle, quiet, and gentle dance. Like the fandango, it is accompanied by castanets and guitar to which the tambourine is added. The bolero is in 3/4 or 2/4 time. The latter is the Cuban variety. It is danced at a moderate tempo.

Ex. 37. Chopin, Frederic: *Bolero,* Op. 19

Ex. 38. Ravel: *Bolero,* Theme A

(Permission for reprint granted by Durand & Cie, Paris, France, copyright owners; Elkan-Vogel Co., Inc., Philadelphia 3, Pa., agent.)

Drum Patterns Accompaniment

Mazurka

The mazurka is a folk dance which originated in the Polish Palatinate of Mazovia about 1750. It was later introduced in France and England. The mazurka attained the realm of art music through the efforts of Chopin, who gave it its stylized characteristics. The mazurka is a dance of moderate tempo in 3/4 time with a variable accent occurring on the third beat.

Ex. 39. Chopin: *Mazurka,* No. 13, Op. 17, No. 4

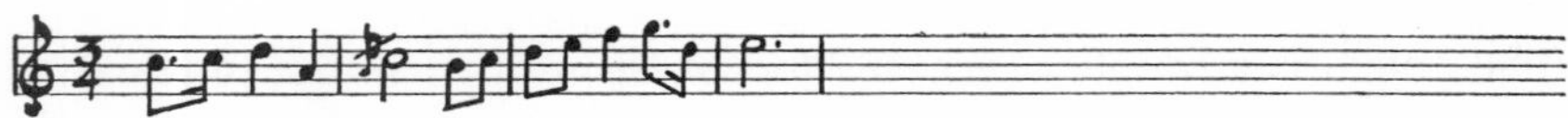

Ex. 40. Scriabin, Alexander: *Mazurka,* Op. 25, No. 3

DANCES IN QUADRUPLE METER

Bourrée

Originally the bourrée was a rustic dance having its inception in the French province of Auvergne. In the middle of the seventeenth century it was cultivated by the court and from there it made its way into the ballet. The bourrée may be found in the French overture and in the operas of Lully and later composers. It is similar to the gavotte but begins on the last quarter of the measure. The bourrée is usually marked

"Allegro," and is in 4/4 time (or alla breve). In the suite the bourrée is found between the sarabande and the gigue.

Ex. 41. Bach: *Partita No. 1 in B Minor,* "Bourrée"

Ex. 42. Britten, Benjamin: *Simple Symphony,* First Movement (Boisterous Bourrée)

Allemande

The allemande is a dance of German origin which appeared around 1550. As a dance, it originally had a metric signature of 2/4, but through evolution it finally became a part of the suite. Here it was employed as the first movement or immediately followed a prelude. As a movement of the suite, the allemande was of moderate speed in 4/4 time and commenced with a short note on the upbeat. In this form it ceased to be danced and became an idealized type.

Ex. 43. Rameau, Jean Phillipe: *Suite in E Minor,* "Allemande"

Ex. 44. Křenek, Ernst: *Little Suite,* Op. 13a, "Allemande"

Fox Trot

The fox trot, of American origin, is based on the two-step and is derived from ragtime. The fox trot appeared around 1912. Ragtime had its origin about 1910 and consisted of syncopated 4/4 measures. The fox trot tends to include such forms of popular dancing called "blues" (circa 1900) which is a slow fox trot, and "swing" (circa 1935) which is a fast fox trot. The *fox trot, cakewalk, shimmy, Charleston, truckin, black bottom,* and *Lindy hop* may be classified under the general heading of jazz. The fox trot is probably the most important form of jazz.

Ex. 45. Levinson, Jerry: *Darkness on the Delta,* Fox Trot

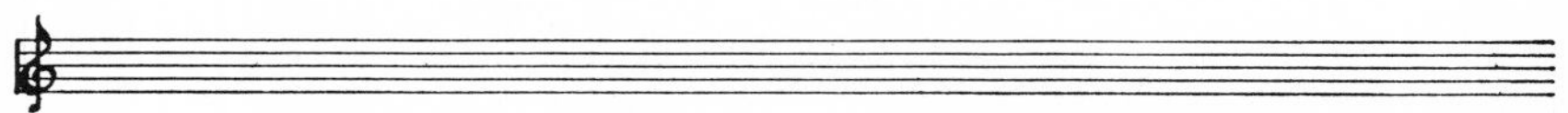

Ex. 46. Carpenter, John Alden: *Krazy Kat,* Ballet, Fox Trot

(Copyright, 1922, by G. Schirmer, Inc., New York 17, N. Y. Reprinted by permission.)

DANCES IN COMPOUND METER

Tarantella

This dance was of Neapolitan origin in the seventeenth century and was associated with tarantism (from the sting of a tarantula spider) and the town of Taranto. In either case, the *tarantella* is a fast dance of ever increasing speed, the music alternating irregularly between the major and the minor mode. In present-day music the tarantella is an instrumental piece in 3/8 or 6/8 time. The tarantella was a popular form around the middle of the nineteenth century.

Ex. 47. Mendelssohn, Felix: *Symphony No. 4,* Op. 90 (Italian), Theme 1

Ex. 48. Walton, William: *Façade, Suite No. 1,* "Tarantella–Sevillana"

(Copyright, 1936, by Oxford University Press, New York 16, N. Y. Reprinted by permission.)

Gigue

The *gigue,* or *jig,* a country dance, is of English origin and flourished as a dance after 1649. The dance was popular in the court of Queen Elizabeth and in France during the reign of Louis XIV. Though early examples have been found in 4/4 time, the eventual evolution was to some combination of threes—3/8, 6/8, 6/4, 9/8, or 12/8—in the eighteenth century. Because of its lively characteristics, the composers of the period chose the gigue as one of the dance movements of the classical suite, where it may be found in its idealized form. The gigue is usually the last movement of the suite.

Ex. 49. Bach: *French Suite No. 4 in E Flat,* "Gigue"

Ex. 50. Debussy, Claude Achille: *Images, No. 1,* "Gigues," Theme 1

(Permission for reprint granted by Durand & Cie, Paris, France, copyright owners; Elkan-Vogel Co., Inc., Philadelphia 3, Pa., agent.)

DANCE INFLUENCE ON NON-DANCE MUSIC

Early Suite Versus the Suite of Bach

Although the introduction of dance rhythms into art music (via the lute players) probably did not occur before the beginning of the sixteenth century, they did have a telling effect in the succeeding years in the formation of an indigenous instrumental style. Dance music provided the essential ingredients for this style, namely, rhythm, and the trend to monophonic melody (see p. 76) with the consequent breaking up of phrases into periods (see p. 184). The periodic division of the phrases into periods was a new feature since choral music had not previously used this technique. By repeating the eight measure period with a different cadence (see p. 184 f.) at the end, a form was developed which was basic to all instrumental and vocal music for centuries to come. Other factors contributed to the new instrumental style: (1) the vertical concept of music (see p. 96 f.); (2) the choice of the Ionian mode (see p. 77) as the vehicle for the new style; (3) the use of the variation idea (see p. 200 ff.) as a means of enlarging a composition; and (4) the idea for further musical expansion—the linking of several dances together.

In the early suite, we find a dance in duple meter—the most common being the *pavane,* followed by one in triple meter, usually the *galliard.* These groups of dances were usually preceded by a very primitive form of *prelude* which provided the means for a display of instrumental technic. The grouping of the contrasting dance movements—prelude, pavane, galliard—led to the suite of the seventeenth and eighteen centuries. In England these groups of dances were called *lessons;* in France, *ordres;* in Germany, *partitas;* and in Italy, *sonata da camera*—chamber sonata. Prior to 1650 the suite contained three movements, the *allemande* (German), *courante* (French), and *sarabande* (Spanish). The *gigue* (English) was added at a later date as an optional dance and was inserted after the allemande or before the sarabande. By the middle of the seventeenth century, the allemande, the courante, the sarabande, and the gigue, moving farther into the realm of art music, had lost their meaning as dances due to the constant weakening of the rhythm on the one hand and by the refinement of the texture and the style on the other. Thus, they lost their utilitarian purpose and became idealized dance forms.

Bach standardized the movements of his suites by employing them in the following order:

Allemande
Courante
Sarabande
Optional dance: *minuet, bourrée, gavotte, passepied, polonaise, rigaudon, anglaise, loure,* or *air*
Gigue

Bach's English Suites and Partitas are preceded by a prelude. His dance movements are in two-part form—binary form (see p. 190)—with each section of about equal length, or with the second section extended. The optional dances are of a contrasting character to the others, but they are simpler and keep the distinctive attributes of true dance music.

It is suggested at this point that the listener compare the dances of several Bach suites (see Appendix V), and, also, compare them with the respective dances by other composers.

Minuet

Of all the pre-classic dance forms, the minuet was the only one to survive the decline of the suite (circa 1750). Appearing in the operas and ballets of Lully and the suites of Pachelbel and others by 1700, its position in the operatic sinfonias of Alessandro Scarlatti and others was generally last. Through a process of evolution, the minuet ultimately became the *minuet-with-trio*, and, as such, was established as the next to the last movement of the symphony by the Mannheim School of composers. Haydn and Mozart retained this position, but gave the minuet greater speed and a lightness which ultimately led to the Beethoven *scherzo*—a movement in 3/4 time, of a symphony, sonata, or quartet, rapid in tempo, with strong rhythm, capricious in character, and often humorous. In listening to the minuet and the scherzo, the listener should not feel frustrated if he is unable to distinguish between some of them; even the experts sometimes find it difficult.

The following example represents the minuet in a later stage of development. The *trio* is the middle section placed between the *minuet* proper and its repetition. The trio derived its name from the seventeenth-century custom of writing for a trio of instruments in the second of the two alternating minuets—Minuet I, Minuet II (trio), Minuet I.

Ex. 51. Haydn, Franz Josef: *Symphony No. 6*, B. & H. No. 94; Third Movement, "Menuetto"

Minuet I

Minuet II—Trio

If you listen carefully, you will be able to hear this third movement Menuetto as three minuets:

Minuet I—Trio (Minuet II)—Minuet I

At this point it is suggested that the listener compare several of the third movement minuets of Haydn and Mozart (see Appendix V), and, also, compare them with minuets by other composers.

Sonata da Camera

While the classical suite was developing in France and Germany, Italy was cultivating the suite as a type of chamber music called *sonata da camera*—chamber sonata. As in the suite, the *sonata da camera* was a group of dances with no rigid order but retaining the custom of being nearly always in the same key. Originally intended as a vehicle for some chamber combination, as opposed to the orchestra, the essential character of the *sonata da camera* was that of the trio sonata in three parts —two upper parts with a thorough bass (see p. 10). Trio sonatas in four voices appeared near the end of the seventeenth century.

The *sonata da chiesa*—church sonata—was a trio sonata which had practically no relationship with the Church. Gradually the dancelike character of the movements was abandoned in favor of freer movements which substituted tempo marking for the dance titles, such as: Adagio, Allegro, or Presto.

Later, the *sonata da camera* and *sonata da chiesa* merged to become the sonata for solo violin with harpsichord accompaniment.

An example of the *sonata da camera* by Arcangelo Corelli is shown here. It was written to be performed by two violins, viola da gamba, and harpsichord. The movements included are: *Preludio, Allemande, Sarabande,* and *Tempo di Gavotte.*

Ex. 52. Corelli, Arcangelo: *Sonata da Camera in B-Flat,* Op. 2, No. 5

French Overture

The *French overture* is an expanded suite in which the dances are preceded by a long preparatory piece called an *overture.* This is a form which gained wide use in the operatic works of Jean Baptiste Lully and other French composers. The Lullian overture contained a slow, pompous, majestic first section, employing a dotted rhythm—♫ ♫ ♫—followed by a second section in a lively—allegro—fugato (see p. 207), and a coda (see p. 192) in the first tempo.

In the example that follows, Bach combines the French overture and its inevitable dotted rhythm with a series of dances. Here the closing section—coda—of the overture is extended into a third movement. The listener will also observe the inclusion of the "Air" for strings after the overture, which, it will be seen, is not in dance form. The work is scored for trumpets, oboes, kettledrums, strings, and continuo. In addition to the overture and the "Air," there is a *Gavotte, Bourrée,* and *Gigue.*

Ex. 53. Bach: *Suite No. 3 in D Major*

Modern Suite

With the exception of the vestiges of the suite found in such forms as the *divertimenti, cassation,* and the *minuet* of the *sonata-symphony,* the suite lay dormant until the last twenty years of the nineteenth century, when it again gained favor. However, this revival set a new pattern for the suite by replacing the traditional dances with a freer grouping which often included ballet and those with national tendencies. Composers found operas and ballets valuable source material for their orchestral arrangements. A case in point, though there are many others, is the following Tschaikowsky example. Here we not only find a freer grouping of dances within the suite, as opposed to the traditional, but the suite constitutes an arrangement of dances, some of which are national in character, from a ballet, *Casse-Noisette*.

Ex. 54. Tschaikowsky: *Nutcracker Suite*, Op. 71a

In the period 1915–1930 we find the suite represented in the contemporary works of composers who rediscovered Bach in the movement called *neoclassicism* (see p. 19 ff.). Their works constitute a throwback to forms and aesthetics which dominated the pre-Bach and Bach eras, hence, their interest in the eighteenth century form of the suite. Idealized versions of modern jazz dances have, of course, been substituted for the traditional ones. The Hindemith Suite is an excellent example of the neoclassic suite.

Ex. 55. Hindemith, Paul: *Suite for Piano, 1922,* Op. 26

(Copyright, 1922, by B. Schott's Soehne, Mainz. Renewed, 1949. By permission of Associated Music Publishers, Inc., New York 36, N. Y.)

Ragtime

"Apotheosis of the Dance"

Wagner considered the Seventh Symphony of Beethoven to be "a human-sphere-dance, the Apotheosis [deification] of Dance herself." Obviously, this remark refers to the spirit of the work and should not be taken literally. Although this symphony does not make use of actual dance forms, there does exist a continuous feeling of rhythmic regularity so pronounced as to cause it to be called by some the Dance Symphony. Here is a striking example of the influence of the dance on absolute music. All sorts of ideas, programmatic and otherwise, have been read into this symphony. But whatever Beethoven's programmatic intent, if any, the music must speak for itself.

Opening with a slow introduction of sixty-two bars, the remainder of the first movement, marked Vivace, contains four themes in 6/8 time, each in a skipping, rhythmic pattern.

Ex. 56. Beethoven: *Symphony No.* 7, Op. 92, First Movement

Introduction

Theme 1

It will be apparent to the listener that the skipping, rhythmic pattern not only generates the theme itself but also the entire main movement, even to the extent of the other three themes of the movement.

Arriving at the *Coda* (see p. 192) near the end of the movement, the listener will observe a syncopated rhythmic pattern of five notes in the bass parts, derived from the first theme, which continues for twenty-two bars while a tremendous climax builds up above it. For this seeming lack of consideration for the listener, it was said by Weber that "Beethoven is now ripe for the madhouse." History has since proved Weber wrong.

Coda

The second movement, because of its somewhat less than fast tempo and its strong rhythmic pattern, has been thought by some to be a wedding march. Others have felt merely that "time marches on," the movement suggesting the unvarying, unrelenting sameness of time itself. However, the pulsating rhythmic figure which generates the theme—hymnlike in character—and which appears as well in other parts of the orchestra, makes rhythm the dominant element of the movement.

The hymnlike theme is supported by a vertical harmonic structure in the key of A minor.

Ex. 57. Beethoven: *Symphony No. 7,* Op. 92, Second Movement

Theme 1

Theme 2, a countermelody, appears with theme 1.

Ex. 58. Theme 2

Theme 3 appears with a return to the key of D major.

Ex. 59. Theme 3

The third movement, marked Presto, is not only faster than the usual Beethoven scherzo, but very much faster than a minuet. The first part of the first theme is somewhat folkish in character.

Ex. 60. Beethoven: *Symphony No. 7,* Op. 92, Third Movement, Scherzo

Theme 1

Theme 2 appears in a slower tempo.

Ex. 61. Theme 2, Trio

The architectural plan of the movement is Scherzo, Trio, Scherzo, Trio, Scherzo, ending with a very short Coda.

The raucous 2/4 dance tune of the fourth movement obviously has the character of an Irish reel. Its bacchanalian character is aided and abetted by the basic and prime source of all music—rhythm. In this movement the apotheosis is reached. Here rhythm is purely physical—one is impelled to movement by the sheer driving force of the rhythm. Contrasted with the second movement, where rapt attention is demanded, the fourth movement seems to say, "Let yourself go!"

Ex. 62. Beethoven: *Symphony No.* 7, Op. 92, Fourth Movement

Theme 1

The second theme, almost as orgiastic as the first, only serves to lead to wilder moments.

Ex. 63. Theme 2

Ex. 64. Theme 3

March

No study of rhythm would be complete without a discussion of a form which, without exception, creates the strongest feeling for physical action—the march. Few can resist its martial qualities or mistake its implications. Its marching tempo and rhythms typified by stirring trumpets and drums, are infectious and full of energy.

The march, indebted to the minuet-with-trio form, usually has one or more trios inserted between a repeated march thus: march, trio, march; or march, trio, march, trio, march. The trio is usually less bombastic than the march itself and is more tuneful in character.

Marches fall into three classifications: (1) *military*, (2) *processional*, and (3) *funeral*. The military march is in quick, lively tempo, in duple meter, and is intended for marching, although this type is often found on band concert programs. The example given here is by the master of the military march, John Philip Sousa. Marches of the military variety serve, primarily, a utilitarian purpose.

Ex. 65. Sousa, John Philip: *Stars and Stripes Forever*

The listener will note that the march does not end with a return to the march, but ends with the trio, thus: trio—theme 3, interlude—theme 4, trio, interlude, trio.

Though the march as an art form dates back to the sixteenth century, it has had a notable effect on serious music, having had its widest use as a ceremonial rather than as a military march. The processional march, which falls into this category, is intended for processions such as occur at weddings, state occasions, commencements, and the like. The tempo is slower and more stately than that of a military march, but the time signature, and the structure remain the same. Composers of opera have, perhaps, made the widest use of this type of march. One of the most outstanding of the processional marches is found in the opera *Die Meistersinger* by Richard Wagner.

Ex. 66. Wagner, Richard: *Die Meistersinger,* Act III, Scene 5

Modern composers such as Gian-Carlo Menotti have also employed the processional march effectively in their works. Such a march is found in an opera written especially for television by Menotti, *Amahl and the*

Night Visitors. Here he employs a processional march for the entrance of the three Kings.

Ex. 67. Menotti, Gian-Carlo: *Amahl and the Night Visitors*

(*Copyright, 1951, 1952, by* G. Schirmer, Inc., New York 17, N. Y. *Reprinted by permission.*)

The Kings afar off

The three Kings wend their way along the mountain road

Appearance of the three Kings on the road

The *funeral march—marcia funèbre*—in duple meter, is a slow, stately, somber march that accompanies the rites for the dead—a dirge.

Of special significance to serious music was the elevation of this type of march to symphonic stature by Beethoven in the second movement of his *Symphony No. 3,* the "Eroica." It is also significant that Beethoven used the funeral march to sound the death knell of his sometime "hero"—Napoleon, to whom Beethoven had originally intended to dedicate the symphony. But when Napoleon, in 1804, made himself Emperor of France, Beethoven, disillusioned, destroyed the dedicatory page and ascribed the work instead "to the memory of a great man."

Certainly the second movement is one of the greatest funeral marches ever composed.

Ex. 68. Beethoven: *Symphony No. 3,* Op. 55, Second Movement

Theme 3

Theme 4

A later example, giving further stature to the funeral march as an art form, is found in the opera *Götterdämmerung* by Wagner. Besides being one of the best-known examples, it remains one of the most beautiful ever written.

Ex. 69. Wagner: *Götterdämmerung,* Act III, Scene 2

The funeral procession begins

As the funeral procession reaches the height, the following theme is heard

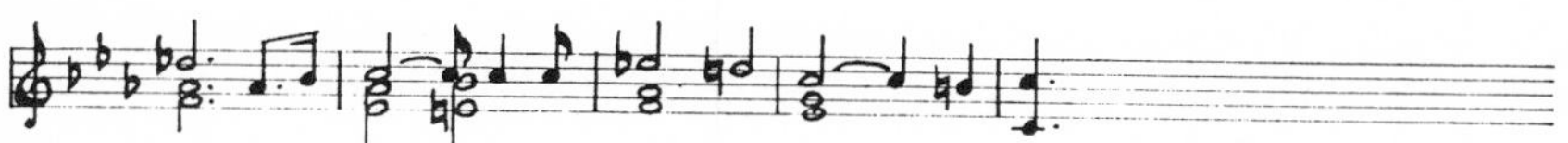

March as Absolute Music

The march as an art form has also made its contribution to the field of absolute music. In the hands of the artist, it becomes a thing of beauty—divorcing itself as it does from any relationship with the utilitarian, though the feeling of action may be as strong as the march intended for the out of doors. Such an example is found in the third movement of the Tschaikowsky *Symphony No. 6*—the "Pathétique." Here the mood of the march is elevated and exalted with telling effect. The march, at first intimated by the oboe, gathers momentum which culminates in a feverish march movement that is as full of splendor as it is overpowering.

Ex. 70. Tschaikowsky: *Symphony No. 6 in B Minor,* Op. 74, Third Movement

Theme 3

Among the modern composers, Prokofieff has often exhibited his fondness for marchlike tempos and rhythms—the "March of the Hunters" from *Peter and the Wolf,* Op. 67; the "March" from the opera *Love for Three Oranges,* Op. 33, being the best known. Prokofieff's abstract use of the march, written for the piano, is shown here.

Ex. 71. Prokofieff: *March,* Op. 12, No. 1

In our foregoing discussion of rhythm, it has been our purpose to show that (1) rhythm is a combination of tempo, accent, meter, and note values so contrived as to create specific patterns, easily recognized and understood by the listener; (2) rhythm can be used to create specific feeling; (3) rhythm, when associated with physical action, becomes largely an end in itself rather than a means to an end—the more subtle the combination of rhythm with melody and harmony, the more its aesthetic value is enhanced; and (4) the dance has been an important and lasting force in the progress of music.

The listener will find the recordings listed in Appendix V, which are to be used in conjunction with the study material of this Unit, to be very rewarding.

The Linear Aspects of Music: Melody and Counterpoint

Why is a melody? This seems like a facetious question. But truly, we are not sure, for melody is one thing to one group of individuals and something else to another. The philosopher speculates while the psychologist investigates.

The Psychological and Aesthetic Aspects of Melody

What we perceive as actual music involves an interrelation of such tonal aspects of music as *interval, scale* (see p. 87 ff.), rhythm (see Unit III), melody, and *harmony* (see Unit V). In other words, isolated tones do not produce music.

Psychologically speaking, when two tones of different pitch are sounded in succession, we perceive an effect which we call a *melodic interval.* The pitch differences of the two tones must be of distinct and significant size so as to be recognized as two different tones. Psychological studies have found that pitch differences between two tones as small as a quarter tone (see p. 118) can be perceived consistently as an interval, and anything less than a quarter tone creates the feeling that the pitch of the same tone is being slightly changed. However, our present system of tuning with its twelve half steps, *semitones,* to the octave precludes the use of intervals of less than a half step.

It is significant that intervals which we perceive with the greatest of ease and precision are those which are the most often used in music. This fact may be attributed, at least in part, to habituation and association.

What we perceive as a melody, then, is a succession of tonal intervals so arranged as to give a feeling of coherence and unity. In a succession of tonal intervals, movement is inherent and implied. But as the tonal intervals proceed one by one, they must create a feeling of continuous movement toward an objective. A melody, then, is the sum of its parts —development realized in fulfillment.

But how or why a succession of tones makes a melody is a moot question. Certain psychological data help us to answer this question. It has been found that: (1) *propinquity*—the nearness of one note to another as opposed to large skips—tends to give greater cohesiveness and continuity to a succession of tones;[1] (2) the *repetition* of its components—thus frequent repetition of the same tones within a sequence—may establish a specific tonal pattern as a melody;[2] and (3) the *finality* which a specific succession of tones may give through a downward movement of tones may create a feeling of conclusion—*cadence*—which is an attribute of melody, though it may be that in this instance we are influenced by what we are used to hearing.[3]

An aesthetic aspect of melody is whether it is beautiful or trite. "The very fact that we speak of some melodies as trite indicates that a tonal sequence can be a melody without producing an aesthetic effect."[4] We may say, then, that for a melody to be beautiful it must be subtle rather than obvious. A subtle melody is one which is crafty, artful, or sophisticated, while a trite or obvious melody is one which leans toward the "popular" and contains elements which are commonly familiar and are used in a common way. A newspaper editor once remarked that he "wouldn't give a nickle for a *tune* he couldn't whistle." To him a tune was good if he could remember and whistle it. Therefore, the less complex and sophisticated the melody the better the editor liked it because, so far as music was concerned, he reveled in the familiar, the sentimental, and the obvious.

As rhythm is the framework of melody, so harmony is the handmaiden of melody—some modern composers notwithstanding. Melody is pre-eminent from a historical, creative, and aesthetic standpoint—Gregorian chant. It is an element of fundamental importance and a test of a composer's artistic qualities. Over the centuries we have in turn glorified melody, harmony, tone color (see Unit VII), and rhythm. Perhaps, now, there is nothing left for composers but to complete the cycle by returning to the soul of music—melody.

The Rhythmic Aspects of Melody

Though melody is a single line of tones, not any line of tones will constitute a melody. In Ex. 72, each tone represents the two fundamental aspects of melody—pitch (see p. 86 ff.) and duration (see p. 135). There is motion in space—pitch—because of the up and down movement of the tones, and there is a certain lasting quality—duration—for each tone. But there is a stagnant quality about this succession of tones because of the lack of rhythmic distinction—they are tones in isolation.

Ex. 72.

To be meaningful, the tones in the preceding example must be organized so that they will not wander aimlessly in space like a free balloon. Melody, to be effective, must have a framework which provides forward motion and direction. Rhythm and meter (see p. 39 ff.)—the lifeblood of melody—supply the motive power for forward motion and direction. Using the same tones as in Ex. 72, notice how, in Ex. 73, life, shape, and direction are achieved by our would-be melody through rhythmic and metric organization.

Ex. 73. Harris, Roy: *Symphony No.* 3, Theme 1

Composers quite often use the same melody but treat it differently, rhythmically, and by so doing, give greater variety to their music.

Ex. 74.

Or, the composer may keep the same rhythmic pattern as in Ex. 73, but change the tones, thus creating a new melody.

Ex. 75.

Having observed the importance of rhythm to melody, let us hasten to say that rhythm is not always essential to melody. Is this a contradiction of what we have been saying, and, perhaps, always believed? The answer is "No," because we have been using the word rhythm in its broadest sense. Let us amend our definition of melody to say that it is a single line of tones which may be without rhythm but never without meter. This implies, then, that "rhythmless" melodies exist. There are many examples, but those below will illustrate the point. Compare them with Ex. 73, 74, and 75.

Ex. 76. Bach: *Art of Fugue,* Contrapunctus IX, Art of Fugue Theme

Ex. 77. Mozart, Wolfgang Amadeus: *Quartet in G,* K. 387, Fourth Movement

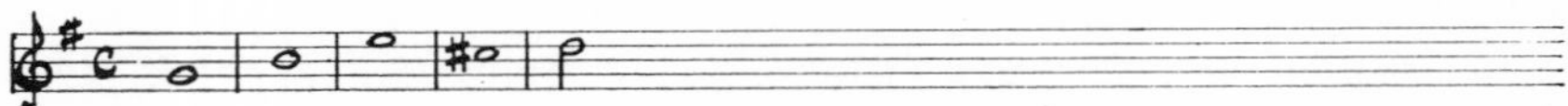

Ex. 78. Brahms, Johannes: *Symphony No. 4,* Op. 98, Fourth Movement

Ex. 79. Mahler, Gustav: *Das Lied von der Erde,* No. 1, "Das Trinklied vom Jammer der Erde"

(Copyright, 1911, renewed 1939, by Universal Edition (London) Ltd. By permission of Associated Music Publishers, Inc., New York 36, N. Y.)

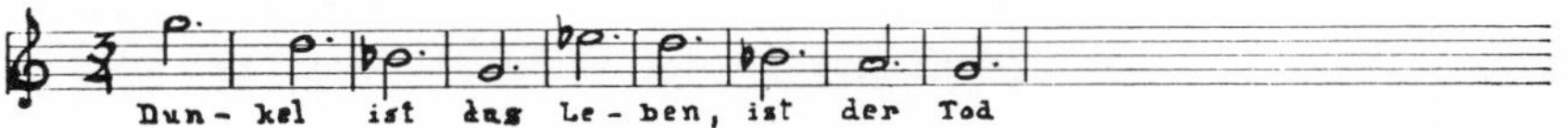

Ex. 80. Wolff, Erich: *Aus der Ferne in die Nacht,* Op. 12, No. 5.

(By permission of Harmonia Publishing Company, Tennent, N. J.)

Compare Ex. 81 with those just given, observing the forward motion inherent in the rhythm and meter.

Ex. 81. Stravinsky, Igor: *Les Noces,* Tableau IV, "Les Repas de Noces," Theme 3

(By permission of J. & W. Chester, Ltd., London, Publisher and Copyright Owner.)

The Climactic Aspects of Melody

We should speak of the effect that *climax* has on a melody. We have seen waves of the ocean that seem to move or reach up to a peak and then gently fall after the crest has been reached. So a melody, to have character, shape, and interest, must rise to a climax at least once during its progress. Melodies which move in stepwise fashion—*conjunct*—

are the more relaxing, while those which move mainly by skips—*disjunct* —create the most tension. Melodies usually make use of both conjunct and disjunct movement in space. The higher notes within a melody usually create the strongest feeling of tension.

Is Ex. 82 conjunct, disjunct, or both? How many climaxes does it have?

Ex. 82. Barber, Samuel: *Essay for Orchestra*, Op. 12, Theme 2

(Copyright, 1941, by G. Schirmer, Inc., New York 17, N. Y. Reprinted by permission.)

There may be a combination of several climaxes which all build to a still higher point of interest.[5]

Does Ex. 83 fit this idea of climax? Again, is it conjunct, disjunct, or both? Does its movement create a feeling of relaxation or tension? Are there other tension points besides the one reached in the climax?

Ex. 83. Britten: *Peter Grimes*, "Four Sea Interludes," Op. 33a, Fourth Interlude, Theme 2

(Copyright, 1945, by Boosey & Hawkes, Ltd., New York 19, N. Y. Used by permission.)

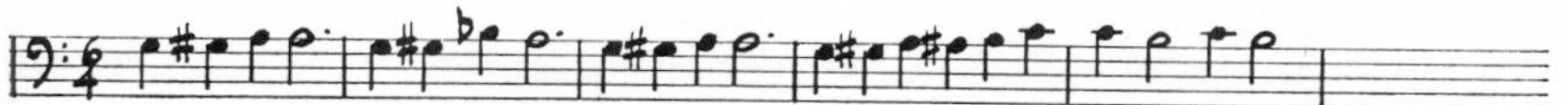

The idea of climax can be applied to whole compositions, as well as to melodies, as in the case of the Ravel *Bolero*, where one climax is added to another and another by first starting the orchestration with the drums, and by adding instrument after instrument, the piece finally reaches its psychological and aesthetic climax near the end where there is a sudden breaking off.

The principle of climax is present to a greater or lesser degree in all of the fine arts.

REALIZATION OF THE MELODIC ELEMENT

Three divergent textures in which the element of melody plays a dominant role may be observed in our music today. Called *monophonic*, *polyphonic*, and *homophonic* (also called *monodic*), these textures roughly outline the progress of music history from the earliest times to the present. Let us examine them singly.

Monophonic Melody

The period A.D. 600–A.D. 1500 is very important to the development of music, especially that of song, for during these years two important styles developed. The first was *monophonic* (a single melodic line without additional parts—harmony—or accompaniment) *sacred music;* the second, *monophonic secular music*—minstrelsy—which developed outside the Church.

The form which monophonic music took within the Church was called the *chant*. *Gregorian chant*—liturgical chant named after Pope Gregory I who gave it its final arrangement and code of laws about the year 600—sometimes called *plainsong* or *plain chant,* is the most important type and remains in use today in the Roman Catholic Church. Gregorian chant is characterized by free flowing rhythm devoid of meter (see p. 39 ff.), beats, or regular phrases. It is sung partly by the choir and partly by a solo voice. The texts are largely prose and are usually taken from The Psalms. The tonal system of the melodies is based on the church modes, or scale patterns.*

The church modes are a series of diatonic scales, in which one of the tones acts as the central tone. This evolved into a system which created scales on *d, e, f, g, a,* or *c,* called, respectively, the Dorian, the Phrygian, the Lydian, and the Mixolydian—authentic modes. The Aeolian and the Ionian—also authentic modes—though never recognized by the Roman Catholic Church, were added later to the eight age-old church modes by Glareanus in his theoretical work called the *Dodekachordon.* Each of the authentic modes had another mode dependent on it called Hypodorian, Hypophrygian, etc.—plagal modes.

The examples show the octave ranges of the authentic and the plagal modes and the *dominant* of each. It should be remembered that the scales represented by the octave ranges shown are diatonic scales, that is, scales consisting of whole and half steps, as represented by the white keys on the piano, the half steps occurring between e–f and b–c.

Ex. 84.

Dorian

Hypodorian

* At the discretion of the instructor, the material on pp. 76–80 may be omitted.

Phrygian

Hypophrygian

Lydian

Hypolydian

Mixolydian

Hypomixolydian

Aeolian

Hypoaeolian

Ionian

Hypoionian

An example of the style of notation used in Gregorian chant is shown in the next example. Notice the four-line staff, the clef sign, and the notes (neumes).

Ex. 85.

(*Examples of Music Before 1400,* ed. by Harold Gleason. *Copyright, 1942, F. S. Crofts & Co., Inc. By permission of Appleton-Century-Crofts, Inc., New York 1, N. Y.*)

Reduced to modern notation this becomes:

Ex. 86.

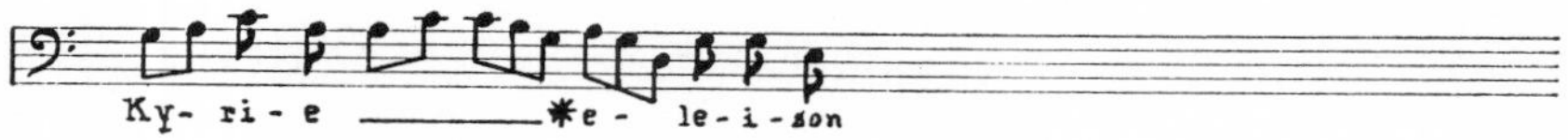

It should be pointed out that Gregorian chant is really a hybrid form resulting from the use of materials from the Jewish liturgy and those of the Greco-Roman period.

The next example shows the use of Gregorian chant in modern composition.

Ex. 87. Respighi: *Gregorian Concerto,* Second Movement (Partitura)

(*Copyright, 1922, renewed 1950, by Universal Edition* A. G., *Vienna. By permission of Associated Music Publishers, Inc., New York 36, N. Y.*)

Other modern composers who have reverted to the use of modal scales are Debussy and Vaughan Williams. The next two examples are in the Aeolian and the Mixolydian modes respectively.

Ex. 88. Debussy: *Children's Corner Suite,* "Jimbo's Lullaby"

(*Permission for reprint granted by Durand & Cie, Paris, France, copyright owners; Elkan-Vogel Co., Inc., Philadelphia 3, Pa., agent.*)

Ex. 89. Vaughan Williams, Ralph: *Pastoral Symphony*, Third Movement

(*Copyright, 1922, by J. Curwen & Sons, Ltd., London. Used by permission of the publishers.*)

Polyphonic Melody

The history of polyphonic melody is essentially the development of choral music. The earliest form of part singing had its origin about A.D. 900. These early attempts at harmony were really the combining of two melodic lines which occurred when men and women sang together, since men's voices are approximately an octave below women's voices. From this beginning a style of music developed which combined two or more melodies according to certain rules. This, then, is the definition of polyphonic music. One of the early forms of polyphonic music was called *organum* (accent on the first syllable).

ORGANUM serves as the connecting link between monophonic where chanting was done in octaves (male and female voices)—called *magadizing*—and the later science of musical composition called *counterpoint.*

STRICT ORGANUM was a form of organum in vogue in the ninth and tenth centuries. There were two kinds of strict organum, simple and composite. Strict simple organum required that the parts move in fourths (diatessaron) or fifths (diapente) in parallel motion. We can see, then, that this device created two melodic lines as shown here.

Ex. 90. Simple Organum at the Fourth from *Musica Enchiriadis*

(*Examples of Music Before 1400*, ed. by Harold Gleason. *Copyright, 1942, F. S. Crofts & Co., Inc. By permission of Appleton-Century-Crofts, Inc., New York 1, N. Y.*)

The upper melodic line was the principal voice—*cantus firmus*—and the lower melodic line was the added voice—*organalis* (duplum). Similarly, organum at the fifth would be as follows:

Ex. 91. Simple Organum at the Fifth from *Musica Enchiriadis*

(*Examples of Music Before 1400*, ed. by Harold Gleason. *Copyright, 1942, F. S. Crofts & Co., Inc. By permission of Appleton-Century-Crofts, Inc., New York 1, N. Y.*)

By doubling the upper and the lower voices a kind of counterpoint was developed called *composite organum.* Here the principal voice was doubled at the octave below and the added voice—the organalis—was doubled an octave above.

Ex. 92. Strict Composite Organum at the Fifth from *Musica Enchiriadis*

(*Examples of Music Before 1400*, ed. by Harold Gleason. *Copyright, 1942, F. S. Crofts & Co., Inc. By permission of Appleton-Century-Crofts, Inc., New York 1, N. Y.*)

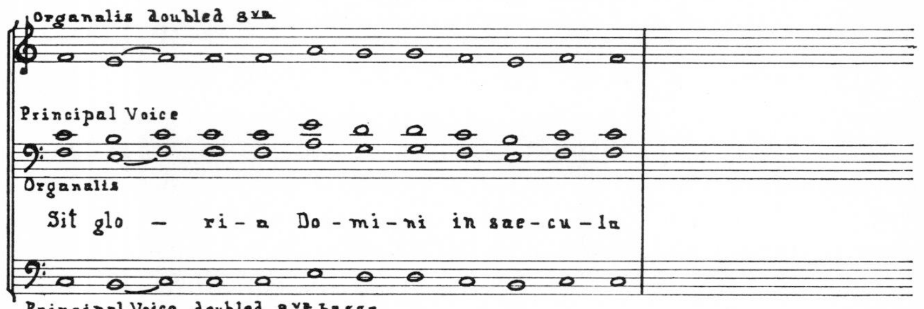

Modern composers have gone back to ancient times for something "new." Below we see how Debussy has used organum for an interesting effect.

Ex. 93. Debussy: *Preludes*, Book I, No. 10; "La Cathédrale engloutie"

(*Permission for reprint granted by Durand & Cie, Paris, France, copyright owners; Elkan-Vogel Co., Inc., Philadelphia 3, Pa., agent.*)

Free Organum. In the eleventh and twelfth centuries a free style of melodic writing was developed called *free organum*. In this style the second voice still followed the principal voice, note for note, but without being restricted to parallel motion, with the result that there was an increasing emphasis on contrary motion. Oblique motion was also permitted and the interval of the fourth was preferred over the fifth since it was believed to be less harsh.

Ex. 94. Contrary Motion Ex. 95. Oblique Motion

The intervals permitted besides the fourth were the major third, the minor third, and the major second.

The next step was permitting two or more notes in the second voice to be written against one note in the principal voice. This device created a chance to compose more freely.

Consonance and Dissonance. To have a condition of *consonance* and *dissonance*—arbitrary terms used for purposes of classification only—melodies must be sounded in combination. Generally speaking, consonance in music is a term used to describe those tones which are considered, by most people, to be relaxing sounds, and dissonance is the term used to describe those which create tension—a psychological as well as an aesthetic consideration. Consonance—relaxation—and dissonance—tension—are affected by such factors as register, dynamics, timbre, spacing, etc. When we compare the music we hear about us every day with that of earlier periods in music history, we can see that our ideas of relaxation and tension have changed a great deal over the centuries. Today, the following give a feeling of rest or repose and are considered to be consonances:

Ex. 96.

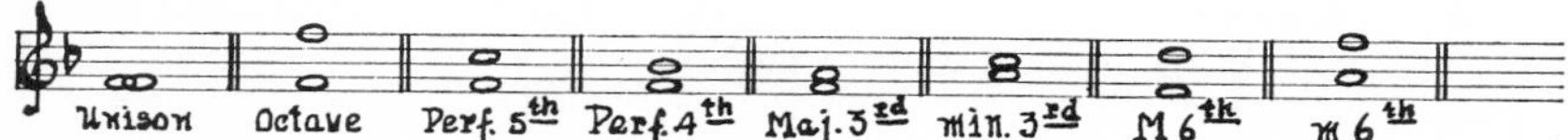

Dissonance is one of the motivating factors of music. The following notes show some combinations which create a feeling of tension or pull toward a point of *resolution*, hence, are considered to be dissonances.

Ex. 97.

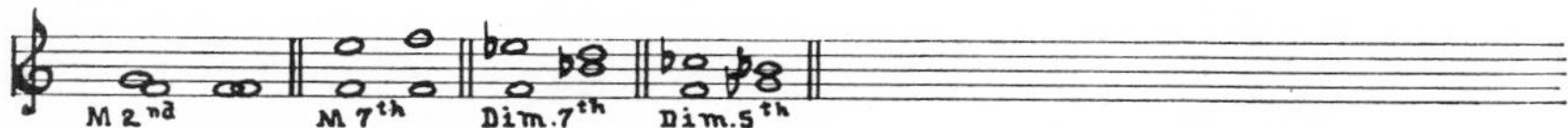

Examples 96 and 97, when combined with certain other tones, may be expanded into what we call chords (see p. 97 ff.), a discussion of which we need not pursue at this point.

Counterpoint. The system of combining two or more relatively independent melodies is called counterpoint. But before this systematization could reach its zenith in the great polyphonic era—1300–1600—certain changes with regard to rhythm and consonance took place. Rhythmically, music evolved from the free flowing style of Gregorian chant and organum to modal rhythms—set rhythmic patterns in triple meter—and finally, to the introduction of duple meter shortly before 1300. In the sixteenth century duple meter became the standard. In sixteenth-century counterpoint, rhythm is the essence of the combination of two or more melodies.

During this period of musical development ideas of consonance changed from a preference for parallel fourths, fifths, and octaves to the use of thirds and sixths in a highly developed system of movement and combination.

Counterpoint, in addition to being the combination of two or more relatively independent melodies, may also be identified as *horizontal* music. Only at the points where the individual horizontal strands of melody coincide, is harmony—or vertical structure (see p. 96 f.)—created. In the polyphonic era composers were not interested in vertical masses of sound as we know them today. Their interest was primarily a melodic one, the harmony being subservient to the free flow of melodies. The vertical structure of music will be discussed in the next Unit.

Imitation. The device known as *imitation* is the essence of contrapuntal music. To gain a quick understanding of this principle we need only to refer to any of the *rounds* with which we are familiar. In Ex. 98 we see that each voice repeats or *imitates exactly* the first voice which has the original theme. When each succeeding voice enters, it too imitates exactly the original theme. This form is called a *canon* and this kind of imitation is called *strict counterpoint*.

Ex. 98. *Row, Row, Row Your Boat*

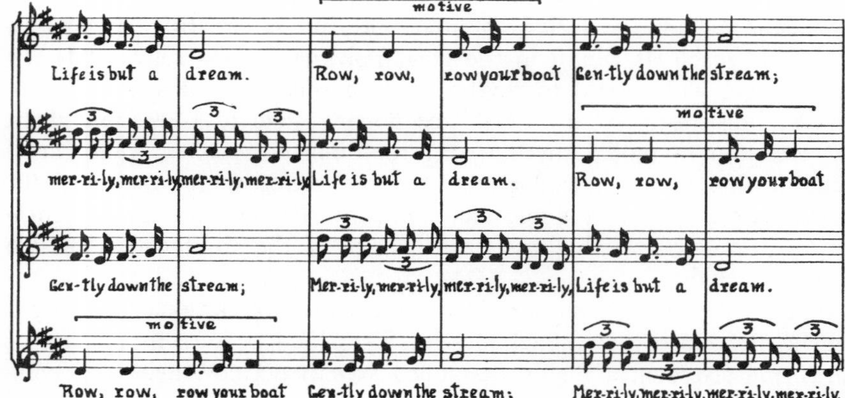

The chief differences between a round and a canon are these: (1) in a round each imitating voice *must* enter at the same pitch level—unison —which is not a requirement of a canon (canon at the unison, the octave, and the fifth are the most common); (2) a round inevitably returns to its beginning, and may be repeated any number of times, whereas a canon is not bound by this rule; and (3) the round has no ending while the canon may have an ending called a coda (see p. 192). So, we may say that all rounds are canons, but not all canons are rounds. There are about nine different types of canon.

Having its first real beginning in the fourteenth century, imitation became the basis of all contrapuntal music of the sixteenth century and reached its zenith in the polyphonic *a cappella* style—choral music without instrumental accompaniment—of Philippe de Monte, Orlando di Lasso, and Giovanni Pierluigi da Palestrina. This period is often referred to as the Golden Age of counterpoint. The accepted forms of sacred music of the Golden Age were the *Mass* and the *motet*, while the *madrigal* was the favored form of secular music. Imitation was the basic device for these forms.

The MASS, a religious rite—the sacrament of the Lord's Supper—of the Roman Catholic Church had its culmination in the form finally adopted in the eleventh century. The Mass is the heart of the Catholic liturgy, and has always been musically important.

There are two main divisions of the Mass: the Proper—*Proprium Missae,* and the Ordinary—*Ordinarium Missae.* The various subdivisions of the Proper, which frequently include psalm texts, change from day to day, depending on the day being celebrated. With the exception of two phrases in Greek at the beginning of the Ordinary, a Latin text is employed throughout the Mass.

Contrasted with the Proper, the Ordinary has a fixed text. The Ordinary has five main subdivisions called, after their initial words: (1) *Kyrie eleison*—"Lord, have mercy upon us," (2) *Gloria in excelsis deo*—"Glory to God in the Highest," (3) *Credo in unum Deum*—"I believe in one God," (4) *Sanctus*—"Holy, Holy, Holy," and (5) *Agnus Dei*—"Lamb of God who beareth the sins of the world."

Example 99 is a portion of a Kyrie and shows how counterpoint is constructed by adding melody to melody. The imitation shown is at the octave and, later, at the fifth. The counterpoint is, however, in a "free" style, since neither the rhythm nor the melody continue in strict imitation of each other. The style of Palestrina is based on the church modes (see p. 76ff.), hence, is called modal counterpoint.

The double G clef shown below in Tenor I and Tenor II is used as a tenor clef, and indicates that the parts lie an octave lower than written.

Ex. 99. Palestrina, Giovanni Pierluigi da: *Mass: Vestiva i Colli,* "Kyrie"

(Examples of Gregorian Chant, *Compiled by G. F. Soderlund. Third Edition Copyright, 1946, F. S. Crofts & Co., Inc. By permission of Appleton-Century-Crofts, Inc., New York 1, N. Y.)*

N.B. The accidentals appearing above the notes may have been employed through the use of musica ficta rules.

The next example shows the use of strict counterpoint by a contemporary American composer. Compare this example with the Kyrie by Palestrina.

Ex. 100. Bacon, Ernst: *Seven Canons,* IV, "The Pelican."
Two-part canon in unison

(Copyright, 1948, by Music Press, Inc. Used by permission of the copyright owner, Mercury Music Corporation, New York 3, N. Y.)

*I and II voices may be: I = women, II = men, or both men or women.

It should be pointed out that up to about 1250 instruments, such as they were, were used only to double the voice part or the parts, or occasionally to sound a tone. Between 1250 and 1600 instrumental music, as such, developed, but it was below the standard set by vocal music.

Homophonic Melody

The form of melody we are now to study was the direct antithesis of polyphonic music. Whereas polyphonic music placed emphasis on the relative independence of each melodic line, *homophonic* music placed its emphasis on one melodic line, which may itself be ornamented, supported by a chordal style accompaniment or one which was more or less embellished, but subordinate and subservient to the melody. This "new music" was a reaction against the restrictions of the purely contrapuntal style of the sixteenth century.

Homophony (also called monody) had its origin in the aesthetics of the late Renaissance, which emphasized naturalism in all forms of art. So it became necessary for the musicians to seek a style which would be more expressive and more direct. Espoused by a group of musicians called the *Camerata,* this new music was based on the ancient Greek music drama. As the result of this "pioneering," lyric expression was based on personal feeling, a form developed in the seventeenth century which eclipsed the original aesthetic ideas of the Camerata. That form was the *opera,* the homophonic features of which were the *recitative* and the *aria.*

Though song—a short composition for solo voice—has been a dominant force from earliest times, it remained for a comparatively recent era to give it impetus, spurred by the subjective lyric poetry of Goethe and Heine. The modern *art song*—an artistic creation of studied simplicity in which the union of poetry and music is consummated in a homophonic form—is the product of the Romantic era. The early nineteenth century saw the union of romantic poetry and music in the songs—*lieder*—of Franz Schubert and, later, those of Robert Schumann and Johannes Brahms. The *lied,* pre-eminently German, became known all over Europe in the last half of the nineteenth century and made a lasting contribution to the subsequent cultivation of the art song in other countries, notably by the romanticists and the modernists of France, England, and the United States.

It should be pointed out that as a result of these aesthetics instrumental music moved, in the seventeenth and the first half of the eighteenth century, to a point equal in importance to that of vocal music. Since 1750 instrumental music has led the way.

PITCH. In the previous Unit on Rhythm, we saw the organization of notes into divisions of long and short. Notes may also be arranged into "high" and "low" according to their position on the great staff, which placement gives them definite pitch. The notes of the great staff are shown in relation to the piano keyboard. Staff notation as we know it had its origin about 1600. Earlier, the staff varied from three to ten lines.

PIANO KEYBOARD AND GREAT STAFF

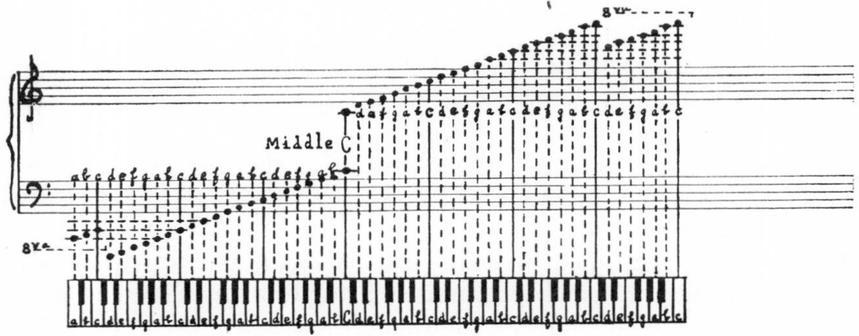

The *G clef* —generally called the treble or "soprano" clef—is placed on the top five lines and arbitrarily makes the second line G. From this sign we can find all of the other notes on the staff. The *F clef* —generally called the bass clef—is placed on the bottom five lines and arbitrarily makes the fourth line F. Notice the addition of the two dots to the sign. In piano music, the G clef is generally reserved for the right hand while the F clef is used for the left hand.

In writing music for other instruments, namely, the *viola,* the *cello,* the *trombone,* the *bassoon,* and occasionally the *double bass,* a *C clef* is used which is a movable clef, but is usually used either on the third or the fourth line but never in a space. In viola music, the treble clef frequently appears to avoid the use of too many leger lines, lines added above or below the staff.

Alto Clef Tenor Clef

The indicated pitch of any note may be altered by placing before it an *accidental, e.g., sharp* (♯), *flat* (♭), *double sharp* (x), *double flat* (♭♭), or *natural* (♮).

The black keys shown on the keyboard are used for both *sharps* (♯) and *flats* (♭) and take their names from the nearest white keys. Thus, C-sharp is the first black key to the right of middle C, while D-flat is the first black key to the left of D. We see, then, that this black key has the same pitch but two different spellings. This "sameness" of pitch and difference of spelling is called an *enharmonic equivalent.* By the same token, B-sharp is also C, etc. Enharmonic change also takes place by spelling D as C-double sharp (x), and also as E-double flat (♭♭). Enharmonic change is applied to intervals and chords for convenience in modulating from one key to another.

A *natural* (♮) cancels, at least for the remainder of the measure, any other accidental.

INTERVALS. As we said earlier, an interval is the difference in pitch between two tones. This difference in pitch is characterized by numbers which describe the staff distance from one tone to the next as:

c–c	c–d	c–e	c–f	c–g	c–a	c–b	c–c′
Unison	Second	Third	Fourth	Fifth	Sixth	Seventh	Octave
perfect	major	major	perfect	perfect	major	major	perfect

When a major interval is reduced in size a chromatic half step, it becomes *minor.* By increasing the size of a perfect or major interval a chromatic half step, the interval becomes *augmented*. When a perfect or minor interval is contracted in size a chromatic half step, it becomes *diminished*. Seconds, thirds, sixths, and sevenths may be made major or minor, augmented or diminished, by the use of accidentals. Unisons, fourths, fifths, and octaves are perfect because each tone exists in the scale of the other.

TONALITY

As a reaction against the church modes employed in the polyphonic music of the sixteenth century, the tonal basis of the seventeenth century was the *major* and the *minor* scales—and consequently major and minor keys—whose derivation may be traced to the Ionian and Aeolian church modes, respectively. The types of scales which have developed from this beginning are called *diatonic*—major and minor, *chromatic*, and *whole-tone*. Broadly speaking, tonality means faithfulness to a *tonic*, that is, to a central tone to which all other tones of a scale are related and around which the melody or chords move.

> It is advisable to guard against the familiar misconception that scales are made first and music afterwards. Scales are made in the process of endeavoring to make music and continue to be altered and modified, generation after generation, even till the art has arrived at a high degree of maturity.[6]

The above named scales do not exhaust the list of all known scales, but are those which have been adopted for use in the music of the Western world.

Diatonic Scales

All major and minor scales are derived from a succession of melodic intervals of a specific pattern laid out according to whole and half steps. In a *diatonic major* scale the pattern is shown by playing all the white keys on the piano from middle C to c¹ thus:

Ex. 101. Diatonic Major

In other words, in a diatonic major scale the half steps must occur between 3–4 and 7–8, all the others being whole steps. There are seven *sharp* (♯) keys and seven *flat* (♭) keys in addition to the one *natural* key just shown. An example of a song in a diatonic major key follows:

Ex. 102. Hopkinson, Francis: *My Days Have Been so Wondrous Free*

(*Copyright, 1951, by Carl Fischer, Inc., New York 3, N. Y. Oliver Daniel, arranger.*)

The note the scale begins on determines the name of the key.

In a *diatonic minor* scale, the half steps must occur between 2–3 and 5–6, all others being whole steps. The essential difference between the major and the minor modes is that in the minor mode, the third step is always a half step lower than its corresponding major—C major, C minor. This pattern is called the *natural* or *pure* minor. By using the white keys again from a^1 to a^2 the scale is as follows:

Ex. 103. Diatonic Minor

In this example the whole and half steps remain in the same position both ascending and descending. Let us see how this scale is used in the following example.

Ex. 104. MacGimsey, Robert: *Shadrack*

(*Copyright, 1931 and 1937, by Carl Fisher, Inc., New York 3, N. Y. Words and music by the composer.*)

There are two other forms of the diatonic minor scale, the *harmonic* and the *melodic*. It will be observed that certain of the accidentals described above will be required in the construction of these scales.

Ex. 105. Diatonic Minor, *Harmonic Form*

Notice that in the previous example the seventh tone has been arbitrarily altered, sharped, and thus the half step is shifted from 5–6 to 7–8. In the harmonic form of the minor the whole and half steps occur at the same places both ascending and descending. Example 107 is an example of an old *spiritual* which employs the harmonic form of the minor scale. See also the use of both the natural minor and the harmonic form in the first eight measures of the Mozart *Symphony No. 40.*

Ex. 106. Mozart: *Symphony No. 40,* K. 550

Ex. 107. Burleigh, Henry Thacker, arr.: *Go Down, Moses*

(By courtesy of G. Ricordi & Co., New York 23, N. Y.)

In the scale shown in Ex. 108, observe the whole and the half steps in the ascending and descending patterns.

Ex. 108. Diatonic Minor Scale, *Melodic Form*

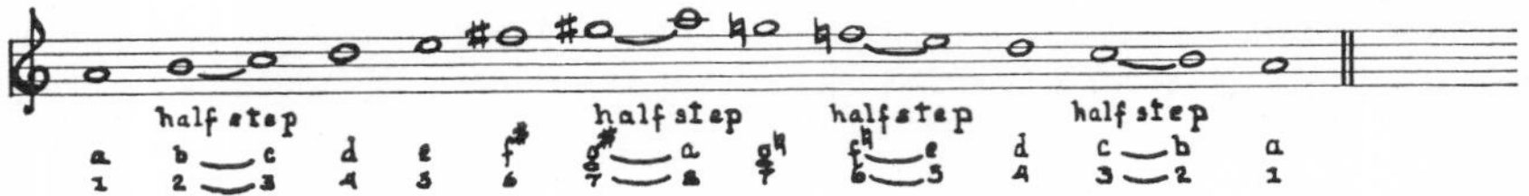

It will be observed in this example that the sixth and seventh tones of the scale have been altered—raised—ascending, while in the descending scale they have been altered—lowered—again, thus making the descending scale a natural minor by restoring the half steps to their original position of 2–3 and 5–6. There are three forms of the minor scale for each minor key, making forty-five scales in all. Does Ex. 109 fit the requirements of the melodic minor?

Ex. 109. Poulenc, Francis: *Poèmes de Ronsard,* I. "Attributs"

(By permission of Huegel & Cie, Paris, France, copyright owners. Theodore Presser Co., Bryn Mawr, Pa., agent.)

Though the *trained* ear is the sole judge, the general principles governing the use of the harmonic and the melodic forms of the minor are these: (1) the implied harmony determines the use of the raised or lowered sixth or seventh degrees of the scale; (2) when 6–7 or 7–6 are used consecutively as *chord tones,* and occasionally when the second of the two is a *nonchord tone,* the harmonic form is used; and (3) when 6–7 or 7–6 are used consecutively and when one or both are *nonharmonic* tones (see p. 106 ff.), the melodic minor is used.

Chromatic Scale

The history of *chromaticism*—as a melodic and harmonic device—dates back to the thirteenth century use of *musica ficta*—the use of extra-modal flats and sharps in the church modes "by reason of beauty" or "by reason of necessity." Their use was so widespread that Pope John XXII issued a Papal Bull in the fourteenth century (1324/5) which not only banned practically all forms of polyphony in the Church, but struck out against its injurious practices. Instead of stemming the tide, it served only to advance the cause of polyphonic secular music in which chromaticism was an essential ingredient.

True chromaticism begins about 1540 with the madrigals of Willaert and De Rore. It continued as a melodic device through the Baroque, the Classic, and the Romantic periods, after which chromaticism was employed both melodically and harmonically to a much greater degree, as we shall see in Unit V.

In the *chromatic*—duodecuple—scale, tones outside the regular diatonic scale are used, the succession of which produces a series of twelve half steps within the octave. A chromatic melody is one in which one or more tones are introduced which are outside the ruling diatonic key. If by the introduction of the chromatic notes a *modulation* (see p. 109 ff.) occurs, the notes are no longer chromatic but belong to the new key.

Ex. 110. Chromatic Scale

The spelling of the chromatic scale is a moot question. Though the lowered fourth degree—G-flat—in the descending chromatic scale—usually called the melodic version—is found in many textbooks, this form is not supported by the practice of composers. Hence, the use of F♯ in Ex. 110. Notice how the chromatic scale is employed in the next example and the use of the raised fourth degree descending.

Ex. 111. Griffes, Charles Tomlinson: *Sorrow of Mydath*, Op. 9, No. 5

Whole-Tone Scale

This scale was an innovation of the last decade of the nineteenth century and, in general, was a revolt against the romanticism of the nineteenth century. This new movement was called "impressionism" and its originator in the field of music was Debussy. While the materials used by Debussy were new, yet the very essence of impressionism was programme music. Musically, impressionism was a forward step, but aesthetically it was a continuance and climax of the programmatic ideas of the Romantic movement. Impressionism had its origin in the pictures of the French painters of the period with whom Debussy was very well acquainted.

Debussy upset many rules and traditions to bring his aesthetic principle to fruition. Chief among the changes was his use of a scale without half steps called the *whole-tone* scale. When constructed, the scale contains but six tones and is limited to two "keys."

Ex. 112. Whole-Tone Scale

It will be observed that by combining the two *pentatonic* scales the chromatic scale evolves. These pentatonic scales are also the source of the whole-tone scale. Note the absence of half steps. Debussy went back to the Chinese for this scale, although the pentatonic scale is not confined to any one country, but appears to be universal, since it is found also in the music of the Japanese, the Irish, the Scotch, the Indians, and the Eskimos. The pentatonic scale may be shown by playing the black keys on the piano.

The use of whole steps only gives each tone of the scale equal function, thus destroying the feeling of a definite tonality—key center, a feeling of "direction" in the melodic contour, and permits the use of irregular and fragmentary phrases. All of this tends to give the music a feeling of vagueness, as when one holds a piece of fine, fragile, translucent china up to the light and then places his hand between the china and the light. What one sees, then, is not the hand itself, but only the image of the hand. This is impressionism.

Notice the use of the whole-tone scale in the following example.

Ex. 113. Debussy: *Cinq Poèmes de Baudelaire,* "Harmonie du Soir"

(Permission for reprint granted by Durand & Cie, Paris, France, copyright owners; Elkan-Vogel Co., Inc., Philadelphia 3, Pa., agent.)

Voi - ci ve - nir les temps où vi - brant sur sa ti - ge

In the next example Debussy uses the pentatonic scale. Compare this with the previous example.

Ex. 114. Debussy: *Nocturnes,* "Nuages," Theme 3

(Permission for reprint granted by Editions Jean Jobert, Paris, France, copyright owners; Elkan-Vogel Co., Inc., Philadelphia 3, Pa., agent.)

Impressionists also used the modal scales to further their programmatic ideas (see p. 28 ff.) while discarding the sonata and the symphony for smaller forms which were more adaptable to pictorial representation.

UNIT V

The Vertical Aspects of Music: Harmony

Webster says that harmony is a "just adaptation of parts to each other; agreement between the parts of a design or composition giving unity of effect or an aesthetically pleasing whole." What are the parts of harmony musically speaking, and how may they be combined to add to our aesthetic experience?

The Psychological and Aesthetic Aspects of Harmony

Harmony is melody in third dimension, and is the sublimation of melody because it enriches a single line of tones. This is not to say that harmony supersedes melody, for it is melody which germinates harmony and gives it movement and form.

Harmony may be said to have three related connotations: (1) the term *harmony* is applied to the simultaneous sounding of three or more tones, it is mass musical sound; the distance between the tones is called harmonic intervals; (2) this definition also applies to a *chord;* (3) to have harmony there must be a succession of chords which are related in some way to each other. When tones are combined, we have a feeling of consonance and dissonance (see p. 81), of repose or tension, satisfaction or dissatisfaction. Harmony forces us to be more conscious of consonance and dissonance because tones are combined rather than stated singly as in a melody. In the previous Unit, we said that a melody may be described as a sequence of tones which were significant because of their relationship to a central tone and which creates a feeling of finality. In harmony, the same principles of progression exist. In consonant chords the tones tend to fuse, which gives the hearer a feeling of oneness with the chord to the extent that he feels identified with it. This is a complete aesthetic experience—for the hearer the chord becomes a thing of beauty.

Over the centuries we have seen how our ideas of what is consonant have changed. Whereas only the unison, fourths, fifths, and octaves were formerly permitted, we have added to these intervals many more which, to us today, seem consonant. How much dissonance can be added to harmony for it to be beautiful remains a moot question at the present time. However, as our tastes change our ideas of what is beautiful may also change. Emerson says, "The love of beauty is taste; the creation of beauty is art."

As we said in Unit IV, dissonance is one of the motivating factors in music because it sets up conflict between tones. A dissonant tone is one which does not belong to a given harmony but belongs to another and, therefore, sets up a rivalry with the prevailing harmony—a psychological aspect. A discord is a tone which does not belong to any harmony. Dissonances tend to enrich the harmony. Since discord does not rule out beauty, a musical composition steeped in discord may be a "beautiful" work of art—an aesthetic consideration.

The old saying that "people like what they know and know what they like" is only too true, because the things which we say we know and like are steeped in familiarity. We have been hearing the same chord progressions for centuries. So it is that we urge you to listen to as much modern music as possible. Through the medium of these Units you will come in contact with the fundamentals of music which will result in your being able to listen to serious music without frustration, and thus be able to develop and improve your taste.

Consonance and Dissonance

We have been theorizing and speculating up to now about consonance and dissonance. Let us now examine some facts in order to understand more completely this phenomenon which is fundamental to most of the harmony with which we are familiar today. This phenomenon is called the *harmonic series,* or *overtone series.* If we were to strike a single string having the pitch of C, called the *fundamental,* we would find that it is not just one tone but a combination of various other tones called *partials.* The fundamental tone C would be divided into the following partials:

Ex. 115. Harmonic Series

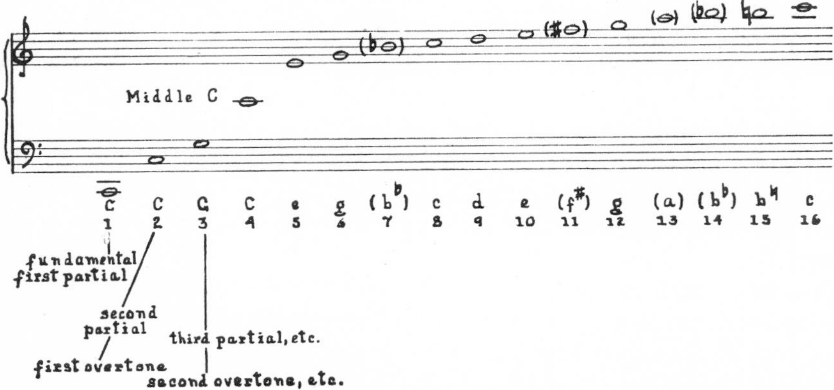

You will see that there are sixteen partials. However, the division does not stop here but continues, the higher partials becoming continually weaker and weaker. In reality, they even extend beyond our limits of hearing. We can now see from the tones shown in Ex. 115, the great possibilities for consonance and dissonance. The first eight tones are the consonant tones, while the next eight are the dissonant ones. Play each set of eight on the piano, holding each key down so that the tones will continue to sound. You now hear how these tones sound when played in succession. Now, strike the first eight together, then the second eight. Which group of eight sounds the better? Why? The first group is the more consonant—blend—because there is less clash—dissonance. Over the centuries, composers have been combining more of the tones contained in the last eight of the harmonic series with the first eight, and with themselves, thus creating a harmony which is increasingly more dissonant. Now, if we take the partials which would result from striking every tone contained within the octave from C to C, we would eventually have all the tones which are contained in the chromatic scale from C to C (see p. 91 f.). Each tone in the chromatic scale is a partial resulting from striking a given fundamental—each fundamental dividing in exactly the same pattern as shown.

THE STRUCTURE OF HARMONY

Both polyphony and harmony had their origin in early organum (see p. 79 ff.). You will recall that in organum tones were combined in unisons, fourths, fifths, and octaves. The preference for these intervals (see p. 87 f.) in combination actually created the first *vertical* structure in music. However, this style of writing did not gain much favor until about the middle of the sixteenth century, at a time when polyphony was at its height with its attendant emphasis on the combination of parallel (horizontal) melodies. Toward the latter part of the sixteenth century music began to appear in which voices moved in *chordal* (vertical) style. The increased interest in the vertical movement of music brought about an expanded concept of tonality (see p. 88 ff.) in the last half of the seventeenth century. This concept made it possible to determine the relationship of the different degrees of the scale to the *tonic* or key center. Whereas, the use of modal scales (see p. 76 ff.) had made music very restrictive, the concept of tonality gave freedom to music through its use of major and minor scales and the resultant use of *modulation*—the movement away from one key and the establishment of a new tonality. Beginning about 1750 and continuing into the twentieth century, music has been concerned with vertical structure on which a single melody was hung, and, which melody was dependent on the effective movement of blocks or chords for its life—called *homophony*. The structural basis of this new concept was called *tertian* harmony, a system based on the interval of the third. Since 1900 this theory has become more and more confused because of "new" theories of harmonic structure, as we shall see later.

The Triad

A triad is the simplest chord in music, and it forms the basis of most of the music we know today. The triad results from the combining of two thirds—a *major triad* consisting of a major and a minor third, a *minor triad* consisting of a minor and a major third—and they are known as "three-note chords." The triads on C shown in Ex. 116 are major and minor respectively, their distinguishing feature being the middle note for which they are named.

Ex. 116.

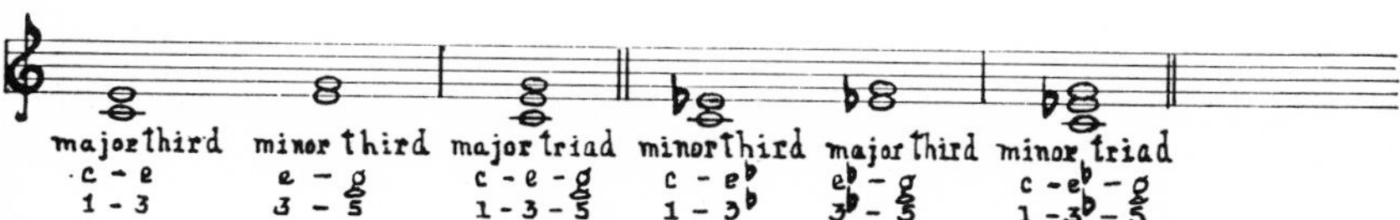

Major and minor triads are classified as consonant, since their intervals are consonant; all other triads, then, are dissonant (see consonance and dissonance, p. 81 and p. 95 f.).

A fourth tone may be added to the triad which is not a new tone but the octave of the bottom tone (root) of the triad.

Ex. 117.

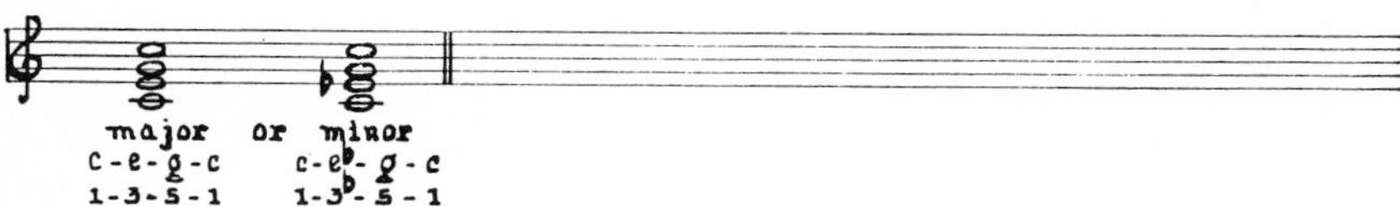

These triads remain triads so long as the fourth note is the same as one of the notes in the triad. Further, the triad remains the same no matter which tone is on the bottom, in the middle, or at the top. The C-major triads shown in Ex. 118 are all the same except for the fact that the notes are arranged differently, and are called *root position*, *first inversion*, and *second inversion* respectively.

Ex. 118.

Statistically, in a study confined to diatonic harmony, Budge has shown that in the period of music literature between 1700 and 1785 which is based mainly on the major and minor scales, of the forty-four various chords counted, the tonic (I) chord with its inversions I^6–I^6_4 ranked first, fourth, and fifth respectively in order of frequency.[1] This fact emphasizes the importance of the tonic triad as a fundamental factor of tonality. Some "ultra" modern music tends to make us appreciate the tonic triad even more.

As triads may be inverted, so may intervals (see p. 87 f.) thus:

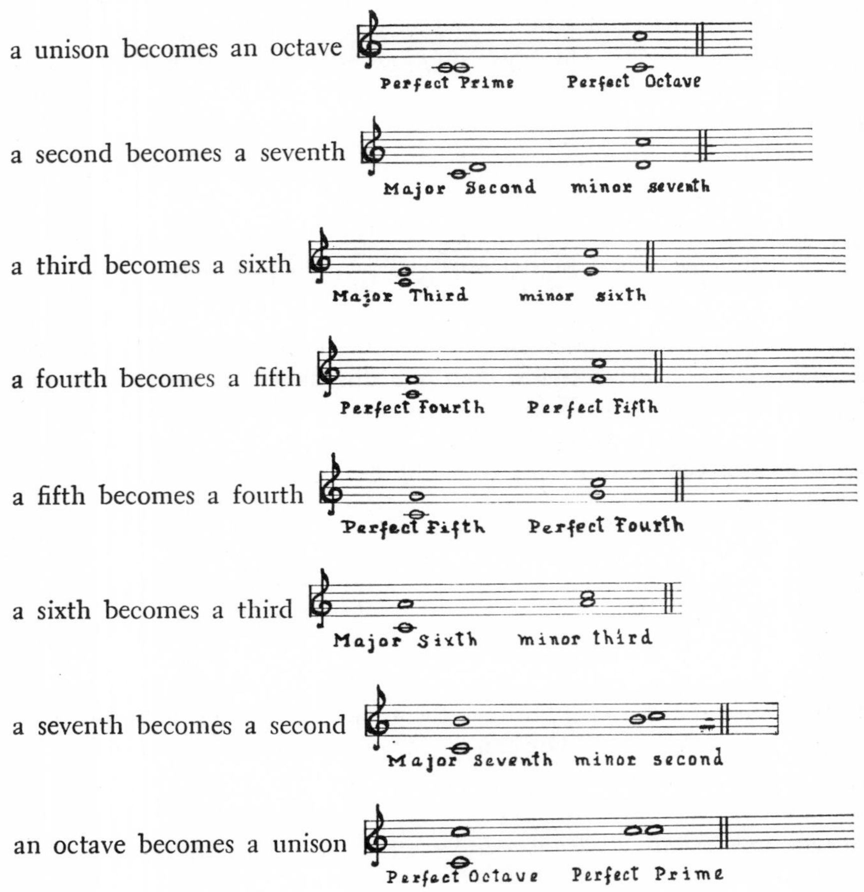

Related Triads

Like each of us who has family relationships, triads have certain other triads to which they are related—some close, some distant. On any of the twelve tones within an octave it is possible to erect a major triad. Of the triads closely related to the tonic triad, we find the first and most important one to be that erected on the fifth tone of the scale —the DOMINANT. Hence, if we construct a triad consisting of a major third and a minor third on G, it will be known as the dominant triad of the key of C. Because of the active tones b and d in this triad it demands resolution to a chord of greater consonance. The dominant triad, then, generates other chords and, consequently, is a tonality-determining factor in music. In the Budge study previously referred to, the dominant triad ranked third in order of frequency.[2]

Ex. 119.

A dominant exists for each of the twelve tones in the octave. It is possible to write music by using only the tonic and dominant, and many compositions have been written using these two triads. The triads use the Roman numeral I for the tonic and V for the dominant. In the simple harmonization shown in the following example observe how the I and V chord are outlined in the melody.

Ex. 120. Schubert, Franz: *Wohin?* (Whither?), Op. 25, No. 2

It can be seen from the preceding scale that the dominant tone from F is C. Therefore, F becomes the second most important tone from C which makes the tone C closely related to both G and F. The relationship may be represented as an equation—G:C = C:F—and stands in the family as brother and sister.

Ex. 121.

The SUBDOMINANT is so-called because it is a fifth below the tonic. This chord is not as strong in function as the dominant because it creates less tension, which fact may be observed by alternately playing the dominant to tonic, and subdominant to tonic, as:

Ex. 122.

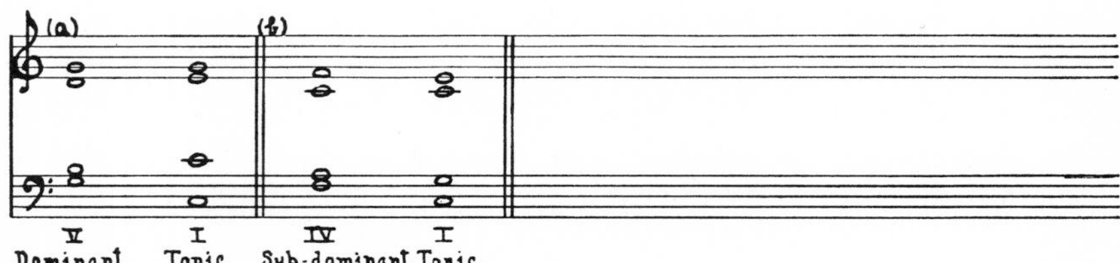

Notice in (a) that G is *common* to both chords, while in (b), C is the *common* tone in each chord. This, then, makes F related to G once removed which makes it have less "pull" or attraction for the tonic principally because the element of dissonance is less.

Remember, too, that every tone of the scale is a dominant or subdominant of some other tone. This fact plays an important part in the principle of modulation (see p. 109 ff.).

Many compositions have been written which use only I–IV–V chords. It should be remembered that these chords occur in all major keys and, of course, have the same functional use. Practice in writing and playing these chords would be to the listener's advantage at this point. Recognizing them by ear is just as important as recognizing them by sight. The notes marked (x) are nonharmonic tones and will be discussed later.

Ex. 123. Irish Air: *Wearing of the Green*

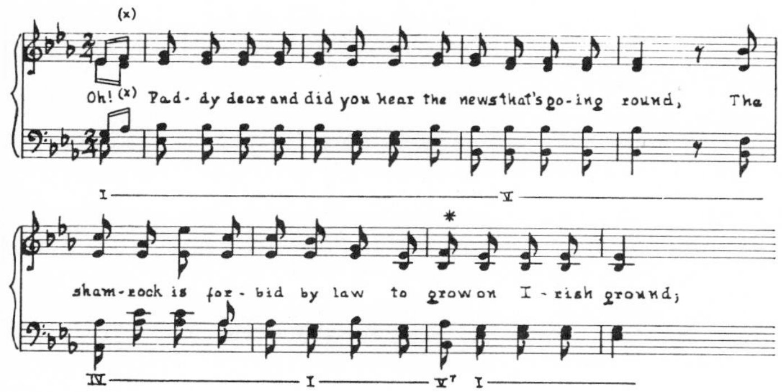

The chord marked (*) is a seventh chord (see p. 104).

If we erect two minor thirds on a root, we have what is known as a DIMINISHED TRIAD. It derives its name from the fact that the triad thus formed will contain a small fifth (b–f) which is itself a *diminished* interval. It is a dissonant triad and, like the dominant, is a chord of motion, creating tension, and requiring resolution.

Ex. 124. Diminished Triad

If we erect a triad on every tone of the major scale we find the following triads with their number, name, and quality.

Ex. 125.

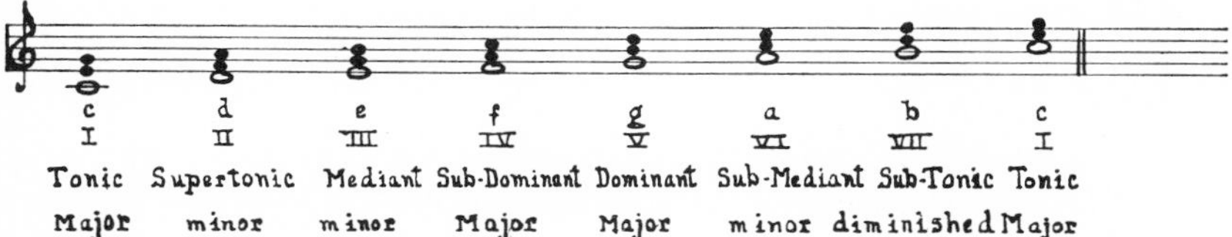

Three different kinds of triads, each with a specific quality, appear in the example just shown. There is still one other kind which results from erecting two major thirds on the root. It is an AUGMENTED TRIAD, taking its name from the large fifth (c–g♯)—an *augmented* interval. Like the diminished triad, it too is classified as dissonant.

Ex. 126. Augmented Triad

As we erected major, minor, and diminished triads on the several tones of a major scale as shown, so we can erect major, minor, diminished, and augmented triads on the several tones of a MINOR scale. In comparing the quality of the triads in Ex. 127 with those shown in Ex. 125, you will observe that the chords once major have become minor—I and IV, while V remains major in both modes (see Ex. 127); VI becomes major in the minor mode, III becomes augmented, while II and VII are diminished in the minor mode.

Ex. 127.

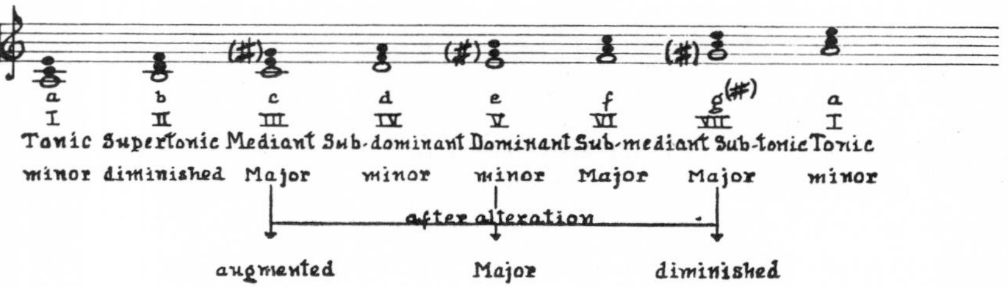

The *same tonality* is inherent in both the scales—the key signature remains the same, only the mode is changed.

Though the minor scale uses the same key signature—signs at the beginning of a composition—of the major scale beginning on the third degree of the minor, it fails to make provision through the key signature for the seventh degree (leading tone) to remain in the usual half-step relationship to the tonic. Hence, it is necessary to alter the seventh degree by an accidental in order to preserve the relationship of the seventh degree to the tonic (see accidental [♯]), thus creating the harmonic form of the minor scale (see p. 89 f.). Thus, the V chord remains major in both modes.

Major and minor scales having the same key note or letter name are called *parallel;* major and minor scales having the same key signature are called *relative;* thus:

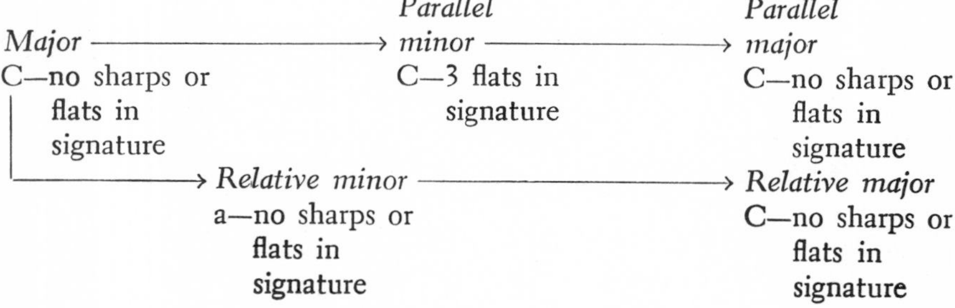

Let us observe the structure and compare the quality of the triads on the root C in this example:

Ex. 128.

It should be noted that the quality of any triad can be changed merely by the addition or the subtraction of accidentals.

The next three examples are parts of two songs and a chorale. See if you can name the different kinds of chords in each.

Ex. 129. Old English Melody: *Greensleeves*

Ex. 130. Foster, Stephen Collins: *Jeanie with the Light Brown Hair*

The notes marked (x) are nonharmonic tones and will be discussed later.

Ex. 131. Bach: *Herr Jesu Christ, du höchstes Gut*

The notes marked (x) are nonharmonic tones and will be discussed later.

For purposes of analysis, Roman numerals are used to identify each chord. Chords tend to progress in the following order:

rare (III → I) rare (IV → VII)

III to I or VI to IV or II to VII or V to I—Key Center

This shows the places where the chords fit best and seem to be more "at home."

The **seventh chord** is a chord of four tones which results when we erect three thirds on a root. This combination of intervals creates a chord consisting of a root, a third, a fifth, and a seventh, the chord deriving its name from the latter interval. The seventh chord sounds harsh—dissonant, and is one of the kinds of chords which helps to give forward movement to music by creating tension or pull. This tension makes us feel that the seventh chord must be *resolved* to a chord of greater consonance. The seventh chord plays a very important part in creating a feeling of tonality. The chord shown next is a *dominant seventh* with its chord of resolution. In the Budge study (*op. cit.*) the V^7 chord ranks second only to the tonic in order of frequency.

Ex. 132.

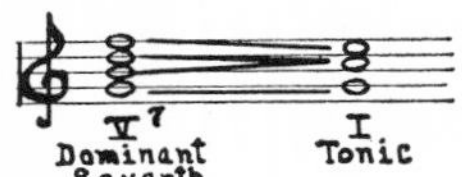

Ex. 133. Wagner: *Tannhäuser,* Act III, "Pilgrims' Chorus"

The notes marked (x) are nonharmonic tones and will be discussed later.

A seventh chord can be created on any degree of the scale by observing the definition of a seventh chord given here. This chord, while used sparingly in the seventeenth century, is used extensively in the music of the eighteenth, nineteenth, and twentieth centuries. Other types of seventh chords are shown herewith.

Ex. 134.

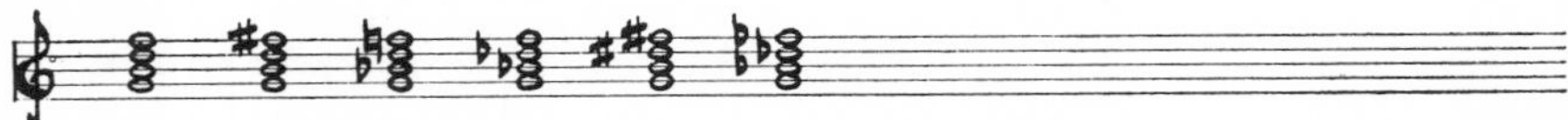

If we add another third to the seventh chord, we have a **ninth;** another added third would give an **eleventh** chord. Add another third to the eleventh chord and a **thirteenth** chord results. Each of the three chords takes its name from the outside interval. We can also build these chords on every degree of the scale and invert them just as we can triads. The ninth, eleventh, and thirteenth chords are much more dissonant and complex than the seventh chords. As triads can be written in major and minor tonalities, so can sevenths, ninths, elevenths, and thirteenths. The ninth chord gained greater use in the nineteenth and twentieth centuries, while the elevenths and thirteenths belong to the twentieth century. In the fifteenth chord shown, it will be observed that the top tone repeats its root. Obviously, then, the limit for the addition of thirds has been reached in the V^{13}.

Ex. 135.

We can see from these examples how the constant addition of dissonant partials of the harmonic series has been utilized, which use has made our "new" music more and more dissonant.

Ex. 136. Franck, César: *Sonata in A major*, First Movement, Theme 1 (for Violin and Piano)

(Reproduced with permission of the publisher, C. F. Peters Corporation, 373 Park Avenue South, New York 16, N. Y., who published the complete Sonata under Peters Edition 3742. Edited by Maxim Jacobsen.)

Note the dissonant effect created by the use of the ninth chord in the preceding example. In four-voice writing, the fifth is omitted, and the chord usually occurs in root position.

Ex. 137. Debussy: *Arabesque No. 1 in E*

(Permission for reprint granted by Durand & Cie, Paris, France, copyright owners; Elkan-Vogel Co., Inc., Philadelphia 3, Pa., agent.)

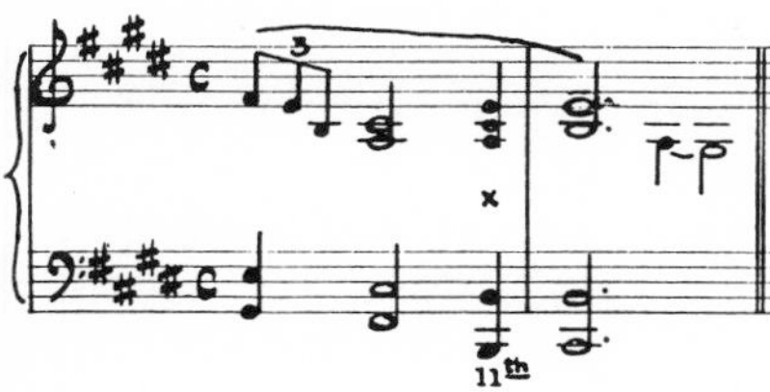

Ex. 138. Debussy: *Pelléas et Mélisande*

Nonharmonic Tones

Tones that are added in any voice as embellishments and which are outside the harmony are called *nonharmonic tones*. These tones are used to give more tension and movement to music. They are of several types.

Passing Tones. These are nonharmonic tones that pass between two chord tones. Passing tones may be used singly or in thirds or sixths.

Ex. 139.

Ex. 140. Bach: *Mach's mit mir, Gott*

Suspension. This is a nonharmonic tone that is delayed in its resolution, thus prolonging the dissonant effect.

Ex. 141.

Ex. 142. Bach: *Wie schön leuchtet der Morgenstern*

Appoggiatura. The movement of a dissonant tone to its note of resolution without previous preparation is called an *appoggiatura.*

Ex. 143.

Ex. 144. Tschaikowsky: *Piano Concerto in B-Flat minor,* First Movement

Neighboring Tone. This is a type of passing tone which does not pass but returns to the harmonic tone which it left.

Ex. 145.

Ex. 146. Bach: *Herr Gott, dich loben alle wir*

The chord marked (x) is the third inversion of the V^7. The nonharmonic tone marked (*) is an appoggiatura.

ANTICIPATION. This type of dissonance is created when a tone of the next chord is introduced before its regular time.

Ex. 147.

Ex. 148. Bach: *Werde munter, mein Gemüte*

ÉCHAPPÉE. The *échappée* (*escape tone*) is a nonharmonic tone which moves stepwise ascending from a chord tone and leaves the chord tone by a leap downward to the next harmonic tone.

Ex. 149.

Ex. 150. Bach: *Ach Gott, wie manches Herzeleid*

PEDAL POINT. This dissonance results from the holding of a tone through a succession of chord changes. The pedal, which begins and ends as a chord tone, is usually on the tonic, subdominant, or dominant note of the key. It is usually found in the bass, and is used more often in instrumental music than in vocal music.

Ex. 151.

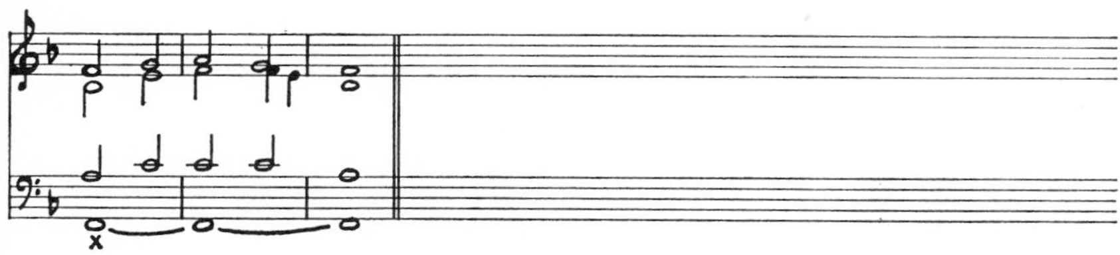

Ex. 152. Bach: *Well-Tempered Clavier,* Vol. I, "Fugue XX," Coda

MODULATION. In music, the movement toward and the establishment of a new tonality is called *modulation.* By modulation, a new key level is attained, which device gives greater variety of harmonic color to a composition. Modulation may be achieved by several means.

Common Chord. By this means modulation is achieved through a chord which is *common* to both keys. The movement may be from major to major, major to relative or parallel minor, minor to minor, or relative or parallel minor to major, depending on the chord selected as the common chord. Because of our system of tuning—equal temperament—it is possible to modulate through the twelve keys from C and arrive again at the key of C. This is achieved by the use of common chords. This movement of chords is shown by the use of a Circle of Fifths. The next example shows a *common* (*pivot*) *chord* modulation. This type may also be called a *diatonic modulation.* (*See next page.*)

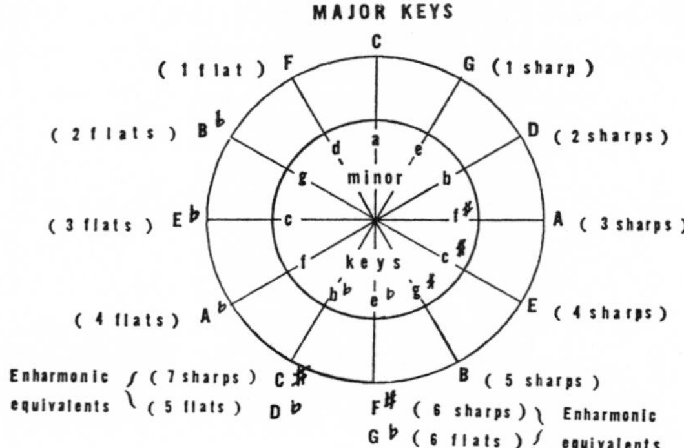

Ex. 153. Mozart: *Fantasia No. 3,* K. 397, "Allegretto"

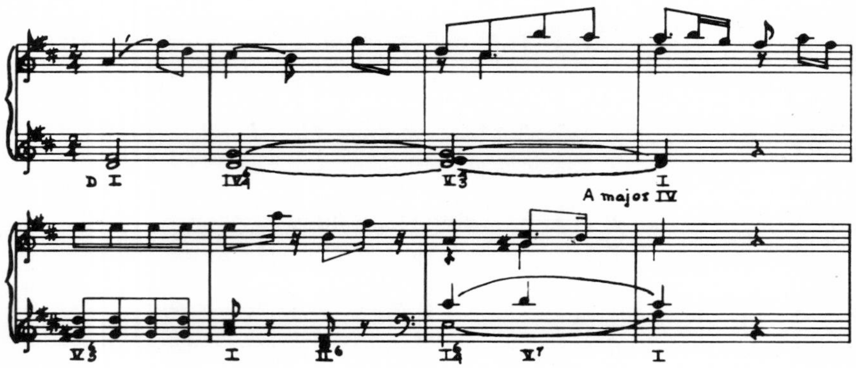

Enharmonic Change. An example of this type of modulation is shown (Ex. 154) at the point marked "x." The black notes represent the enharmonic change. The notes contained in this chord are called *enharmonic equivalents*—the same sound with different spelling of the chords.

Ex. 154.

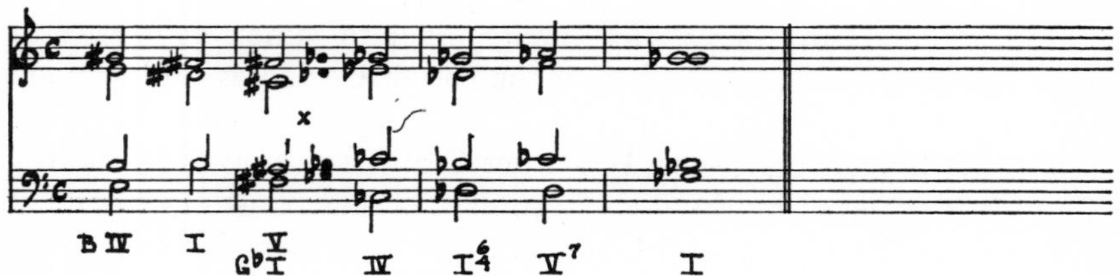

Chromatic Alteration. Chromaticism is the use of tones or chords outside the diatonic key. To modulate by this means is merely to arbitrarily alter by accidentals—sharp, flat, or natural signs—one or more tones of a chord in order to get into a new key. The following example is one of the more common ways of modulating by chromatic alteration. Notice also the chromaticism in the melodic line.

Ex. 155. Chopin: *Mazurka,* Op. 68, No. 4 (Posthumous)

The listener should realize that other types of altered chords may be used in the course of a composition. The *Neapolitan Sixth* (Ex. 156) is to make us aware of the fact that these chords exist largely for the purpose of modulation. The N6 is usually found in the first inversion.

Ex. 156. Beethoven: *Sonata,* Op. 14, No. 1, "Rondo"

The material presented in this Unit contains the essential ingredients of what may be termed conventional harmony. Its structure is a composite of (1) consonance and dissonance, (2) chords and related chords, (3) sevenths and altered chords, (4) ninth, thirteenth, and fifteenth chords, (5) nonharmonic tones, and (6) modulation. The listener would do well to spend considerable time in the study of the foregoing material and in listening to the records listed for this Unit in Appendix V before proceeding to the greater complexities of the next Unit.

UNIT VI

New Tonal Concepts

Over the past several centuries, our harmonic system has been based on a concept of tonality which operates on the premise that tones tend to revolve around a key center. Since 1900 this philosophy has been overthrown by the rejection of this harmonic system in general and the established ideas of consonance and dissonance. Ernst Toch has this to say:

> In order to discuss these terms [consonance and dissonance], we must first put aside their popular connotations of 'beautiful' and 'ugly.' The identification of the 'dissonance' with 'cacophony' or, for that matter, with any aesthetic consideration whatsoever does not touch the technical significance of the term. Nor does the wholesale rejection of contemporary music of any epoch because of its 'dissonances' differ in any way from the wholesale rejection of any innovation in any field of art or science before its general acceptance.
>
> So let us disregard any aesthetic considerations and approach the question from a purely technical viewpoint.
>
> Dissonance can exist only if and where there exists consonance. The two terms are interconditioned as are big and small, light and dark, warm and cold. All these antagonistic concepts which suggest diametrical contrasts, are quite useful indeed as handy communication symbols of our everyday language. In reality, however, the terms of each pair are only different gradations of the same quality, or idea, or phenomenon. Physics does not know warmness and coldness, but just 'heat,' which covers the whole range from the lowest measurable or conceivable temperature ('degree of heat') to the highest. A certain definite temperature, felt as a chill if suddenly occurring in the tropics, will be felt as real heat in the arctic regions. Man is a huge giant as against the microbe, yet himself a microbe in the face of a glacier. Between these two arbitrarily selected sizes are innumerable others, filing progressively by in an endless row. In the light of light there are countless shades of shade. At what point does dark, the small, the cold cease and the light, the big, the warm begin?[1]

This statement, which was quoted at some length, represents in essence the thinking of such theorists and composers who, in more recent years, have introduced us to a harmonic system distinguished by an absence of tonality and replete with dissonance (see *atonality,* p. 114 ff. and *polytonality,* p. 116 f.). The listener is encouraged to keep an open mind and, after sufficient listening, to let his ear tell him what to accept, for the ear is the final judge and jury of what it will accept as beautiful and psychologically agreeable and satisfying. The psychology of music and aesthetics will not be violated if we accept "ultra" modern music on its own standards rather than by the old. However, it is likely that the foregoing statement refers to the element of taste rather than to a change in the psychological and aesthetic aspects of consonance and dissonance.

We have discussed the use of chromaticism melodically and harmonically. While the chief function was to add more melodic and harmonic color, it did, at the same time, hasten the breakdown of tonality. This collapse became apparent with the advent of Debussy's whole-tone scale (see p. 92 f.) which established the aesthetic principle called impressionism. Also, *modality*—a reversion to the church modes of the Middle Ages and the Renaissance—again interested the composer. We need, now, to become familiar with these new styles not only because they exemplify new trends in tonal construction, but because they represent the music of our time.

The "Mystic Chord"

Scriabin was another innovator of the twentieth-century impressionism of whom we should speak briefly. Instead of chords built on thirds, as in the case of Debussy, Scriabin evolved a six-note chord built of fourths (which is the reason for including it under the heading of new music) called the "mystic chord." Up to now our harmonic structure has been built on the interval of the third—tertian harmony. Now we find a completely new idea. A scale built on C would look like the following:

Ex. 157.

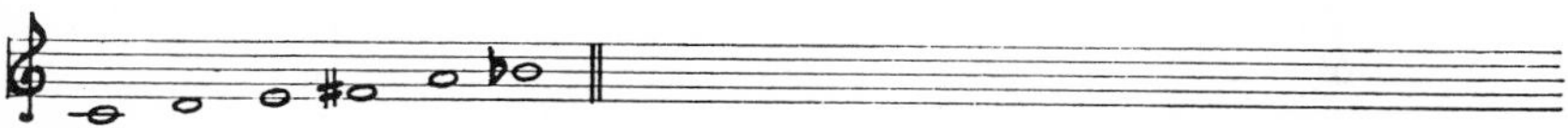

The "mystic chord" which would result from such a scale is shown below:

Ex. 158.

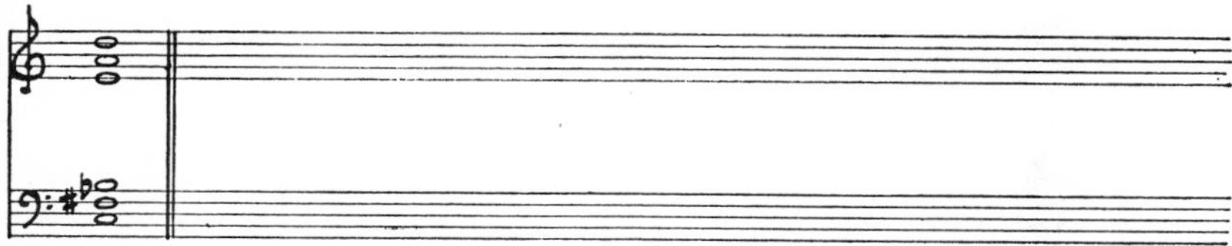

If the listener will refer to the harmonic series shown on page 95, he will see that the scale and the chord derive from the partials beginning with

8 and progressing through 14. If we analyze the intervals of this chord from the bottom up, we find an augmented fourth, a diminished fourth, an augmented fourth, a perfect fourth, and a perfect fourth. This is a new kind of sound and the listener should practice hearing it by itself before he tries to recognize it when combined with other sounds. In the following example the mystic chord is identified in the measure marked "x."

Ex. 159. Scriabin: *Quasi Valse,* Op. 47

(Used by permission of The Boston Music Company, Boston 16, Mass., copyright owners.)

The spelling of this chord is b-flat–e–a-flat–d–g–c. In this chord, dissonance—or a wider conception of consonance—is its essence which, in turn, tends to obliterate a feeling of a tonal center to which we have been conditioned over the years.

Atonality

About the same time that Stravinsky was breaking with the chromaticism of the late nineteenth century, an even stronger and more radical revolt was taking place in Europe in the person of Arnold Schoenberg, whose aesthetic principles may be summed up in the word *expressionism.* The expressionist school led by Schoenberg, whose most noted disciples were Alban Berg, Anton von Webern, and Ernst Křenek, did not accept the realism of Debussy and his followers, but promoted the aesthetic principle of *subjectivism.* That is, an attempt at a psychological approach—one might say to create in music an "impression" of an "impression." Hence, this music becomes abstract and introverted, and produces music which throws tradition to the winds by employing an extremely complex and discordant texture with disjointed melodic lines and forms. The vehicle for the development of Schoenberg's style was the *tone row.*

The tone row, sometimes called the twelve-tone technique, is really not a scale at all but an arbitrary arrangement of the twelve tones from the chromatic scale—duodecuple scale. The tones may be used in any order as material from which to construct a melodic (?) and harmonic framework. All keys and key centers are abandoned and the melodic line

—and consequently the harmonic structure which results—destroys any feeling of tonality. The music, then, is said to be atonal.

Here is a prearranged set of tones from the chromatic scale which forms the basis of a composition:

Ex. 160. Křenek, Ernst: *Twelve Little Pieces*, Op. 83

Original form = O (twelve-tone series on which the following pieces are based)

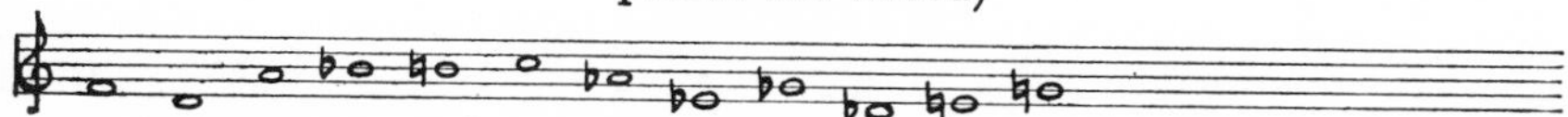

Inverted form of O = I (obtained by changing ascending intervals to equivalent descending ones and vice versa)

Retrograde form of O = R (obtained by proceeding from the last tone to the first)

Inverted form of R = RI (obtained from R by the same procedure as I from O, or reading I backward)

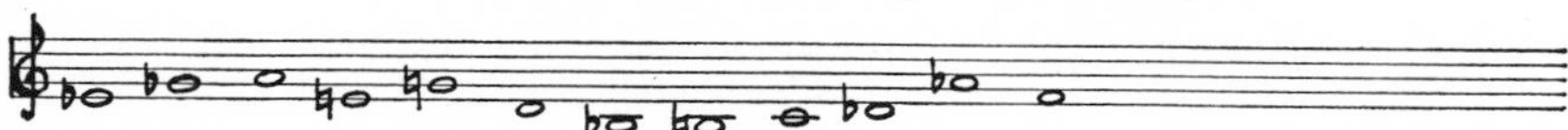

♭ and ♯ are used equivalently.

The different forms of the series are used in building the twelve pieces according to the following scheme:

1. O—*Dancing Toys*
2. I—*Peaceful Mood*
3. R—*Walking on a Stormy Day*
4. RI—*The Moon Rises*
5. O + I—*Little Chessmen*
6. O + R—*A Boat, Slowly Sailing*
7. O + RI—*Streamliner*
8. I + R—*Glass Figures*
9. I + RI—*The Sailing Boat, Reflected in the Pond*
10. O + R + RI—*On the High Mountains*
11. O + I + R—*Bells in the Fog*
12. O + I + R + RI—*Indian-Summer Day*

The use of the tone row demands a constant restatement in its original form, or in various modifications, which may be accomplished by inversion—turned upside down, retrograde motion—read backward, retrograde inversion—upside down and backward, or by transposition to any step of the chromatic scale. Thus, a tone row may be used in as many as forty-eight different ways.

In the next example, the use of the tone row is readily seen. The tone row has been numbered for convenience.

Ex. 161. Schoenberg, Arnold: *Suite*, Op. 25, "Menuet"

Atonal music has been described as eye music rather than ear music, and as harmony out of control. In musical aesthetics the ear must always be the final judge and jury rather than the science of mathematics. Perhaps evolution is more to be desired than revolution.

Polytonality

The device of neoclassicism is polytonality, the vehicle is contrapuntal texture. Neoclassicism had for its purpose the rejection of romanticism and impressionism, and represented an even more radical approach to music than that of Debussy.

The term neoclassicism literally means *new classic,* and infers the imposition of modern harmonic devices on forms of the eighteenth century, or forms of still earlier periods. In short, a rediscovery of Bach of whose style contrapuntal texture is the essence. Though Ferrucio Busoni was the father of neoclassicism, it was Stravinsky who made this aesthetic felt round the world. Paul Hindemith and Darius Milhaud, among others, have embraced this movement.

Polytonality—a term used to designate the simultaneous use of more than two keys, but now used to cover bitonality as well—is largely the combining of the traditional tonal material. Instead of writing in one tonality at a time—for example, the key of C—composers combined two tonalities, or even three, in a composition. Thus we might find, in a piano composition, the key of A-flat in the left hand against the key of D in the right hand. Of course, by striking these two chords together it may be readily seen that the essence of this technique is dissonance, wherein a feeling of tonic (key center) is obscured. However, consonance in the traditional sense is to be found in each part.

Nowhere is there a better example of the technique of polytonality than in Stravinsky's ballet *Petrouchka,* where the key of F-sharp is superimposed on the key of C. Laid out side by side these two keys have a familiar look.

Key of C—c d e f g a b c d e f
Key of F♯— f♯ g♯ a♯b c♯ d♯ e♯ f♯

You will notice that the chromatic scale is formed when these two keys are combined. Compare this with the tone row.

Ex. 162. Stravinsky: *Petrouchka,* Tableau 2, "Chez Petrouchka"

(Copyright by Edition Russe de Musique. Revised version copyright 1947, 1948, by Boosey & Hawkes, Inc., New York 19, N. Y. Used by permission.)

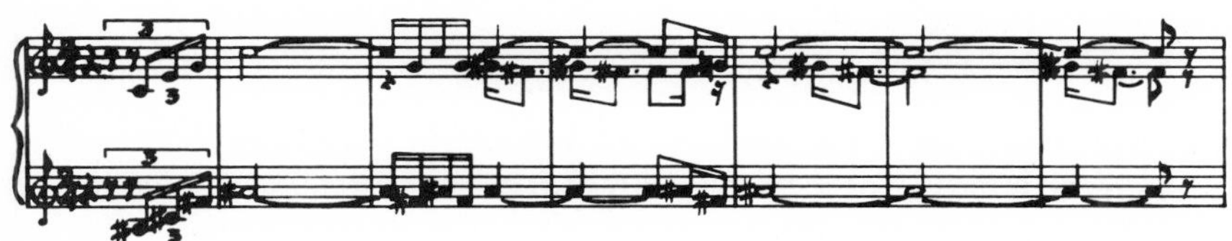

Pan-diatonicism

Literally the word means all or everything diatonic. Like polytonality, pan-diatonicism is a "fellow traveler" in the neoclassic movement. In this style the diatonic scale again comes into its own as tonal material. The essence of this method is the unrestricted use of the several tones of the diatonic scale in its pure form, that is, without chromatic alteration. Major keys are the favored mode with the "simpler" keys being given the preference to avoid the excessive piling up of sharps and flats.

In Ex. 163, it will be observed that the tonic of the key of F is used against its dominant. Let us lay these two keys side by side and see how they look together.

Key of F—f g a b♭ c d e f g a b♭ c
Key of C— c d e f g a b c

Here no chromaticism actually exists, but dissonance still prevails though, perhaps, to a lesser degree.

It is readily seen here, when compared with the two keys used in the polytonal example, that the diatonic scales are the essence of pan-diatonicism.

Ex. 163. Stravinsky: *Sonata for Two Pianos,* First Movement

(*Copyright, 1945, by Associated Music Publishers, Inc., New York 36, N. Y. By permission.*)

NEW TONAL HORIZONS

The Schoenbergian revolution has made it more difficult for the contemporary composer to communicate with the listener. The cohesive qualities of melody as evidenced in the music of the nineteenth century—which was tonal and hummable—are, for the most part, rejected, and the listener is now left without a frame of reference. The musical language of the twentieth century requires the listener to put the past in limbo and forces upon him a higher degree of concentration.

The Microtone System

As atonality with its use of the chromatic scale broke down traditional harmony and tonality, so the use of microtones—intervals smaller than the half step, such as the quarter tone, the sixth tone, the eighth tone, and the sixteenth tone—may eventually in turn do away with the principle of atonality. Already there have been several pianos constructed on the principle of quarter tones, and some music has been written utilizing this system. In this "new" music, the quarter tones are evenly distributed throughout the octave. This, of course, opens up new harmonic and melodic fields for the use of dissonance (or consonance, depending on your viewpoint). We need only examine the music of the early Greeks (quarter tone) and Hindus (smaller intervals) to find that microtones have been used before. Among those who have experimented with microtones are Alois Hába, Charles Ives, John Eaton, and Harry Partch.

The Hindemith System

Hindemith, in his *Craft of Musical Composition,* bases his theory on a system of twelve tones selected from the overtone series. The twelve tones chosen by Hindemith are c, d♭, d, e♭, e, f, g, a♭, a, b♭, b, c, which he sets down according to what he calls "tensions" in the following order: c, c, g, f, a, e, e♭, a♭, d, b♭, d♭, b. (Compare this series with that of Schoenberg as shown on page 116.) Hindemith's intervals are then combined according to their relative strength: octave, perfect fifth, perfect fourth, major third, minor sixth, minor third, major sixth, major second, minor seventh, minor second, and major seventh. Any of the twelve tones of the series can become a tonal center. As Scriabin's "mystic chord" contains the tritone—an augmented fourth or diminished fifth—so Hindemith uses the tritone to make the movement of chords convincing. Hindemith includes a table in which he has classified all the ultramodernistic chords as well as those of traditional harmony. He is one of the leading protagonists of neoclassicism. His style is smooth, clear, logical, and scholarly. Hindemith has been a leader in a movement which has been called *Gebrauchsmusik*—social or practical music for amateurs. Simplicity was the watchword for this music, aimed primarily at youth rather than the concert hall. We may see today the results of this "youth movement" in such works as Hindemith's *Let Us Build a City,* a cantata; Weill's *Down in the Valley,* a one-act opera; and Britten's *Let Us Make an Opera.*

The Schillinger System

We mention briefly here the *Schillinger System of Musical Composition,* which is an application of the science of mathematics to music. This system only carries to an extreme the principles of certain mechanical compositional devices long used by composers; i.e., augmentation (see p. 182), diminution (see p. 182), strict imitation (see p. 82), and so forth. Composers have always applied mathematical concepts to a limited area of composition, whereas Schillinger applies them to the whole process. By choosing certain "formulas" the composer is able to write in any style, new or old, which uses our present materials. So far, the system has been used by arrangers and composers who are expected to turn out arrangements and compositions on a production basis for the music industry and films. In these fields the system has had wide acceptance; in fact, it has become a necessity. Whether the serious composer will ever embrace the system remains to be seen.

The Schenker System of Analysis

In the years prior to his death in 1935, Heinrich Schenker evolved a system of analysis based on the premise that tonality (see p. 88) is the expression of but a single key. Obviously, then, this premise rules out the principle of modulation (see p. 109) as found in the traditional textbooks on theory and analysis. Schenker's system analyzes would-be modulations as belonging to the fundamental tonal center. In the light of this, certain chords and chord structures are given new labels, emphasis, function, and direction. While Schenker's premise was applied to eighteenth- and nineteenth-century music, it has been shown that it need not be limited to the music of these periods.

Music from Electronic Instruments

Up until the time—the nineteenth century—that "modern" electrical science discovered a basically new means of producing music, musical sound was created by other mechanical means or by air pressure. Energy had to be supplied by the performer in order to set the sound waves in motion, which were then carried to the ear through the medium of the air. Today it is not only possible to *amplify* musical sound but it is possible to *create* it by means of electrical impulses. The success of these electrical systems is due largely to an ingenious little device called the vacuum tube*, which made not only the radio and later television possible but also other electrical methods of producing and reproducing music which will be described briefly.†

The science of electronics has been applied to such instruments as the piano and bowed string instruments—violin, violoncello, and double bass; and to such fretted string instruments as banjos, mandolins, and guitars—more notably the steel guitar, which is used extensively in dance orchestras. In order to adapt these instruments for the electrical production and reproduction of musical sound, some modification in mechanical construction has been necessary. For example, the soundboard is eliminated in the piano, and the bowed and fretted string instruments have a simplified body structure. In each case, these deficiencies have been made up by means of a pickup and amplifying system. In the electronic instruments named, the musical sounds created by the vibrating strings are converted into electrical impulses by means of a pickup system and sent through wires to the amplifier, which increases their strength and sends them on to the loudspeaker, where they are reconverted into sound waves for our ears to hear.

Further experimentation has produced an electronic pickup for wind instruments. The pickup is attached to the instrument and is activated by the column of air on the inside of the instrument. The electrical impulses from the pickup are sent through wires to an amplifier and in turn are

* Subsequently miniaturized and followed by the transistor and its subsequent microminiaturization.

† For more detailed discussion, the reader is referred to the books on this subject listed in Appendices II and III.

relayed to the loudspeaker. This pickup is likely to have its widest use in combos and dance bands.

In the case of the electronic organ, musical sound is produced by wind-blown reeds—by mechanical energy, or by means of electrically generated frequencies (see p. 135). In the former, the musical sound is converted into electrical impulses by means of a pickup from the vibrating reeds, which have been activated by air pressure supplied by a fan in the instrument. These impulses are amplified, and sent on to a loudspeaker which in turn completes the cycle by converting the amplified impulses to sound waves again.

The second type of electronic organ generates sound from electrical impulses. Here, the sound is generated from a series of small motor-driven metal discs which produce alternating current at frequencies which correspond to those of the tempered scale (see p. 109).

Through scientific development it is now possible to eliminate the pipes of a pipe organ by taking characteristic tones from the finest existent pipe organs and installing them in a pipeless organ. To do this the sound waves are photographed as they emerge from the mouth of each pipe and then engraved on copper plates. Twenty-four plates are needed, two for each of the twelve tones of the chromatic scale. The plates are then mounted, one on each end of a kind of tube containing a scanner which turns at a fixed speed and generates an electromagnetic reproduction of the note or notes being scanned. The electrical impulses are sent on to an amplifier and in turn are fed to loudspeakers. The tones from the twelve tubular generators are activated by depressing the levers of a keyboard. Thus the tones of a great organ may not only be reproduced but be preserved indefinitely.

The sounds of bells weighing many tons may be reproduced by a device called the electronic *carillon.* With this instrument, bell sounds are produced by two methods: (1) a set of coiled steel rods or (2) loosely suspended lengths of piano wire. In either case, the carillon is played by means of a keyboard which controls electrically operated strikers. An amplifying system with volume controls completes the unit.

Electronics has also been applied to another percussion instrument. The sound of the *chromatic timpani* resembles favorably that of the conventional drum. In reality, it is thirteen drums in one, since its thirteen bass-viol strings may be sounded at the same time. These strings are stretched over a rectangular frame and are tuned in half steps. Played in the conventional manner, the strings set up vibrations which are picked up, amplified, and sent on to the loudspeaker.

We need only mention here two other applications of electrical science to music: (1) the *theremin*—a space-controlled instrument—and (2) the photoelectric process, which is employed in the sound track of modern motion-picture film.

SCIENTISM IN MUSIC

With the amalgam of composer-mathematician-scientist, the decades following 1950 may well be called the *age of scientism* in music. The scientific and technological advances—especially in electronics and acoustics—which spawned the space age have been extended to the field of music, engendering new artistic styles, forms, and media, all characterized by one word—experimentation. The contemporary musical scene is marked by diversity, a fact observable in other art forms of the twentieth century.[2] There is no apparent interest in a unified style or style system. Music, like the other arts, has become more and more abstract and uncommunicative. As the Apollo 8 astronauts' spaceship freed them from earth's gravitational force, so electronic music is freeing the composer from the gravitational influence of the elements inherent in our traditional Western music. (See Plate XII.)

Music from Electronic Tape

Simply stated, electronic music is (1) existent sound electronically modified or transformed, or (2) sound electronically generated. Its methods, materials, and techniques produce an utterly new and different musical language which requires a notational system replete with symbols, graphs, and diagrams to represent pitch, timbre, and other elements of sound,[3] and requiring a specialized terminology. Like the scientist, the composer of electronic music must discover and construct,[4] his music thus becoming objective and impersonal.[5]

In a discussion of electronic music, mention must first be made of Edgard Varèse. Though his early studies in mathematics and science pointed toward an engineering career, he later turned to music.* In the field of composing his search for new sonorities and new sounds evolved into what he called "organized sound." He anticipated in the twenties the experimental composers of the fifties with his prophetic work with percussion and bell sonorities in his composition *Ionisation*. It was scored for forty-one percussion instruments, including tubular chimes, celesta, piano; an assortment of Latin-American instruments; and two sirens, for which he indicated the *theremin* could be substituted. His *Ionisation* is a *tour de force* in pure sonority and rhythm. With this work he truly set the stage for the era of electronic music which was to follow.

He reached a creative stalemate with the materials at his disposal, and it was not until the later 1940's that his interest in composition was reawakened by the advent of *musique concrète* (see below) and its new rhythms, colors, and sound effects made possible by electronic tape. One of his most important compositions, *Déserts*—completed with the aid of the Musique Concrete Studio in Paris—combined live and electronic

* He came to the United States in 1915 and became an American citizen in 1926.

Plate XII—Abstract Expressionism. *Number 8*, 1949. Pollock, Jackson—1912-1956. Seeking to project an immediate emotional expression within the technique of abstraction, Pollock was the creator of a revolution in modern art which made him and American art known around the world. (Courtesy, Roy R. Neuberger.) Photo by Geoffrey Clements.

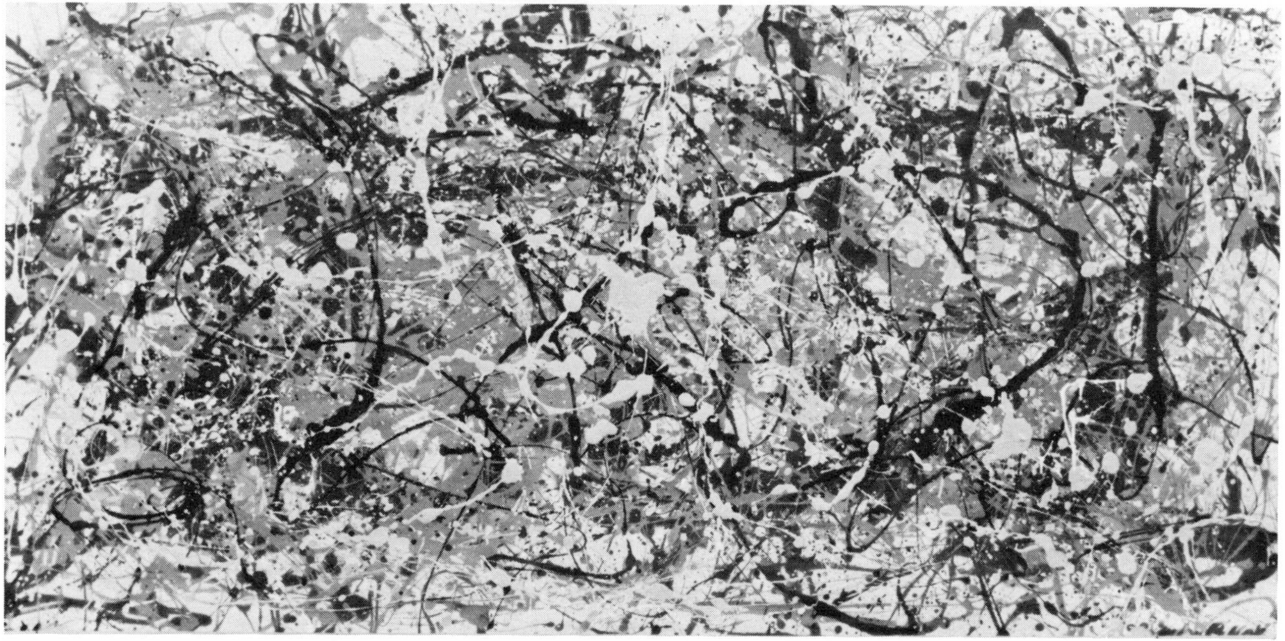

sounds (mixed media). The première performance in Paris in December, 1954, created something of a sensation.

Poème Électronique, written by Varèse for the Phillips 1957 Pavilion at the Brussels Fair, required four hundred and twenty-five loudspeakers arranged stereophonically to give a spatial effect to the music. Though lights devised by the architect Le Corbusier were used in conjunction with the music, each operated independently.

The introduction of the tape recorder to the musical scene has given the musician-composer-experimenter a new medium for musical expression. The earliest experimentation in composing with tape recorders was done in Paris. In 1948 Pierre Schaeffer brought to the public, through Radiodiffusion Française, the première demonstration of music for tape recorder in a program called "Concert Noises" in which sounds of the railroad (*Étude aux Chemins de Fer*), the kettle (*Aux Casseroles*), and the beat of the heart (*Aux Tourniquets*) were individual numbers.

Musique Concrète, which may be said to be representative of the French School, is a type of music for tape of which such French composers as Boulez, Henry, and Messiaen are proponents. In this music, ideas are superimposed on already existing sounds. For these men, the source of sound is not an important factor; the result has only to be sonorous and rhythmically interesting. Music, speech, or more unusual sounds are their materials.

Two groups of composers have emerged in this country as protagonists of tape music. One group, composed of John Cage, David Tudor, Morton Feldman, *et al.,* have catalogued a wide variety of sounds from which they select appropriate items according to a set of complex principles contained in the ancient Chinese Book of Changes, *I—Ching.* The combination and distortion of these sounds are by chance. The numbers on Chinese dice are assigned to the several elements in composition. The dice are then thrown; the resulting numbers determine which elements in a compostion are to be used and how. That which is created by chance methods rather than by calculation is called *aleatory* music.

Cage has sought a medium of musical expression which would free him from any ties with the past, even the twelve-tone system with which he was originally identified. To this end he has embraced the total abstraction of *musique concrète,* of which *Williams Mix* and *Fontana Mix* for magnetic tape are examples. The latter employs the element of chance.

Cage's avant-garde tendencies led him to *Dadaism*—a movement of the 1920's which joined the art of music with the absurd. His *Variations* V is an example of *audio-visual* music in which he combines Dadaistic visual stage effects with music by coupling electronic equipment, noisemakers, loudspeakers and orchestral instruments with TV images and film clips which are visible on a screen. The chief performer is a flashily dressed bicyclist who rides through electronic transmitters, producing odd sounds which are amplified and sent on to loudspeakers placed strategically in different parts of the auditorium.

Cage and Hiller (see p. 27) have collaborated to produce HPSCHD* (Harpsichord reduced to computer language)—a mixed-media extravaganza. It is of such proportions that it may be likened to a three-ring, theatrically artistic circus. This music-and-light show, designed to fill huge spaces—gyms, stock pavilions, Madison Square Garden, or the Astrodome—employs computer-generated music; fifty-one tapes, many of which were composed by *I—Ching* chance procedure; fifty-nine amplified channels each with speaker; motion-picture and slide projectors; and seven amplified harpsichords with live performers visible on raised platforms in the center of the pavilion. Mozart's *Introduction to the Composition of Waltzes by means of Dice* forms the fundamental material for the harpsichordists, a trio of whom play fixed versions, while others play sections in any order assisted by computer versions of this and other Mozart fragments. In addition to his own solo, each harpsichordist may play any of the other solos, while a lone performer may play any Mozart he chooses. The mix creates a microtonal sea of largely unrelated sound which produces no order, and only minuscule repetitions of material may be perceived. Sound and imagery have been extended and juxtaposed *ad infinitum.* Though the listener and/or viewer may be seated for the performance, freedom of movement—which Cage believes is inherent in this society and this art—is a necessity if one is to have the intended welter of experiences and events.

Also representing the American School and working in close association are Luening and Ussachevsky, professors at Columbia University. These men have the distinction of being the first composers to have their tape music performed in the United States. This première performance was given in New York at the Museum of Modern Art on October 28, 1952. On the program were Ussachevsky's *Sonic Contours* and Luening's *Low Speed, Invention,* and *Fantasy in Space.* Further collaboration produced *Incantation* and *Rhapsodic Variations for Tape Recorder and Orchestra,* the latter having been commissioned by the Louisville Orchestra and premièred there on March 20, 1954.

In composing music for tape, Luening and Ussachevsky have utilized music having its source in conventional instruments, the voice, and any other available sounds. They believe that the artistic validity of their music lies in time-tested compositional devices which, through a long process of evolution, have given shape, dimension, and structure to music. Evidence of this is contained in such terminology as "acoustic relationships," "acoustic harmony," and "sonority forms." (See Plate XIII.)

* Premièred at the University of Illinois, May 16, 1969.

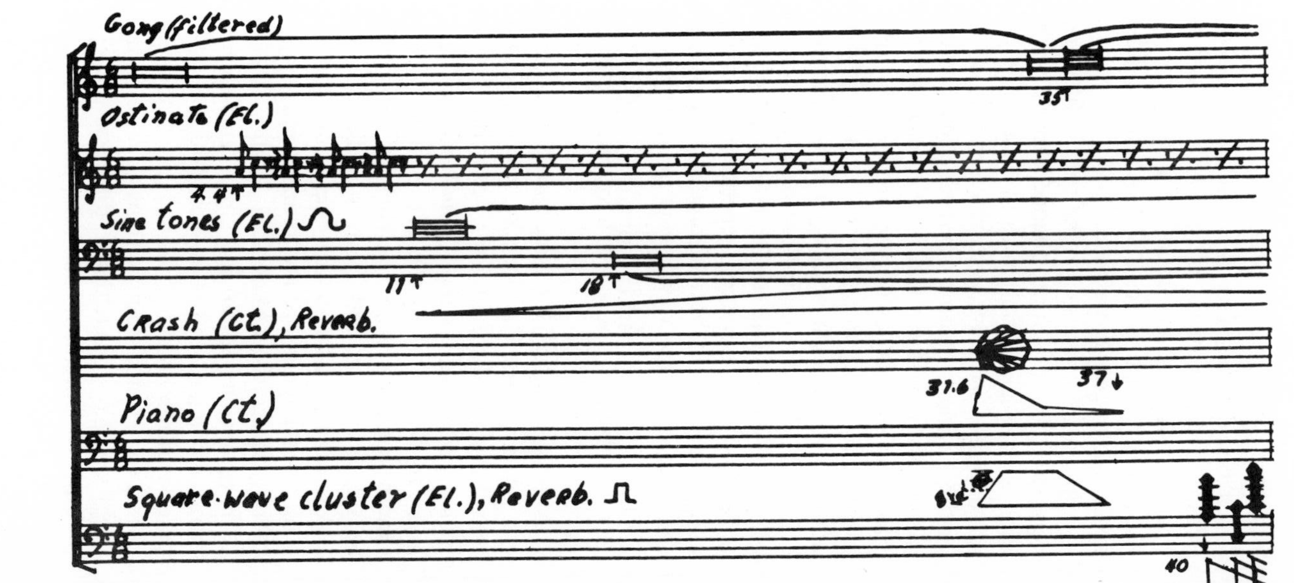
Gong (filtered)
35
Ostinato (El.)
4.4
Sine tones (El.)
11
18
Crash (Ct.), Reverb.
31.6
37
Piano (Ct.)
Square-wave cluster (El.), Reverb.
40

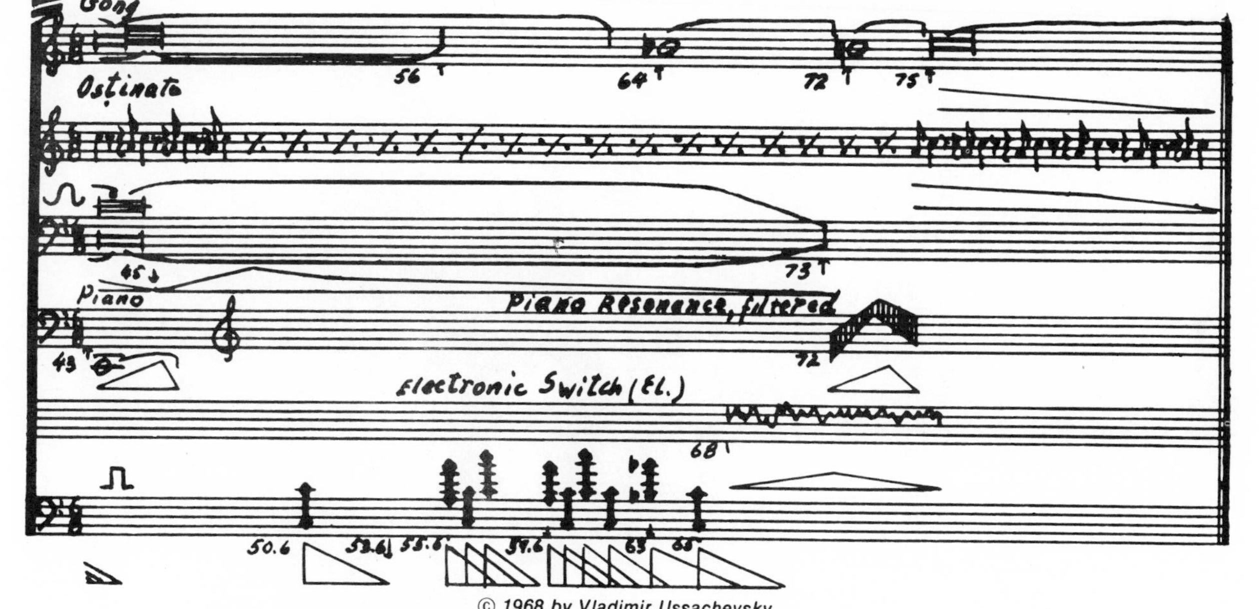

Plate XIII—Score for *Dramatic Pantomime,* Part Three of the four-part suite Four Miniatures. Ussachevsky, Vladimir—1911- . "This score combines musical notation with a few specially designed symbols representing either nonpitch sounds or clusters covering delimited pitch areas. As used, such note values are generalizations rather than exact indications of durations. Arabic numerals specify the time in seconds at which each sound enters or is terminated. Triangular symbols below the staff lines are dynamic indications describing the envelope of a given sound or sound pattern. Origins of the sound materials are indicated and further categorized as electronic (El.) or concrete (Ct.)."—Vladimir Ussachevsky. (Copyright © *Music Educators Journal* November, 1968. Reprinted with permission.)

The German School, which represents the third wave of experimentation in electronic music, is centered in the Cologne studio of the West German Radio under the direction of Herbert Eimert. Stockhausen has established himself as the leading protagonist of this group. The Cologne School believes that true electronic music must be derived from electronically generated sound. For them, *sinusoidal sound*—pure sound devoid of overtones—is of the essence. Their aesthetics are based on those of Webern, whose idea of pure music was the absolute control of its every facet. Unlike the French and the Americans, who have adhered to the usual compositional techniques—canon, imitation, augmentation, diminution and retrograde—the Germans have extended the Schoenbergian idea of the tone-row, limited to pitch, to include complete serialization of all compositional elements; namely, duration (which includes rhythm), timbre (tone color), dynamics (attack), and density (structural complexity). Boulez and Stockhausen have also experimented with aleatory music. (See Plate XIV.)

Plate XIV—Serialism, *Habitat 67*. Safdie, Moshe—1939- , Architect. "This modern design signifies something new in urban living. It departs from the conventional block type apartments and instead is made up of individual units, piled up so that the lower unit provides a roof garden for the one above it." (Courtesy, Expo 67, Montreal, Canada.)

Though the materials and ideas may vary from group to group, the method for projecting them on tape is fundamentally the same. First, the sounds to be used for replaying or distortion are put on a strip of magnetic tape. A fantastic number of variations may be achieved from one tone by electronic manipulation. By employing various speeds, any tone may be raised or lowered several octaves by passing it over the magnetic sounding head. The frequencies used correspond to the audible frequency range of the human ear. Additional effects are achieved by: (1) playing the tape backward; (2) mixing two or more tapes to change the texture, and/or the polyphonic texture; (3) sequential splicing of small portions of tape are combined to create rhythmic patterns, melodic lines, and unrelated sonorities; (4) electronic distortion; (5) modifying the tone color by means of filters, and (6) using echo chambers.

A completed composition will have merged the tapes of several recorders into a single tape, which in turn may be joined to others to produce a master tape—all of which implies tape doctoring and splicing for musical continuity. The composer finds this a time-consuming and arduous task.

The future holds the answer to the success or failure of this medium of musical expression. The performer is eliminated, since the merchandising will be directly from "factory—the composer—to consumer." Dancers find its rhythmic capabilities intriguing. Radio, television, motion pictures, and "pop" music have accepted this new medium.[6]

Music from the Electronic Synthesizer

Through experience and technological advances, the French and American experimenters have come to interest themselves in electronically generated sound. In America, with the advent of the RCA Sound Synthesizer in 1955, the proponents of electronic music at Columbia University—Luening and Ussachevsky—and those at Princeton University—Sessions and Babbitt—joined forces, with the aid of a Rockefeller grant, to establish in 1960 the Columbia-Princeton Center for Electronic Music. Though not giving up tape, Ussachevsky since 1967—upon the invitation of the Bell Telephone Laboratories in New Jersey—has interested himself in the multimillion-dollar GE 645 computer. There he works with men who are both mathematicians and composers.

A synthesizer is a system of electronic instruments which produce and control sound. It is not a computer. There are many synthesizers, but there is only one RCA Synthesizer. It is capable of creating any sound known to man provided man can specify its components. The advantage of the synthesizer over tape is that the composer composes directly into the machine, and what he produces can be tested before he punches the tape. Thus the ear and the synthesizer work in direct relationship. If the sound is not what the composer wants, he can alter it immediately by adjusting

Plate XV—Moog Electronic Music Synthesizer. Walter Carols, seated at the Synthesizer, has "at (his) left an 8-track recorder which tapes directly from the Synthesizer's output. Above the Synthesizer keyboards are the circuit modules which can be interconnected (as shown here) to generate tones with any desired qualities. Tones are monitored through the loud-speaker barely discernible at the right." (*Saturday Review*, January 25, 1969.) Photo by Laura Beaujon.

the switches to make a new sound. A score is required in advance and nothing is left to chance. The synthesizer is also capable of superimposing one sound upon another—standard in tape doctoring—transforming live sounds, and programming wholly original scales.

Babbitt, a composer-mathematician, Conant Professor of Music at Princeton University and one of the directors of the Columbia-Princeton Electronic Music Center, has been interested in the electronic media since 1939. In the late forties, he was extending Schoenberg's serial principles as applied to pitches to the total serialization of all musical elements—duration (including rhythm), register, dynamics (attack), and timbre (tone color)—but insisting that pitch remains the most essential aspect of musical structure. He also believes the serious electronic composer is interested in supplementing and increasing the resources of music, not supplanting them. Babbitt still composes for live performers.

Of particular interest is the successful electronic realization in performances of *Switched-On Bach,* Bach's most famous short works, by physicist-musician Walter Carlos and musicologist Benjamin Folkman—on a Moog Synthesizer. Like an organ, this instrument is played with the hands and feet, but the sound is produced by means of a complex amalgam of oscillators, filters, generators, and amplifiers. The instrument gives greater clarity and definition to Bach's polyphony than are possible for live musicians. Some believe that placing the electronic medium in the mainstream of traditional music is only putting an old picture in a new frame. But if composers become interested enough to compose new music for it, the Moog (or rival equipment) could be the means of taking electronic music out of pure abstractionism. (See Plate XV.)

Music from Electronic Computers

Another method of composing has made its appearance on the musical horizon. "Illiac," a high-speed electronic digital computer normally used by scientists to solve highly complex problems, has "composed," with the aid of two research workers, Professors Lejaren Hiller and Leonard Isaacson, the *Illiac Suite for String Quartet.* This work is the result of a selection of random numbers of musical materials produced by the machine. Random numbers were given the violins, viola, and cello. After the automatic computer had selected the numbers, they were transcribed into musical notation, and the completed composition was performed by a group of live musicians on the campus of the University of Illinois in August, 1956. The musical experiments, represented by the movements of the suite, range from the simple to the highly complex.[7]

Stochastic Music is a term introduced into musical composition in 1955 by the Greek-born mathematician-physicist-philosopher-architect-musician Iannis Xenakis. Coming from the Greek, *stochastic* means point of aim or target, and has its source in an important treatise on the theory of probability (1713) by Jacques Bernouilli.[8] In brief, the theory states that the law of large numbers implies that the more numerous the phenomena, the more they tend toward a defined limit.* Hence, the problems of chance are rigidly controlled. In aleatoric music, one leaves the choice to the performer, whereas in Xenakis's stochastic music, every note is calculated by complex mathematical formulas. In the following compositions, Xenakis has used the IBM 7090 computer for what he calls a family of works: *ST/10* for ten instruments, *ST/4* for String Quartet, *Atrées* for ten players, *ST/48* for forty-eight players, *Stratégie* for two orchestras, and *Eonta* for piano and five bass instruments. With these and other works—*Métastaseis* for an orchestra of sixty-one players and *Pithoprakta* for fifty instruments—it will be seen that Xenakis seeks to perpetuate with new sonorities and finesse, rather than eliminate through electronic means, the instruments of the modern orchestra. His music is characterized by "galaxies" of events in sound—glissandi—like "clouds" in space made up of an infinite number of particles which he controls by applying the theory of probabilities. Some see his compositions as musical architecture having its source in planes, lines, and curved surfaces.

After first introducing the calculus of chance as *Stochastic Music*, Xenakis has gone on to develop the "Mathematical Theory of Games" titled *Strategic Music*, and later a "Set Theory and Mathematical Logic" titled *Symbolic Music*.[9]

Xenakis is known in the U.S.A.—he became a French citizen in 1965—not only by his music but through an affiliation with the University of Indiana as Associate Professor of Mathematical and Automated Music, and with the Berkshire Music Center at Tanglewood (Lenox, Massachusetts).

Spatial and Directional Music

Some avant-garde composers have sought a stereophonic effect by the strategic placement of performers or loudspeakers in the auditorium. Henry Brant experimented with the placement of performers in various parts of the concert hall with his composition *December*. Stockhausen envisions a spherically shaped concert hall with the sound coming from all directions for what we might call "sound in the round," of which *Gruppen* for three orchestras and *Carré* for four orchestras and four choirs are indicative. Also contributing to the field of spatial and directional music is Xenakis, whose *Terretektorh*[10] is written for a large orchestra of eighty-eight players whom he scatters among the audience, making it necessary to perform the work in a large ballroom. Xenakis considers the present-day theaters and concert halls inadequate for modern music, and believes that a new kind of architecture will have to be devised. His

* The basis of insurance calculations and statistical forms.

Polytope[11] for four identical orchestras requires each of the four to be placed at a cardinal point in the concert area.

The success of *Don Rodrigo,* an opera partly aleatory and partly twelve-tone, by Alberto Ginastera* and *The Visitation* by Gunther Schuller, an opera which fuses jazz and the twelve-tone technique into what the composer chooses to call "third-stream" style, has established the artistic and aesthetic effect of spatial or directional music.

The Moving Finger writes; and, having writ,
Moves on: nor all your Piety nor Wit
  Shall lure it back to cancel half a Line,
Nor all your Tears wash out a Word of it.

—From *The Rubáiyát of Omar Khayyám*

* In *Bomarzo,* Ginastera utilized the serial technique, electronic music, tone clusters, aleatory and microtonal music.

UNIT VII

The Acoustical Aspects of Music: Tone Color

Color is inherent in nature. It is an essential factor in daily living. Color to the artist means the use of reds, greens, purples, browns, pinks, black, white, and grays. To the musician, color is something entirely different. Let us explore the phenomenon of color in music.

The Psychological and Aesthetic Aspects of Color

The word *color* as applied to music can have several different meanings. Color here applies to the *quality* or timbre of a tone of the same pitch when sung by different kinds of voices or sounded by various musical instruments. But before we examine the various vocal and instrumental colors, we must first study some of the psychological and aesthetic properties of sound and tone.

We live in a world of sound—radio, phonograph, films, television, instruments, voices, sounds of nature, and industrial sounds—but have you ever stopped to consider what causes sound? The shaking or tremulous motion of the air or a specific body is called *vibration*. Vibration causes *sound*. Sound produces a *sensation*—a psychological factor, which in turn creates a feeling within us—the aesthetic factor. Even though the sound which causes the sensation and resultant feeling produces no outward sign of response in the individual, we are, nonetheless, affected by it. It is relatively easy to analyze sound but much more difficult to analyze and measure feeling. The first we can describe in objective terms, while the latter is entirely subjective.

To provide the experience of sensation and feeling there must be (1) the vibrating object, (2) air or some medium to carry the vibration, and (3) the ear to receive the vibration. The ear in turn transforms the vibrations into sensation which the brain then identifies as sound and as a specific kind of sound. This specific sound may be one of two kinds. If the to-and-fro motion—vibration—is irregular, the resultant sound is noise—as in hitting a table. If the to-and-fro movement is regular, the resultant sound is a musical tone. The scientific study of the physical properties of musical tone is called *acoustics,* the elementary aspects of which we need to consider here.

There are four attributes of musical tone: *frequency, amplitude, timbre,* and *duration.* This acoustical terminology may be reduced to the following easily understood terms:

ACOUSTICAL TERMS	PSYCHOLOGICAL TERMS
Physical	*Sensation*
frequency	pitch—high or low tones
amplitude	intensity—loud or soft tones—volume
timbre	quality—tone color of voices or instruments
duration	time—lasting quality of tones

The relative highness and lowness of tones—*pitch*—is dependent on the number—*frequency*—of vibrations per second. The faster the vibration, the higher the pitch of the tone; the slower the vibration, the lower the pitch of the tone. The ear is capable of receiving these vibrations in any quantity from about 20 to 20,000 per second. The relative loudness or softness of tones—*amplitude, intensity,* or *volume*—is dependent on the distance the vibrating body moves in its to-and-fro motion. The greater the distance, the louder the tone; the shorter the distance, the softer the tone. It can be observed that amplitude has nothing to do with pitch by striking the key of the piano hard and then gently. The tone is loud and then soft, but in each case the pitch remains the same. The unit for measuring intensity is called a *decibel.*

Duration may be described as the length of time it takes for a tone to fade out after being sounded. This is a very important factor in the rhythm of music because rhythm depends on the lasting quality of tones. The higher the tone, the sooner it fades. This is the reason that there are no dampers for the highest tones of the piano.

Timbre—quality, color—is the one attribute of tone which makes it possible for us to distinguish between instruments and voices when they sound the same pitch. Few, if any, of us would be unable to distinguish between a tone sounded on a trumpet and the same note struck on the piano; nor do our ears have to be blessed with a great degree of sensitivity for us to distinguish between the color of two trumpets or two violins. You probably have observed that even though two automobiles of the same make which have come off the same assembly line will not have the same sound, or even operate exactly the same. So it is with all musical instruments or voices. In fact, the same instrument played by two different people will have a somewhat different color depending on the performer's skill. Another analogy would be for two painters of equal competence using the same colors to paint the same scene. While the broad outline would be the same, the details and shadings would vary from one painting to another. The aesthetic impact on the viewer, or listener in the case of music, would also be different.

However, in music the psychological (sensation) or the aesthetic (feeling caused by sensation) impact is not very great on the hearing of just one tone or an isolated color. Rather, it is differences in pitch, loudness, duration, and color of one tone combined with the same attributes of another tone which increase our feeling of pleasure or, perhaps, displeasure.

The Physical Aspects of Tone Color

Have you ever wondered what it is that makes instruments or voices sound different? The color of an instrument or a voice is due to a number of factors. First, there is the matter of the *overtone series,* which we discussed briefly in the previous Unit (see p. 95 f.). A physicist can show, by the use of resonators, that when a tightly stretched string is plucked, it is, at the same time, a combination of many sounds. He can also show, by the use of the same string, that it will vibrate in halves, thirds, fourths, fifths, etc., at the same time. When the string vibrates as a whole, it produces a tone which we call the *fundamental* or *first partial.* The name we give to the pitch, *i.e.,* C, D, B-flat, etc., is the name of the fundamental which is the loudest of the combination of tones we are hearing. The weaker tones produced beyond the fundamental are called *partials, overtones,* or *harmonics*. Let us check on the physicist to see if this phenomenon is true. The presence of these partials can be shown simply by depressing and holding the following keys on the piano without striking them: C, c, g, c, e. Now, strike hard the first key, C, and you will hear that by sympathetic vibration the rest of the partials also sound. Check your own discovery now by holding down other keys and striking the C fundamental. Notice that there is no sympathetic vibration in the other strings. What does this prove? Simply that the strings do vibrate in segments which are the multiples of the fundamental. The same phenomenon can be shown to exist in an open or closed pipe when a column of air is forced into it. The presence or the absence of partials in a string or pipe accounts for the color—timbre or quality—of a tone. A pure tone, one without partials, can be produced only by an electronic device or a tuning fork. The more partials present in a tone, the richer or more complex is that tone. The distinctive color of an instrument or a voice, then, is dependent on the number and the intensity of the partials present in each fundamental which that instrument or voice is capable of sounding.[1]

The tone color of a sounding body is further dependent on the following factors: (1) how the tone is produced—struck, plucked, bowed, or by a forced column of air; (2) its material and shape; (3) the force exerted on the sounding body by bowing, striking, plucking, or amount of air pressure; (4) the length, thickness, amount of tension and elasticity of the sounding body; and (5) the kind of resonator employed to reinforce the tone. The tone color of instruments and voices is further affected by the natural structure of the listener's ear; foreign noises such as those produced by whatever means the vibrating body is set in motion—bow, hammer, air, etc., and those in the area where the listening is taking place—reverberation, squeaky seats, shuffling of feet, and so on. Tone color is also influenced by temperature. We are never completely free of these foreign noises, consequently we cannot tell what *true* tone color actually is. Tone color, then, is a mixture of the fundamental, the presence or the absence of partials, and physically produced noise. The skilled performer reduces the noise element to a bare minimum which, of course, enhances the aesthetic experience of the listener.

The importance of a good *vibrato* to the total effect of tone color is quite often underestimated by the performer and listener alike. Seashore defines the *good vibrato* as "a pulsation of pitch, usually accompanied with synchronous pulsations of loudness and timbre, of such extent and rate as to give a pleasing flexibility, tenderness, and richness to the tone."[2] In other words, there is a simultaneous deviation of pitch, loudness, and tone color. The average speed of a good vibrato is 6.5 times per second within the width of a semitone. Artistic singing requires the presence of the vibrato in the voice, and it exists on practically all tones employed by the singer. The good vibrato has become an essential for all performers of string and wind instruments. Soloists on string and some wind instruments have used the vibrato for years. Until recently the use of the vibrato has been limited to the string section of the orchestra. The time has arrived for the entire wind section of the orchestra to use the vibrato whether automatic or artificial. Not to use it will stamp the instrumentalist as being incompetent. All pipe and electronic organs employ a *tremulant* stop to provide a mechanical vibrato which is actually a fluctuation of loudness rather than pitch. The voice, the only *natural* instrument, has employed the vibrato for centuries, and the aesthetic appeal which a fine voice has is due in large part to a well developed vibrato. A fine voice is unmatched in emotional appeal, flexibility, and variety of tone color. So it is that string players imitate the voice vibrato by rocking the finger back and forth while pressing the string to the fingerboard. We are able to listen with ease and pleasure rather than strain to the performer with an evenly developed vibrato because it has an emotional impact on us as listeners. To be correctly produced, the vocal vibrato must be involuntary rather than voluntary. The so-called vocal tremolo is a voluntary vibrato which results from improper muscular co-ordination, and is generally between seven and ten pulsations per second. When the listener and the performer become conscious of the vibrato, it is then a poor vibrato and becomes objectionable. Do not confuse a good vibrato with a tremolo. The former is much sought after by the artist and listener, the latter is undesirable. Neither should a good vibrato be confused with a trill. The vocal vibrato is thought to be the result of nervous and muscular energy. The vocal and instrumental vibrato has great psychological value both for the listener and performer in the expression of feeling because of its life and warmth. Seashore says that "in cultivating the vibrato avoid a simulated feeling; try to cultivate the power to feel music genuinely."[3]

VOCAL TONE COLOR

Since primitive man the voice has been the basic musical instrument. It still remains in that position, since more people, whether amateur or professional, sing today than play instruments. More vocal literature than instrumental is in existence. There are more choruses in churches, schools, and communities than orchestras or bands. Singing abounds on phonograph records, television, and radio. Some study singing seriously while others study for their own amazement. The voice teacher finds it exceedingly difficult to develop a voice, for it is a complex structure. The process must be carried on largely through the ears of the teacher and those of the student, since the vocal apparatus of the student cannot be seen nor can it be taken apart to be examined and reassembled. The teacher has recourse only to demonstration, explanation, and word pictures. Voice teaching, then, becomes a subjective rather than an objective thing. The voice student tries to imitate and translate the understanding of words into appropriate action. Yet, in spite of these difficulties, many learn to sing well, thanks to intelligence, talent, a voice of natural beauty, excellent teaching, and hours of practice. Voice teaching has not yet been subjected to scientific experimentation, and remains empirical—dependent only on experience or observation—in its approach to the subject. It is not the purpose of this discussion to give the listener a method for learning to sing, but rather to give him information which will lead to better understanding and appreciation of singing, singers, and teachers of singing.[4]

Let us see how the voice is produced. First of all, the voice must be thought of as a double-reed wind instrument. This "double reed," which we call the *vocal cords,* is situated near the top of the windpipe. The vocal cords are set in vibration by air pressure from the lungs and are the determinants of pitch. The cavities—throat, mouth, and head—which lie above the vocal cords add resonance to the overtones. These overtones, which we have previously discussed, are responsible for the vowels and the tone color of the various classifications of voices. To improve the tone color, the number and intensity of the overtones must be increased. To do this the singer seeks to "place" or "focus" the voice in the head. In doing so, he learns how to co-ordinate the lower-chest, and upper-head registers, so that from his lowest to his highest tone the color will match. In addition to mastering the production of the vowel sounds, he must also master the consonants, especially those at the beginning and endings of words.

Of the greatest importance is the way the singer controls his diaphragm, throat, tongue, lips, and jaw, and such other factors that have a bearing on tone production.

Classification of Vocal Tone Color

We have found out through our study that tone color is dependent on the action of the vocal cords, the resonators—number and intensity of the overtones present—and the vibrato. The classifying of a voice, then, is not based on its range, but rather its tone color. (Most scientists and vocal authorities will agree on this point.)

It seems almost trite to say that there are two large classifications of voices, namely, male and female. More important are the subclassifications which are used to describe women's and men's voices. Though the range does not determine the kind of voice, it is, nevertheless, interesting to see how high and low the average singer in an organized choral group is expected to go. It must be remembered that the artist, operatic and concert, often exceeds these ranges. Men's voices are approximately an octave lower in pitch than women's voices, due to the longer length and size of the vocal cords. In both women's and men's voices the longer and larger the vocal cords, the lower the pitch and the darker the tone color.

WOMEN'S VOICES*

Ex. 164. Ranges for Choral Works

MEN'S VOICES*

Ex. 165. Ranges for Choral Works

* For subjects marked with an asterisk, additional information of a technical nature is supplied in Appendix IV.

Seating Plan and Voice Distribution for a Chorus of 60 Voices

Sopranos	Basses / Tenors	Altos
I–12 Sopranos–20 II–8	I–4 Basses–14 II–10 I–6 Tenors–10 II–4	I–7 Altos–16 II–9

ORCHESTRAL TONE COLOR

Originally, instruments were used to double the voices, play the same part, because there was no music in existence written especially for instruments. Gradually this situation changed and instruments became more independent of the voices. The early instruments were crude in construction and sound. Between 1600 and 1750 instrumental music achieved an equal footing with vocal music because of the composition of more music for instruments alone and in combination, the improvements made on the instruments themselves, and the improved technique of the players. Since 1750 instrumental music has surpassed vocal music in importance. However, no single instrument is capable of the shadings of color or emotion of the human voice, and the orchestra as a whole, thrilling and great as it is, is limited by this very fact. Composers have felt this inadequacy and have, from time to time, included various combinations of voices in their symphonic works. Like singing, variety of tone color is the essence of orchestral sound.

Orchestras have not always been their present size. The early orchestra around 1700 was small in comparison to the large quantity and variety of instruments in a Richard Strauss score. The modern symphony orchestra is the direct result of the want and need for greater variety of tone color. However, at the present time, composers seem to be reverting back to the small orchestra, perhaps for economic reasons. How far this trend will go remains to be seen.

We have already discussed the physical aspects of tone color in a general way. We need now to classify the instruments of the orchestra and to describe individually their physical, mechanical, and tonal characteristics. First of all, orchestral instruments are divided into four classifications, *string, woodwind, brass,* and *percussion,* each classification containing several kinds of instruments (see Appendix IV). On page 143 f. is a chart showing the four classifications, with the instruments of each being grouped as they would appear in an orchestral score. In addition, the chart shows the method by which instrumental sound is set in vibration, and whether or not a specific instrument sounds what the player reads from the score. For example, if the trumpet in B-flat reads "C," he sounds one whole step lower—B-flat; likewise the horn in F sounds a fifth lower than he reads. These and other instruments, then, are called transposing instruments. A good rule to remember is that any transposing instrument will sound the note which corresponds to the name of that instrument when asked to play a written "C."

Classification of Instrumental Tone Color

As in the case of voices, it is very difficult to describe the tone color of the various musical instruments with words. The records for this Unit listed in Appendix V provide their own description. There are, however, a few things which we need to say concerning specific instruments which will help you to understand them better.

The physical aspects of tone color which we discussed on pages 136–138 must be applied here specifically to the tone color of instruments. The listener is also reminded that as in voice, the distinctive color of an instrument is further dependent on the number and the intensity of the partials present in each fundamental which that instrument is capable of sounding.

To help you to visualize the placement of the instruments in an orchestral score—which may number thirty staves or more—we will again study them in the order in which they appear, reading from top to bottom. You will remember that we have already divided them into four classifications, namely, woodwinds, brasses, percussion, and strings. By referring to the chart you will see that the woodwinds, the brasses, and the strings represent a choir of soprano, alto, tenor, and bass voices. Though the harmony tends to be complete in each of these sections, it may be enlarged by the addition of other voices from other sections of the orchestra.

Chart Showing a Widely Used Seating Plan by Symphony Orchestra Conductors

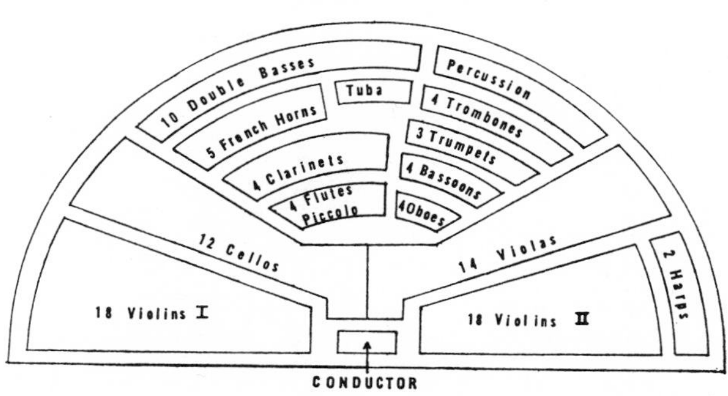

Chart of Orchestral Tone Color as Shown on a Score Page

	Corresponding Vocal Range	Strings			Membranes, Rods, Plates, Bells Struck	Winds				
		Keyboard	Bowed	Plucked		Single Reed	Double Reed	Sharp-Edged Hole	Cupped Mouthpiece Lips	Transposing Instrument
Woodwinds (Reeds)										
Piccolo	high soprano							x		
Flute	soprano							x		
Oboe	soprano						x			
English horn	alto						x			x
E-flat clarinet	high soprano					x				x
Clarinet in B-flat and A	soprano					x				x
Bass clarinet in B-flat and A	bass					x				x
Saxophone in E-flat	alto					x				x
Bassoon	tenor						x			
Contra bassoon	bass						x			
Brass										
Horn in F (French horn)	alto								x	x
Trumpet in B-flat	soprano								x	x
Tenor trombone	tenor								x	
Bass trombone	bass								x	
Tuba	bass								x	

Percussion										
Definite pitch										
Timpani					x					
Glockenspiel					x					
Xylophone					x					
Chimes—Bells					x					
Vibraphone					x					
Celesta		x								
Indefinite pitch										
Bass Drum—Snare Drum and other percussion					x					
Organ (Pipe)		x				x		x		
Piano		x								
Harp				x						
Strings										
Violin I	soprano I		x							
Violin II	soprano II		x							
Viola	alto		x							
Violoncello	tenor		x							
Double bass	bass		x							

Woodwinds*—Reeds. In these instruments the column of air in the pipe may be set in vibration by blowing air across an opening—the embouchure, as in the case of the flute and the piccolo—or by blowing the air across a *reed*—as in a clarinet, a saxophone, an oboe, or a bassoon. In the case of reed instruments, the reed vibrates in resonance with the column of air in the pipe, thus greatly reinforcing the tone. However, in the flute or the piccolo, the tone is created by the natural vibration period of the column of air in the pipe. The pitch (frequency) of woodwind instruments may be changed by opening and closing the finger holes which are bored in the instrument. By covering or opening these finger holes the player is able to lengthen or shorten the pipe. The same may also be accomplished by increasing the air pressure or by changing the position of the lips and the tongue against the embouchure; this is called *overblowing.* In overblowing, one of the partials becomes so prominent that the fundamental drops out. Hence, the player can produce a complete scale from the lowest to the highest note of the instrument.

In the eighteenth century (Haydn, Mozart, Beethoven) the woodwinds were of secondary importance, but in the nineteenth century they assumed a place of equal importance.

Brass Instruments*—Wind. This family of instruments is so called because they are made of brass or other metal. The sound in brass instruments is produced through pipes of varying lengths by means of cupped or funnel-shaped mouthpieces also made of metal. Remember that it is not only the material from which the instrument is made which gives it its distinctive tone color (see discussion of tone color, p. 140 f.). In the brass family, the lips serve as the reed and, thus, the vibrating source of sound. This vibration enters the instrument through the cupped mouthpiece, where the air column is set in vibration, amplifying the original lip vibration and giving the tone its distinctive color. In the brass family a large number of overtones is utilized, the design of the mouthpiece having a great deal to do with the number of overtones present in a specific fundamental. The lips are capable of producing only a small number of natural tones, called open tones, but with the aid of valves, crooks, or slides, additional tones can be produced, making a complete chromatic scale a reality. All the tones on a brass instrument sound through the bell. The tone color of brass instruments can be varied by the embouchure —lip and tongue technique. Because long lengths of tubing are required for brass instruments, the tubing is coiled for ease in handling and playing. Two thirds of the length of the French horn and the tuba is of conical bore and they overblow at the octave, while two thirds of the length of the trumpet and the trombone is of cylindrical bore and they also overblow at the octave.

* See footnote, page 139.

Plate XVI—A *Woodwind Ensemble.* (Left to right) Flute, oboe, bassoon, French horn, clarinet. (Courtesy, Eastman School of Music and the University of Rochester. Louis Ouzer, Photography.)

Plate XVII—A *Group of Brasses. Foreground:* French horns, trumpets. *Rear:* trombones and basses. (Courtesy, Eastman School of Music and the University of Rochester. Louis Ouzer, Photography.)

Plate XVIII—*The Eastman Wind Ensemble*, Dr. Frederick Fennell, Conductor. (Courtesy, Eastman School of Music and the University of Rochester. Louis Ouzer, Photography.) Compare the instrumentation and the seating arrangement in this photograph with that of a symphonic band.

Plate XIX—*The Console of a Large Pipe Organ,* showing: 4 manuals (keyboards); stops, and pistons; pedal organ (keyboard); swell, great, and crescendo pedals; foot pistons. (Courtesy, M. P. Möller, Inc.)

It has remained for the twentieth century to give equal, if not first place, to the brass instruments largely through increased technique in jazz arrangements and the efforts of such symphonic stalwarts as Stravinsky, Bartók, and Hindemith. It remains, however, for the symphonic brass players to develop their technique to the point of men in the dance orchestras. The brass in the dance band often soars to heights and achieves effects which the symphony men are at present incapable of reaching.

Percussion Instruments.* The next group of instruments shown in a full orchestra score are the percussion instruments. This family consists of instruments which are played by either striking or shaking them, the sounds resulting being classified into those of definite pitch and those whose pitch is indefinite. The vibrating media of percussion instruments

* See footnote, page 139.

Plate XX—A *Group of Pipes in a Division of the Organ*. St. George's Church, New York City. (Courtesy, M. P. Möller, Inc.)

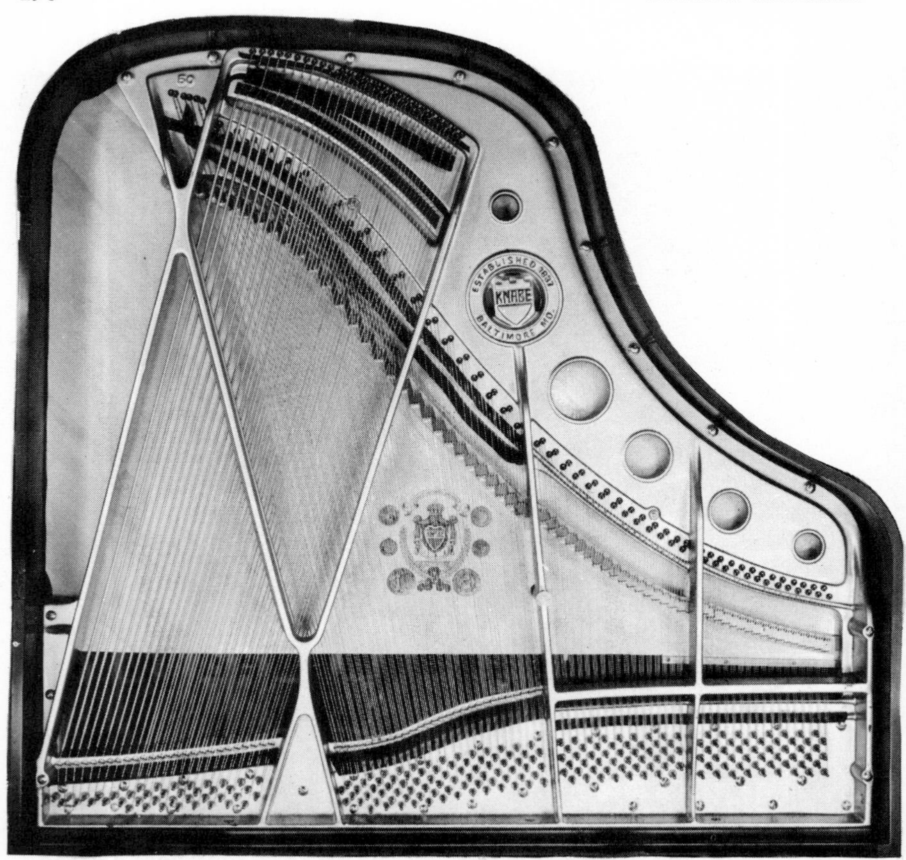

Plate XXI—*An Inside View of a Grand Piano,* showing: sound board, plate, strings, tuning pins. (Courtesy, Æolian American Corporation.)

are membranes, rods, plates, or bells, the upper partials of which are inharmonic, that is, the upper partials are not an even multiple of the fundamental and are, therefore, out of tune with the fundamental, and so clash with it, tending to create noise. So it is that the composer uses these instruments with great care.

While percussion instruments which have definite pitch can be used as melodic instruments, their primary function, like the rest of the instruments of the percussion group in the orchestra, is that of marking the rhythm. Hence, they are often called rhythm instruments. Percussion instruments are also used for color effect.

Organ (Pipe), Piano, and Harp. These instruments are inserted here because of their position in the orchestral score. The organ, the piano, and the harp are adequately discussed in Appendix IV.

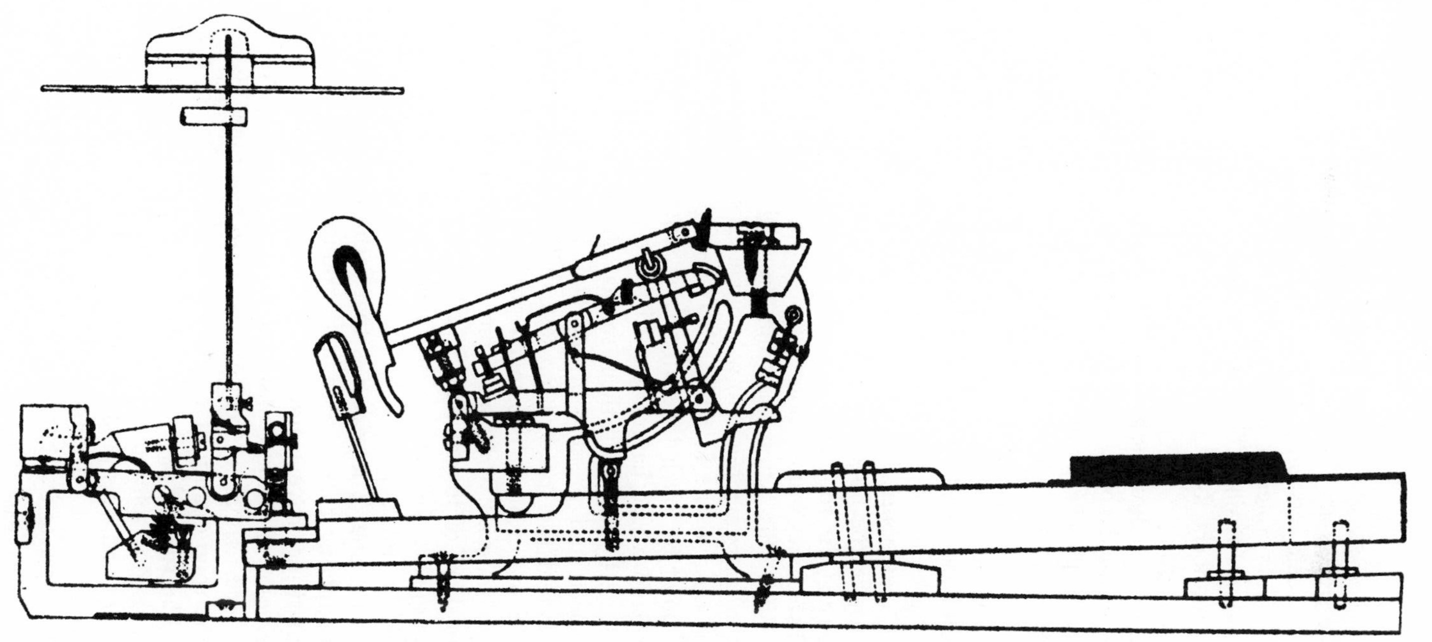

Plate XXII—A *Cross-section of a Grand Piano Action*, showing: key, hammer, backcheck, damper. (Courtesy, Æolian American Corporation. Photograph by Gary Eisenhart.)

Strings.* Last, but by no means least, are the strings on the score page. The strings are the backbone of the symphony orchestra. Not only because of their versatility, but because, from a psychological standpoint, the ear is more tolerant of string tone than it is of the brasses, woodwinds, and percussion. This fact is true musically speaking and in the point of numbers. In a modern orchestra of one hundred players, over half are strings.

In our earlier discussion in this Unit of the physical aspects of tone color, we learned about some of the acoustical properties of a vibrating string. Let us pursue the discussion still further. Not only is the tone color of stringed instruments dependent on whether they are bowed, plucked, or struck, but the point at which this occurs affects the tone color. For example, if the string is bowed or plucked at its midpoint, the tone has a more hollow sound. If the performer wishes a brighter tone, he must play near the end of the string. So by playing near the bridge of the instrument (*sul ponticello*) he strengthens the higher harmonics, and by playing nearer the fingerboard (*sul tasto*) the higher harmonics are weakened, causing the tone color to be less brilliant. You may have heard the sound that comes from a violin when played by the wood of the bow (*col legno*). With this type of bowing the higher partials are strengthened, giving the instrument a "tinny" sound. This is caused by the hardness of the wood and the fact that the wood of the bow is round, allowing only its point to touch the string. The same hard, metallic sound comes from a piano whose hammers need to be replaced, filed, or pricked with a special needle to soften them so that the tone will be more mellow.

The speed and pressure of the bow influence the tone color to the extent that, if the speed is too fast and the pressure too light, whistling harmonics are created. Too much pressure, without increasing the speed, tends to "squeeze" the tone from the string, giving it a raspy quality. Also, the kind of material used in the manufacture of strings influences the tone quality. In the case of a metal string, the thinner it is the more brilliant the tone, because a thin string will produce higher partials than a thick one. The reason is that a thick string cannot divide into as many segments, therefore cannot produce the higher harmonics. Likewise, gut strings have a different tone color from metal strings.

Tone color of stringed instruments is also influenced by the materials used to give resonance (reinforcement) to the tone. Have you ever compared the tone quality of a spinet piano with that of a large upright or grand? The spinet has a very small, thin sound because the soundboard which is used to reinforce the tone is quite small. The upright has a larger soundboard and thus produces a tone of better substance and body. Likewise, the grand piano sounds even better than the upright because of the still larger area of its soundboard. With instruments of the violin family,

* See footnote, page 139.

Plate XXIII—*A String Ensemble. Foreground, left to right:* violin I, violin II, cello, viola. *Rear, left to right:* double bass, harp. (Courtesy, Eastman School of Music and the University of Rochester. Louis Ouzer, Photography.)

the shape and the thickness of the bridge has a bearing on their tone color. The grain of the wood in the belly of the instrument, the size, thickness, the arch of the soundboard, and the shape and size of the "f" holes have a bearing on the tone color of the instrument. The position and thickness of the sound-post which is fixed between the top and bottom panels of the body influences the tone color. If the sound-post is positioned too far from the bridge, or if it is too thick, the tone will be less brilliant. The bass-bar performs a dual purpose. It conducts the vibrations to the entire belly of the instrument and reinforces it to allow for the pressure on the belly caused by the tension of the strings.

When a "wolfnote"—the coincidence of a certain pitch with a strong vibration form in the belly of the instrument—occurs, and all stringed instruments have them to a greater or lesser degree, it has been found that the fault lies in the design of the instrument.

The Orchestra—Its Growth

In the little more than three hundred years from *c.* 1600 to the present, the orchestra has grown from one of meager size and tonal resources to one of large proportion, and almost unlimited tonal color. We need but to compare the requirements for the following two compositions to verify this fact.

Giovanni Gabrieli	Richard Strauss
"Sacre symphonie"—*c.* 1600	"Eine Alpensinfonie"—1918
	2 Piccolos
	2 Flutes
	3 Oboes (Eng. hr. alt.)
	1 Heckelphone
	3 Clarinets
	1 Bass Clarinet
Bassoons	3 Bassoons
	1 Contra bassoon
Cornetti	8 Horns (4 alt. with 4 tenor tubas)
	4 Trumpets
Trombones	4 Trombones
	2 Tubas
	4 Timpani
	Bass Drum
	Snare Drum
	Cymbals
	Triangle
	Gong
	Cowbells
	Wind-machine

Giovanni Gabrieli	Richard Strauss
	Thunder-machine
	Glockenspiel
	Celesta
	Organ
	2 Harps
Violins	Violins I–II
	Viola
	Violoncello
	Bass
Voices	Off Stage
	12 Horns
	2 Trumpets
	2 Trombones

An examination of orchestral scores of representative composers of the several periods of music history, *i.e.*, pre-Bach, Baroque, Classic, Romantic, and Modern periods, reveals to us the continual reaching out for new colors and effects. Depending on one's viewpoint, it might be called progress or orchestral extravagance. During three centuries the color pendulum has been swinging to the right, but appears now to be starting its movement to the left. Though both were composed in the same year, 1918, the Strauss "Alpensinfonie" and the Stravinsky "L'histoire du Soldat" are in direct contrast in the resources required:

"L'histoire du Soldat"

1 Clarinet	1 Cornet	8 Percussion	1 Violin
1 Bassoon	1 Trombone	(1 player)	1 Double bass

The present trend seems to be pointing in the direction of economy of resources demanded by composers not only for musical reasons, neoclassicism and the rediscovery of Bach, but also because of the economic strain placed on present-day orchestras. An examination of the later scores of Schoenberg, Hindemith, and Stravinsky will reveal a more conservative use of orchestral color.

The Composer's Attitude Toward Tone Color

Have you ever tried to paint? How did you go about choosing and mixing your colors? These questions can also be asked of a composer. For a direct and specific answer, let us go to a well-known contemporary composer of established reputation—Aaron Copland:

> . . . not every musical theme is born fully swaddled in a tonal dress. Very often the composer finds himself with a theme that can be equally well played

Plate XXIV—*The Eastman-Rochester Orchestra*, Dr. Howard Hanson, Conductor. (Courtesy, Eastman School of Music and the University of Rochester. Louis Ouzer, Photography.) Compare the seating arrangement and instrumentation in this photograph with that found on page 141.

on the violin, flute, clarinet, trumpet, or half a dozen other instruments. What, then, makes him decide to choose one rather than the other? Only one thing: he chooses the instrument with the tone color that best expresses the meaning behind his idea. In other words, his choice is determined by the expressive value of any specific instrument. That is true in the case not only of single instruments but also of combinations of instruments. The composer who chooses a bassoon rather than an oboe in certain instances may also have to decide whether his musical idea best belongs in a string ensemble or a full orchestra. And the thing that makes him decide in every case will be the expressive meaning that he wishes to convey.

At times, of course, a composer conceives a theme and its tonal investiture instantaneously. There are outstanding examples of that in music. One that is often quoted is the flute solo at the beginning of *L'Après-midi d'un Faune* (*Afternoon of a Faun*). That same theme, played by any other instrument than the flute would induce a very different emotional feeling. It is impossible to imagine Debussy's conceiving the theme first and then later deciding to orchestrate it for a flute. The two must have been conceived simultaneously. But that does not settle the matter.

For even in the case of themes that come to the composer in their full orchestral panoply, later musical developments in the course of a particular piece may bring on the need for varied orchestral treatments of the same theme. In such a case, the composer is like a playwright deciding on a dress for an actress in a particular scene. The stage shows us an actress seated on a bench in a park. The playwright may wish to have her clothed in such a way that the spectator knows as soon as the curtain rises what mood she is in. It is not just a pretty dress; it's an especially designed dress to give you a particular feeling about this particular character in this particular scene. The same holds true for the composer who "dresses" a musical theme. The entire gamut of tonal color at his disposal is so rich that nothing but a clear conception of the emotional feeling that he wishes to convey can make him decide as between one instrument and another or one group of instruments and another.[5]

PART III

Synthesis of Musical Elements

UNIT VIII

Juxtaposition of Musical Elements

The psychological, aesthetic, and sensuous impact of a composition is the sum total of all we have said about each of the elements of music, and of all that we hear in music. The sum total of these elements the composer uses to create a mood, the initial impression being sensuous. As we have seen, this appeal may be subtle or obvious. It should be remembered, also, that during the course of a composition the listener is likely to be conscious of the fact that one element predominates. That is, melody may be the dominant element of the moment while rhythm may predominate later on. Yet, while this may be happening, we must be consciously aware of the other elements which are, at the same time, functioning to fashion a perfect whole.

In the previous Units we have analyzed and critically examined these elements—through example, by sight and sound—in order to understand better their function within the framework of a whole piece of music. It is relatively easy to dissect a completed work, but more difficult to create it piece by piece so that it functions as a whole. No one is more conscious of this fact than the composer. In this Unit, then, we propose to study the means by which a composer pyramids the elements for maximum psychological and aesthetic effect.

To achieve this effect, the composer uses a device we may call *juxtaposition.* Webster says that "juxtaposition is placing or being placed side by side." For our purpose, we are not only going to place the elements side by side but superimpose one on the other—pyramid. We shall be primarily concerned with rhythm, melody, harmony, and color. The compositions chosen for study were selected not only for their psychological and aesthetic appeal, but to show the increasing complexity of structure as the elements are juxtaposed.

RHYTHM

We have learned in Unit III that rhythm, in its broadest sense, is the movement of a piece of music. This indicates the passage of time, and time is the canvas on which musical "images" are drawn by means of melody and harmony. Rhythm systematizes; it controls the duration of tone itself, whether it be in melodic or harmonic combinations. As well as being easy to perceive, rhythm acts like a drug on the emotions which calms or excites. But rhythm, like drugs, must be used judiciously.

To start our building process, let us begin with a group of notes. Rhythmical in a sense, they are certainly uninteresting as they stand. Clap the following series of notes, giving *equal* stress to each note:

♩ ♩ ♩ ♩ ♩ ♩ ♩ ♩ ♩ ♩ ♩ ♩ ♩ ♩ ♩ ♩

Now let us systematize these same notes by placing regular *accents*. Clap again, this time putting in the accents as shown in the following:

♩ ♩ ♩ ♩ ♩ ♩ ♩ ♩ ♩ ♩ ♩ ♩ ♩ ♩ ♩ ♩

We see now that we have four groups of four notes, which may be divided into groups, called measures, which command a time signature of 4/4. Clap, using accents and counting the basic underlying beat of 1, 2, 3, 4.

1 2 3 4 1 2 3 4 1 2 3 4 1 2 3 4

We now feel four pulsations to each measure because of the accents on the first of each group of four notes. These accents give the notes movement in time within each note, duration as well as the length of time required to play or sing the entire group of notes.

On the last pattern, let us superimpose another rhythmic pattern:

pattern 2

pattern 1

1 2 3 4 1 2 3 4 1 2 3 4 1 2 3 4

In this example we have the underlying pulse of 1, 2, 3, 4, in every measure, and the regular rhythm of the quarter notes to which is added another rhythmic pattern. Together, they give us a feeling of two rhythmic patterns moving simultaneously in time. With your foot, tap the basic pulse of pattern 1 while you clap the rhythm of pattern 2, and count the beats of each measure. Has your interest and appreciation been increased through the recognition of the superimposed rhythm?

Now, keeping the above in mind, let us move to another phase of juxtaposition.

MELODY

You have noticed that the rhythmic patterns shown are devoid of any semblance of what, in Unit IV, we described as melody. These rhythmic patterns would become very monotonous and boring if it were not for the element of melody. Also, as we saw in Unit IV, just any series of tones won't make a melody. Let us look at the following example:

Ex. 166.

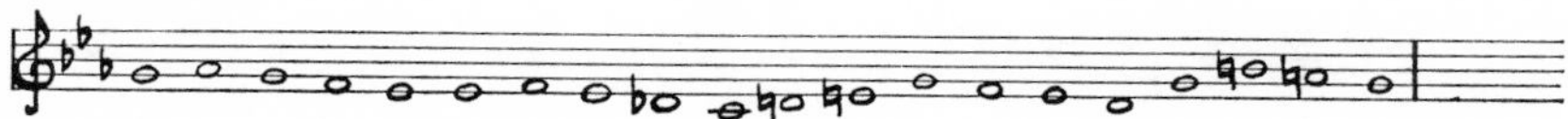

Sing or play this sequence of tones and you will see that they need to be systematized to give them character and meaning. This is just what rhythm does to a melody. Notice what happens when the rhythmic pattern is superimposed on this series of tones. Sing or play this melody, keeping the basic pulse of pattern 1 going simultaneously.

Ex. 167.

Melody moves in lines forming strands of tones which might be considered as running horizontally through the musical structure. In addition to the horizontal movement, we also have the up-and-down movement of the tones from lower to higher to lower, etc. One might call this feature a "two-way stretch" of the musical fabric. Consciously or subconsciously, the ear follows this time line in much the same manner as the eye follows the notes on the printed page. This process is relatively easy when only one melody—homophony (see p. 85 f.)—is utilized. For the ear, the process becomes increasingly more complicated as two or more melodies are combined as in polyphony (see p. 79 ff.) and requires repeated listening.

HARMONY

We generally think of harmony as the vertical building of tone combinations (see p. 96 ff.). These tone combinations may be likened to blocks of sound and serve as "chord posts" on which melodic strands are hung. Music which depends primarily on this element of the chord for its effect may be classified as harmonic in style. The hymns which we find in our church hymnals come under this classification.

To the melody which we used in Ex. 167, let us now add a harmonic structure.

Ex. 168.

The blocks of sound or chord posts which we mentioned can now be seen and heard in objective form. The series of notes which we used in Ex. 167 seemed to be an independent melody but now are fused with a substructure and become a part of the vertical harmonic fabric. Hence, the melody itself is not an independent melody; its existence as a melody is entirely dependent on the harmonic and rhythmic movement of each chord. But even though the top note of each chord is fused with the substructure, the ear is able to follow it satisfactorily. If you were to ask yourself whether the melody which results from the movement of the chords is vocal or instrumental, your answer should be vocal, because the melody can readily be sung. Examine now, some well-known hymns and folk songs as further examples of harmonic, and therefore, homophonic style (see p. 83 f.).

For practice, analyze the chords in the example given.

You may have recognized Ex. 168 as the first four measures of *Prelude*, Op. 28, No. 20, by Chopin. This *Prelude* is based on the repetition of a five-note motive. Variety is achieved by means of harmonic modulation. Notice also that the climaxes seem to occur on the third beat of the measure with the greatest climax occurring in the fourth measure. Basically this *Prelude* is harmonic in style and the "pull" of the chords adds to the feeling of movement.

COLOR

This poetic miniature by Chopin is one of twenty-four such *Preludes* which he wrote for the piano. The chord structure and general mood of the music is indicative of the Romantic period. With Chopin, the prelude lost its original meaning in that it was never intended to be an introductory piece. The twenty-four *Preludes* exist as separate entities—functionless, autonomous music. This same type of prelude may be found in the works of Scriabin, Debussy, and Rachmaninoff. In the case of Bach, his forty-eight *Preludes* are each followed by *Fugues*. In addition to being one of the earliest types of keyboard music, the prelude emerged as a characteristic form separate and apart from vocal influence. The prelude is, generally speaking, instrumental in classification and frequently pianistic in character.

Let us reconstruct another piece of music from its elements.

RHYTHM

Again we start with a basic pulse of four beats to the measure,

Pattern 1

1 2 3 4 1 2 3 4 1 2 3 4 1 2 3 4

on which we superimpose the following rhythmic pattern:

Pattern 2
Pattern 1

1 2 3 4 1 2 3 4

While you tap with your feet the basic pulse of pattern 1, clap the rhythm of pattern 2. Observe how pattern 2 creates an altogether different feeling of movement. Here we have juxtaposed a series of sixteenth notes on a movement of four quarter notes.

MELODY

Examine the following sequence of tones. You probably feel that, as a melody, they are uninteresting as they stand.

Ex. 169.

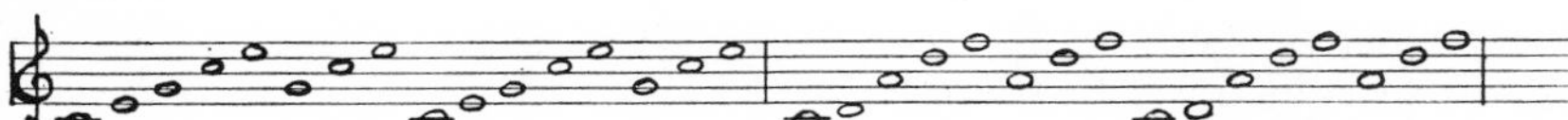

But let us systematize these tones for character and meaning by juxtaposing patterns 1 and 2. Sing or play the following "melody" keeping the basic pulse of pattern 1 going simultaneously.

Ex. 170.

At once they take on new life and meaning. But is there a real melody inherent in these tones? Before answering this question, let us proceed to an examination of its harmonic structure.

HARMONY

While harmony is the basic element in Ex. 170, we recognize it this time as a series of broken chords rather than being blocks of chords as in Ex. 169. To reduce these broken chords to block chords would not only defeat the whole idea of this piece of music but would involve changing the rhythmic character of the piece, thus robbing it of its meaning, character, and mood. If you have not already recognized the few measures in Ex. 170, we should tell you that they are taken from "Prelude No. 1" of the Bach *Well-Tempered Clavier*.

Sometimes composers appropriate other composers' music for their own purposes. The next example below represents such an appropriation. Let us see what Charles Gounod has done to the Bach *Prelude*. Compare the following example with Ex. 170.

Ex. 171.

First, Gounod transposed the notes an octave lower; secondly, he changed the rhythmic character of the harmonic structure; thirdly, he added a melodic line which he derived largely from the harmonic structure; fourthly, he added a set of words.

Find the notes in the piano accompaniment which serve as the tones of the melodic (?) line. Now play the piano part, accenting these notes. Notice also how the rhythmic character of the accented notes has been changed to further the melodic idea. Actually, *accent* belongs to rhythm, not to melody or harmony. Has the harmonic content been strengthened or weakened by the addition of this "melodic" line?

If we compare the Chopin *Prelude No. 20* with the Bach *Prelude No. 1,* we find that the melodic line of the former is dependent entirely on the movement of the chord posts, while the "melody" of the latter moves about with a great deal of rhythmic, melodic, and harmonic freedom, and is dependent largely on accent for its life, thus creating a subconscious feeling that a melody exists. Gounod has juxtaposed a synthetic melody on an essentially rhythmic and harmonic fabric.

COLOR

Originally, *Prelude No. 1* by Bach was written for a stringed keyboard instrument—*clavichord* or *harpsichord.* These instruments differed greatly in tone quality and mechanical features from the present-day piano—pianoforte (see p. 272 f.). Today, since the piano has become the basic stringed keyboard instrument of the twentieth century, we generally hear this *Prelude* played on that instrument. The original prelude is definitely pianistic in character. The Bach-Gounod adaptation—the *Ave Maria*—loses its original color by becoming a song. As a song, it is melodic in style. As a piano composition it is harmonic in style. If sung by a soprano, it has one color; if sung by a contralto, it takes on another—likewise a tenor or a bass. When we compare the climaxes of these two pieces, we find that the Bach *Prelude* has one climax, located seven bars from the end. The Bach-Gounod *Ave Maria* has in all about seven climaxes. It would seem, then, that Gounod, in his *Ave Maria,* misconceived the whole idea of Bach by transforming a harmonic keyboard work into a melodic vocal composition. However, the *Ave Maria* provides us with an excellent example of juxtaposed elements. Whether Gounod was justified in making this adaptation is a moot question, yet this was a favorite pastime of composers of the nineteenth century.

In the following example the music becomes somewhat more complex because of the introduction of new devices.

RHYTHM

To start with, our basic rhythmic pattern is again quarter notes, and the measure signature is C—4/4.

Pattern 1 C

1 2 3 4 | 1 2 3 4 | 1 2 3 4 | 1 2 3 4

On this basic rhythm two different rhythms are superimposed.

Pattern 3

Pattern 1 C

Pattern 2

1 2 3 4 | 1 2 3 4 | 1 2 3 4 | 1 2 3 4

To get the full effect of this rhythmic structure, divide the class into three sections. Section 1 claps the rhythm of pattern 1, section 2 claps pattern 3, while section 3 is subdivided so that one part claps the rhythm of the upper rhythm of pattern 2, and the other part claps the lower rhythm. Observe how, in the preceding patterns and those which follow, rests play a part in the movement of music. Some eight bars later in our composition, the preceding rhythmic patterns shift to the following, where we find an additional rhythmic pattern has been superimposed:

Divide the class in the same manner as previously described and clap the rhythms as shown. Now do you feel the complexity of the rhythmic structure? This should make you aware of the fact that it is possible to juxtapose one or more rhythmic patterns on a basic beat. When composers superimpose contrasting rhythms, we say that the music is polyrhythmic.

MELODY

Again let us start with a sequence of tones.

Ex. 172.

The composer transforms these into the following melodic line which he superimposes on the basic rhythmic pattern of 4/4 ♩ ♩ ♩ ♩:

Ex. 173.

Eight bars later a countermelody is introduced, using a different melodic line and rhythmic pattern. The melody just shown is transposed to the bass clef while the countermelody is introduced in the treble clef.

Ex. 174.

The melody represented by pattern 3 is vocal and typically lyric in style, while the countermelody of pattern 4 is definitely instrumental in style. However, the melody of pattern 4 is a type of instrumental writing which can be executed by a gifted *coloratura soprano* (see Appendix IV). Sometimes we refer to passages like this as *coloratura*. The melody of pattern 4 is used merely as decorative material and plays no vital part in the evolution of the theme—pattern 3—itself.

HARMONY

Although the opening sixteen bars of this composition are harmonic in style, like the Chopin example, the seventeenth bar begins a rhythmic pattern which is the generating force of this section. In the next example the harmony is delayed by the use of rests, creating in its movement a simple guitar-like accompaniment. The harmony is subservient to the rhythm. While the lyric melody of pattern 3 is dependent on the harmonic structure for its life, it maintains its rhythmic independence.

Ex. 175.

Eight bars later the composer further shows his craftsmanship by introducing a countermelody which we have already described. This countermelody stretches the rhythmic and harmonic fabric still further to make the music not only more complex, but it adds immeasurably to the psychological and aesthetic effect.

Ex. 176.

Although notes have now replaced the rests in pattern 2, the eighth-note movement has been maintained and the rhythm remains the generating force. Observe, though, that the chord posts have been simplified. Notice, also, the dissonances which are created by the passing tones. Listen for the deceptive cadence (see p. 175) which occurs in measure 25. Variety is achieved by means of melodic and rhythmic manipulation.

In Ex. 176 we find melody superimposed on melody, two melodies superimposed on the same harmonic structure, and the harmony superimposed on a motivating rhythmic pattern. The melodies, though rhythmically free of the accompaniment and of each other, are, nevertheless, dependent harmonically. This example affords us an excellent study of the increasing complexity of juxtaposed elements.

COLOR

The examples which we have just been studying are taken from the "Prelude" to Act I of the opera *La Traviata* by Verdi. The "Prelude," likewise the entire opera, is scored for orchestra. In Ex. 175 the lyric melody is sung by the violins while the accompaniment is supplied by the lower strings. In Ex. 176 the violins take the countermelody while the clarinet, bassoon, and cello sing the melody. The accompaniment is supplied by violas and basses. This "Prelude" is a good example of the juxtaposition of string and woodwind color.

Though the première of *La Traviata* was something of a fiasco, later revisions and subsequent performances have made it a favorite with opera audiences. However, the music critics have not always shown a corresponding respect for the work. The Italian love for the sentimental and the romantic is in evidence throughout this generally obvious music.

In the foregoing examples we have gone into considerable detail to show the pyramiding of rhythm, melody, harmony, and color. In the following examples we intend to discuss the juxtaposition of one element on itself. However, the listener is urged to continue on his own the juxtaposition of the elements in the manner we have shown.

In Ex. 177 a most interesting bit of juxtaposition takes place. This comes about by the pyramiding of chordal harmonies of different keys, sometimes referred to as *polyharmony.*

JUXTAPOSED HARMONY

To see how polyharmony is used, let us note the following example:

Ex. 177. Stravinsky: *Petrouchka,* "Fête Populaire de la Semaine Grasse," Theme 2

In this we note the chord of B-flat major superimposed on that of G minor, the chord of A minor superimposed on that of G minor, etc. These chords in block style are reminiscent of the Chopin *Prelude,* Ex. 168.

If taken together, these chords may be analyzed as triads, sevenths, ninths, and thirteenths. If this is done, the polyharmony is obscured. However, we may assume that this was not Stravinsky's intention, since in *Petrouchka* satire and caricature were uppermost in his mind. Certainly from an aesthetic and psychological point of view, the idea of chords in different keys being juxtaposed is much more harsh, brash, and satirical. This, then, was the effect Stravinsky was trying to achieve.

Beginning with the thirteenth chord, note the use of successive 6-4 chords. Examples of polyharmony may also be found in the "Dance Russe" of the ballet.

JUXTAPOSED RHYTHM

Though the purpose of Ex. 177 was to show the use of polyharmony, it is well to note that Stravinsky employed a rhythmic device which stamped him as a progressive. In the first tableau of the *Petrouchka,* we find the following time signatures in successive measures: 3/4, 5/8, 8/8, 7/8, 5/8, 7/8, 5/8, 8/8, 7/8, 5/8, 3/4, 2/4, 3/4, 2/4, 7/8, 5/8, 7/8, 5/8, 3/4, 7/8, 5/8, 7/8, 3/8, 5/8, 7/8, 5/8, and 3/4. There are also many instances of polyrhythm in *Petrouchka. Polymetric* measures also occur. A run-down of the score will show the piccolos and the oboes playing in 5/8 while the rest of instruments are playing in 2/4 in the same measure; or the piccolos and the oboes in 8/8 and the rest in 3/4 meter, etc. This device, of course, creates cross accents.

JUXTAPOSED MELODY

Also of interest in the *Petrouchka* ballet is the way Stravinsky makes use of a device called *polytonality* (see p. 116 f.).

In the tableau "Chez Petrouchka," Stravinsky juxtaposes melodies in the key of F♯ major and C major. This is writing which is definitely melodic rather than harmonic in style. The next example shows Stravinsky's use of the *tritone*—augmented fourth or diminished fifth. Here the bitonal melodies are an augmented fourth apart.

Ex. 178. Stravinsky: *Petrouchka,* "Chez Petrouchka"

The juxtaposition of tonalities is quite common in modern music. We would, however, like to make clear that while polyharmony and polytonality are similar, they differ in that the former applies to the simultaneous sounding of *chords* in different keys, the latter applies to juxtaposed *melodies* in different keys.

COLOR

Though originally intended for piano and orchestra, the work, after some changes and additions, finally saw the light of day (Paris, June 13, 1911) as the *Petrouchka* ballet. In this ballet, Stravinsky has juxtaposed not only the elements of music but also scenes, incidents, and emotions—in this case anguished love and jealousy—from the drama of life. *Petrouchka* is masterfully orchestrated and represents a bold departure from previously accepted orchestral sound—new, or at least different sonorities, harmony, and rhythms. *Petrouchka* is scored for the following:

2 Piccolos	Bass drum
2 Flutes	Cymbals
4 Oboes (1 English horn)	Tam-tam
4 Bassoons (1 contra bassoon)	Triangle
4 Horns in F	Tambourine
2 Cornets	Snare drum
2 Trumpets	Bells
3 Trombones	Celesta
1 Tuba	Piano
Timpani	2 Harps
	Xylophone
	Strings:
	Violin 1–2
	Viola
	Cello
	Double bass

We move now to a method of juxtaposition which had its origin in the sixteenth century but reached its zenith during the eighteenth century in the contrapuntal works of J. S. Bach. Based on counterpoint, this method of juxtaposition resulted in a form (?) called the *fugue* (see p. 205 f.). Harkening back to the pyramiding of horizontal melodies (see Unit IV, p. 81 ff.), the fugue represents the coming of age of imitative counterpoint. The pyramiding of melodies also implies the juxtaposition of rhythms, and rhythm is the driving force of the fugue.

JUXTAPOSED MELODY

Example 179 is a four-voice fugue. The entrance of the theme is clearly marked for easy recognition. Note how the space between each statement of the subject is filled in with free counterpoint derived from melodic motives and rhythmic patterns of the subject. Unity is achieved not only through the successive statements of the theme but by these melodic and rhythmic motives which tend to recall to the mind the subjects themselves.

Ex. 179. Bach: *Well-Tempered Clavier,* Fugue No. 1

The entrance of the second voice, stated in the dominant key, is a *real answer,* transposed exactly, to the first statement of the subject. A *tonal answer* is one in which the imitation is not exact. That is, certain melodic steps are changed—a fifth becomes a fourth or vice versa.

We see in this fugue, as in all polyphonic music, that rhythm remains the driving force. Notice also the polyrhythm which occurs because of the melodic imitation. Bach's success with polyphonic music can be traced largely to the psychological and aesthetic value of his fugal subjects—themes, melodies. Harmony is created only at the points where the individual horizontal strands of melody coincide. A fugue may be described as horizontal music.

In Ex. 179 variety is achieved through frequent modulations. There is continuous repetition of the subject to provide unity. In the middle portion of the fugue the restatements of the subject are not as widely spaced as in the exposition, one coming closely on the heels of the other.

JUXTAPOSED COLOR

We are probably more aware of the juxtaposition of color than we are of juxtaposed rhythm, melody, and harmony. Yet, of all the elements of music, we are probably more inclined to take the use of color for granted.

Of the fine arts, the use of color in painting more nearly corresponds to the use of color in music. Color breathes life into music. Color provides the means whereby music is objectified so that it may be heard and experienced. Color contributes immeasurably to the thrill of music. The composer juxtaposes colors just as the artist does. Color is the means by which the composer communicates with the listener. Color helps to give definiteness to music.

In Unit VII we listened to instruments and voices of various colors singly, and in combination. In the example that follows, we shall see how the composer uses color to help build a mounting emotional climax. Though all of the elements are drawn on to fashion the psychological impact of this composition, three—rhythm, melody, and color—are relied on heavily by the composer. Harmony and form are only a means to an end, the end being the slow and gradual sensuous buildup to an all-consuming climax.

"BOLERO"

Ex. 180. Ravel: *Bolero*

(Permission for reprint granted by Durand & Cie, Paris, France, copyright owners; Elkan-Vogel Co., Inc., Philadelphia 3, Pa., agent.)

CHART SHOWING THE JUXTAPOS

Th. 1 = Theme 1 RPa = Rhythmic Pat
Th. 2 = Theme 2 RPb = Rhythmic Pat

Measure	10	20	30	40	50	60	70	80	90	100	110	120	130	140	150	16
Piccolo															149 Th1	----
2 Flutes	5 Th1	----	21 RPa	----	----	----	----	75 ----		95 Th1	----	111 RPb	128 ----		147 RPa	----
2 Oboes													129 RPb	----	146 ----	
Oboe d'am.								77 Th1	----	93 ----						
Eng. horn													129 RPb	----	146 ----	
E♭ clarinet						59 Th 2	----	75 ----								
2 B♭ clarinets			23 Th 1	39 ----									125 RPb		147 RPb	----
Bass clarinet															147 RPb	----
2 Bassoons					41 Th 2	57 ----		75 RPa	----	93 ----					147 RPb	----
Contra Bsn.																
4 Horns in F										93 RPa	----	111 ----			149 Th 1	
4 Trumpets										95 Th 1	----	111 RPa	----	----	147 ----	
3 Trombones																
Tuba																
2 Soprano Sax.														131 Th 2	147 ----	
Tenor sax.												113 Th 2	129 ----			
3 Timpani																
2 Snare drums	RPa	----	----	----	----	----	----	----	----	----	----	----	----	----	----	----
Cymbals																
Tam-Tam																
Celesta															149 Th 1	----
Harp				39 RPb	----	----	----	75 ----							147 RPb	----
Violin I									89 RPb	----	----		129 RPb	----	146 ----	
Violin II								75 RPb	----	92 ----		111 RPb	128 ----		147 RPb	----
Viola	1 RPb	----	----	----	----	----	----	----	----	----	----	----	----	----	----	----
Cello	1 RPb	----	----	----	----	----	----	----	----	----	----	----	----	----	----	----
Str. bass								75 RPb	----	----	----	----	----	----	----	----

Bolero

ition of Instrumental Color

tern (a) .... = Instrument Continues

tern (b) Blank = Instrument Silent

0	170	180	190	200	210	220	230	240	250	260	270	280	290	300	310	320	330 340
165 ---				203 Th 2	215 ----	221 Th 1	239 Th 1	....	257 Th 2	269	275 Th 2	290	293 Th 1	....	311 Th 2	....	335 RPa
165 ---		183 RPa	....	203 Th 2	....	221 Th 1	239 Th 1	....	257 Th 2	....	275 Th 2	....	293 Th 1	....	....	....	335 RPa
167 Th 1	....	183 ---		203 Th 2	219 RPb	221 Th 1	239 Th 1	....	257 Th 2	....	275 Th 2	....	291 RPa	....	....	....	335 RPb
167 Th 1	....	183 ---															
167 Th 1	....	183 ---		203 Th 2	219		239 Th 1	....	257 Th 2	....	275 Th 2	....	291				335 RPb
167 Th 1	....	183 RPb	....	203 Th 2	218	221 Th 1	239	....	255 RPb	....	275 Th 2	....	291 RPa		311 Th 2	....	335 RPb
....	....	....	....	....	218		237 RPb	....	254 ---	269 Th 2	273 RPb	290 Th 2	291 RPb	....	....	....	....
....	....	182		201 RPb	....	....	....	....	....	....	....	....	....	....	....	....	....
		183 RPb	....	....	....	....	....	....	....	....	....	....	....	....	....	....	....
165 RPa	....	....	....	....	....	....	....	....	....	....	....	....	....	....	....	....	....
165 RPb	....	182 ---		201 RPa	219				257 Th 2	269	273 RPb	....	293 Th 1	309	311 Th 2	....	....
		185 Th 2	....	201					255 RPb	....	275 Th 2	....	291 RPb	....	311 Th 2	....	....
									255 RPb	....	....	....	....	....	....	....	....
							237 RPb	....	....	....	275 Th 2	290	293 Th 1	309	311 Th 2	....	....
				203 Th 2	219		239 Th 1	....	255 RPb	....	....	287 Th 2	293 Th 1	309	311 Th 2	....	....
					219 RPb	....	....	....	....	....	....	....	292	300 RPb	....	....	....
....	....	....	....	....	....	....	....	....	....	....	....	....	....	....	....	....	....
																	335 RPb
																	335 RPb
165 ---																	
....	....	....	....	....	218		237 RPb	....	....	....	....	....	....	....	....	....	....
165 RPb	....	182		201 RPb	219	221 Th 1	239 Th 1	....	257 Th 2	....	....	....	293 Th 1	309	311 Th 2	....	335 RPa
....	....	....	....	201 RPa	219 RPb	....	239 Th 1	....	257 Th 2	269 RPb	....	....	291 RPa	....	....	....	....
....	....	183 RPa	....	201 RPb	....	....	....	....	....	269 Th 2	....	....	291 RPa	....	....	....	....
....	....	....	....	....	....	....	....	....	....	....	275 Th 2	....	291 RPa	....	....	....	....
....	....	....	....	....	....	....	....	....	....	....	....	....	....	....	....	....	....

The *Bolero* is built on the themes and rhythmic patterns just shown. The composer mounts these themes and rhythms on a form we call *theme and variations* (see p. 200 ff.). There are eighteen variations, with each variation being introduced by a different instrumental color or combinations of color. Variety is achieved only through the use of color.

The two themes illustrated are never juxtaposed, but there is juxtaposition of the melodic rhythm with that of the rhythmic patterns (a) and (b). The rhythmic patterns (a) and (b) are also juxtaposed. Though basically in the key of C, the *Bolero*, at measure 327, suddenly modulates to the key of E major. The emotional climax, though reached at this point, is allowed to continue uninterrupted to the end where there is a sudden falling off.

The chart on pp. 176–177 is intended to help the listener to visualize the architectural plan of the composer. At the same time, the listener can, at a glance, observe exactly what elements are being juxtaposed in any given measure throughout the composition. The chart will also give the listener an idea of the magnitude of music in general and that of the composer's mind in particular.

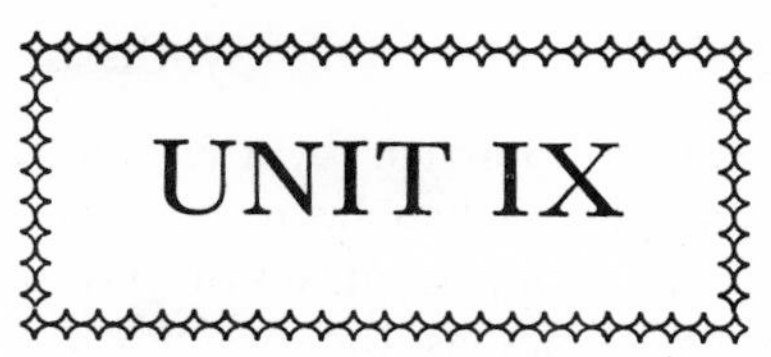

UNIT IX

The Architectural Aspects of Music: Form

Architects work with forms. They start with lines which, when used in certain ways, create squares, triangles, rectangles, which in turn create rooms, which in turn may result in a house of certain design. So, too, music deals with forms. But what is form in itself, and how may it be studied?

Form is the agent by which *order* is given to art, thus making it more easily grasped. Without form, art would be a chaotic combination of materials and parts. In music there are two different aspects to the study of form: (1) form *in* music and (2) forms *of* music. The study of these two aspects is approached in the following manner.

TWO METHODS OF APPROACH TO THE STUDY OF FORM

The first method involves aesthetic speculation, which in turn results in a philosophy of art. To the philosopher form is an abstract, subjective thing which cannot be studied in a systematic, concrete fashion. Form can be measured only in terms of the feeling of delight experienced by the individual in viewing a work of art as a whole.

> The concern of art, like that of science, is with the world as form, or with abstract experience. But whereas science seeks to understand a form either in terms of its constituent parts or by relating it to other forms and thus classifying it, art accepts the form for whatever measure of delight it may have to offer.[1]

Musically speaking, a composition possesses form when it is consistent, orderly, well balanced, and symmetrical.

The second method is an extension of the first. It is the perception of *forms* within a form. Forms are the substance of form objectified by example, form which becomes concrete by analysis. It is in this sense that form concerns us here. The manipulation of these forms involves an intellectual and artistic approach by the composer. The listener becomes one with the composer when he re-creates the form through analysis. The study of forms of music makes it possible for the listener to recognize such structural types as the overture, minuet, sonata, rondo, variation, etc. Here the composer has manipulated his materials according to a previously established pattern in a thoroughly free and personal manner.

All experience begins with forms, with organized wholes, which are at first vague and shadowy outlines because their component details are as yet indistinct. They are like a woodland which is only a blotch on the horizon until the traveler has come close enough to see the individual trees. When this latter happens the woodland is still a form, designated as being this or that thing. So forms, natural phenomena, grow in definiteness as the details that constitute them increase in clarity on repeated contact. It is by this process of getting to know a thing by coming increasingly closer to it that we learn what to do with it and about it.[2]

It should be remembered that no great composer allows himself to become a slave of form. Further, there are compositions which are not conceived in terms of a previously established pattern. Smetana says that "the music creates the form." Furthermore, long periods of experimentation are often necessary in the development of a specific form, e.g., sonata or rondo.

The term *style* (see p. 210 ff.) should not be confused with form. Webster says that style is a "distinctive or characteristic mode of presentation, construction, or execution in any art." For example, compositions may have the same form but differ in style (e.g., the symphonies of Mozart and Beethoven).

THE GENERAL PRINCIPLES OF FORM IN ART

In every work of art there are certain aesthetic principles which must be utilized in just the right proportion in order to convey a completely satisfying experience to the observer or listener. Form in art involves a balance between *unity* and *variety*, the essence of which is just the right *balance* and *symmetry* of and within its parts. Unity is achieved by judicious repetitions of the basic idea in the same or varying devices and implies systematic co-ordination. Variety implies the introduction of new details or the alternation of contrasting ideas. Variety appears to be in direct opposition to unity but the skillful artist must not completely divorce himself from either.

Though unity and variety are the most difficult to achieve, they are, at the same time, the most important principles. Let us see how they may be applied to music.

ACHIEVING UNITY IN MUSIC

The composer may achieve unity by the use of a *motive* (motif). It is the smallest structural unit in music capable of expressing a musical idea. The motive in music may be likened to a word in language. It is possible to express a musical idea with a motive of as little as two notes if the two notes are quite distinctive as to rhythm and/or interval relationship. The constant repetition of the motive is the first principle in musical construction and is analogous to unity in the principles listed previously. The motive is the driving force of music which gives movement and life to a composition.[3]

Through this constant repetition of the motive, whole sections may be developed. The motive not only binds the music together but through it the composition itself takes on form. It should be pointed out, however, that the motive is but one of the means the composer has of securing unity.

The following examples give definition to the term:

Ex. 181. Beethoven: *Symphony No. 5 in C Minor*, Op. 67, First Movement

Ex. 182. Tschaikowsky: *Symphony No. 6 in B Minor*, Op. 74, First Movement

Ex. 183. Franck: *Symphony in D Minor*, First Movement

Ex. 184. Mozart: *Symphony No. 40 in G Minor*, K. 550, First Movement

Motive (or Phrase) Development

The motive may be developed in one of the following ways: (1) Repetition of the motive on the same scale degrees. The repetition may be exact or modified, melodically, rhythmically, or harmonically.

Ex. 185. Mozart: *Symphony No. 40*, K. 550, First Movement

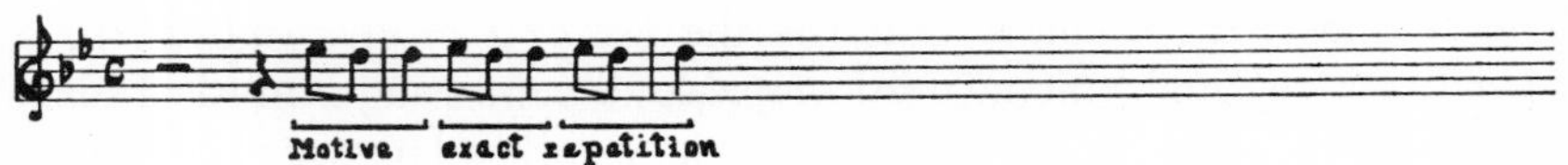

(2) SEQUENCE. The use of the motive on different scale degrees. The sequence may be exact or modified rhythmically, melodically, or harmonically.

Ex. 186. Beethoven: *Symphony No. 5*, Op. 67, First Movement

(3) AUGMENTATION. The lengthening of the note values of the motive.

Ex. 187. Tschaikowsky: *Symphony No. 6*, Op. 74, First Movement

(4) DIMINUTION. The shortening of the values of the motive. In the next example, the diminution occurs through the *alla breve* or cut time which in performance cuts the note value in half.

Ex. 188. Wagner: *Die Meistersinger*, Overture

(5) EMBELLISHMENT (extension). The addition of notes to the motive.

Ex. 189. Tschaikowsky: *Symphony No. 6*, Op. 74, First Movement

(6) THEME. This is the subject or basic idea with which the composer works. It is the dominating essence of the work of art. In many cases the statement and working out of the theme or themes becomes the work itself.

ACHIEVING VARIETY IN MUSIC

Deviation and Return

The composer achieves variety (contrast) by means of *deviation*—the addition of opposing but reciprocal *materials* and *tonalities* to arouse and maintain the listener's interest—and *return*. Though the following discussion confines itself to deviation and return, it should be pointed out that these devices per se will not alone achieve variety; they are but a means to an end.

We have seen how, by the constant repetition of the motive, unity is achieved. While this in itself gives the music coherence, it is necessary for a work of art to have contrast; otherwise it tends to become monotonous. The composer must say something new but inevitably related to what has already been said. This in itself creates contrast of ideas which, when heard side by side, lay themselves out in a kind of architectural pattern (form). In listening or observing smaller pieces of music, we will discover that they seem to fall into divisions of about equal length. These divisions have been called *phrase, period, double period,* and *phrase group*. We should point out that these divisions are not the only means the composer has of securing variety. Their purpose is one of punctuation. The divisions serve as the vehicle for variety, not the forms themselves.

The Phrase

In relation to the motive the phrase is the next largest structural unit. The phrase in music is likened to a series of words in language which expresses a unit of thought but one which requires another thought to make it complete. In music the phrase—a *harmonic* as well as a *melodic* unit—may contain repetitions of the same motive or a combination of several motives, and is usually four measures in length.

Ex. 190. Paganini, Niccolo: *Caprice,* Op. 1, No. 24, *in A Minor*

Ex. 191. Tschaikowsky: *Symphony No. 6,* Op. 74, First Movement

Ex. 192. Franck: *Symphony in D Minor,* First Movement

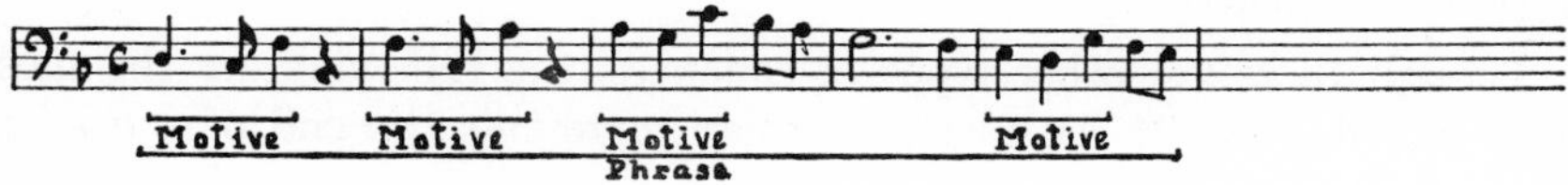

Ex. 193. Mozart: *Symphony No. 40,* K. 550, First Movement, Theme 2

The Period

In language a complete thought is expressed in a *sentence.* In music the sentence is called a *period.* The period usually consists of two four-measure phrases. A *parallel period* is one in which the second phrase begins like the first. A *contrasting period* is one in which the second phrase has a different beginning.

Ex. 194. Haydn: *Symphony No. 6,* B.H. No. 94, First Movement

Ex. 195. Beethoven: *Sonata No. 8 for Piano,* Op. 13, Second Movement

Ex. 196. Chopin: *Ballade II,* Op. 38

Ex. 197. Beethoven: *Symphony No. 9,* Op. 125, Fourth Movement

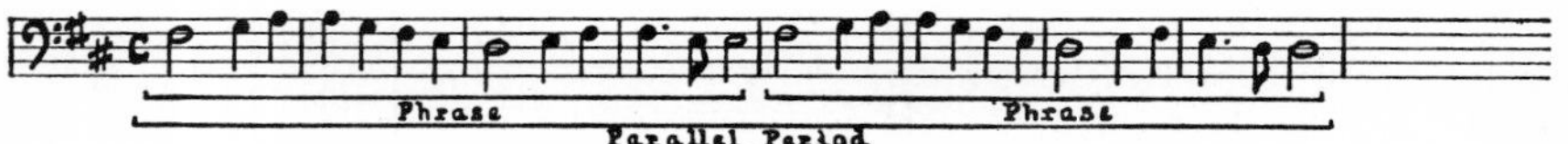

The first phrase of a period is called the *antecedent phrase,* generally ending with a *half* or *imperfect cadence* (usually V). The second is called the *consequent phrase,* generally ending with a *full* or *perfect cadence* (usually V or V^7 to I). The cadence is to music what punctuation marks are to language; they serve to separate one phrase from the next. The cadence is one means of giving form to music.

Types of Cadences

Though there are other types of cadences, the following are the most common. In Ex. 194 the fourth measure represents the end of a musical idea but the effect of the half cadence is indecisive and is therefore an imperfect cadence. In the eighth measure the cadence effect is much more final and is called a perfect cadence. All cadences are judged *aurally* as to their degree of finality. To distinguish between imperfect and perfect cadences the listener has but to decide whether the cadence is weak, hence the music must go on, or strong, thus signifying a satisfactory ending. The following example shows the use of the imperfect and the perfect cadence as well as the period form in music.

Ex. 198. Beethoven: *Sonata in E-Flat,* No. 18, Op. 31, No. 3, Second Movement

The *plagal cadence* is another type which may be employed. This cadence is often found at the end of hymns as the *Amen.*

Ex. 199. Handel: *Messiah,* "Hallelujah Chorus," No. 44.

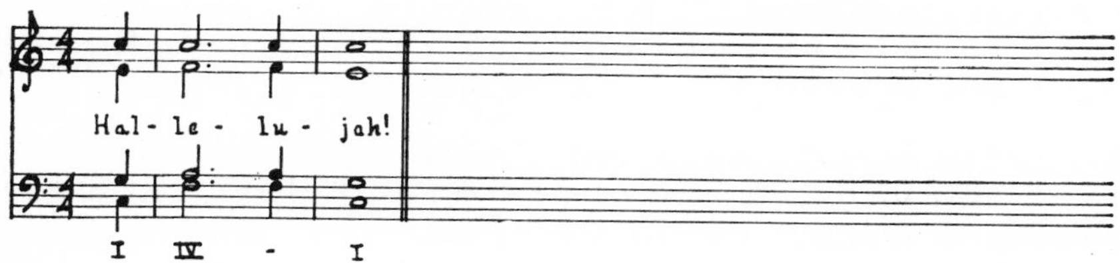

The *deceptive cadence* is one more type of cadence which we should consider. This cadence, usually made on VI, is used to create greater tension by delaying the normally expected tonic chord. It will be observed that this cadence is inconclusive, hence, in the truest sense, is not a cadence at all.

Ex. 200. Handel: *Xerxes*, "Largo" (Ombra mai fu)

Irregular Phrases

While the foregoing is illustrative of the regular phrase, which is four measures in length, it should be pointed out that if every piece of music were constructed in this manner the result would be monotonous. We should remember that variety is just as essential as unity or balance. Therefore, we find many examples of irregular phrases in music. Phrase irregularity arises from two causes: (1) phrases which are inherently not four measures in length—by inserting a cadence before it is normally due or by omitting a cadence, and (2) phrases which, due to melodic manipulation of the phrase, may be extended beyond the normal length of four measures. Note the insertion of the cadence in the third measure of this example:

Ex. 201. Brahms: *Sapphic Ode*, Op. 94, No. 4

The following example employs a deceptive cadence in measure 4 to give the effect of a bridge, thus lengthening the phrase to six measures.

Ex. 202. Carey, Henry: *America*

Phrases are also irregular in length because of the repetition of a complete phrase or a portion of it. In the example that follows, the extension is made by a repetition of measures 3 and 4.

Ex. 203. Mendelssohn: *Songs Without Words,* No. 37, Op. 85, No. 1

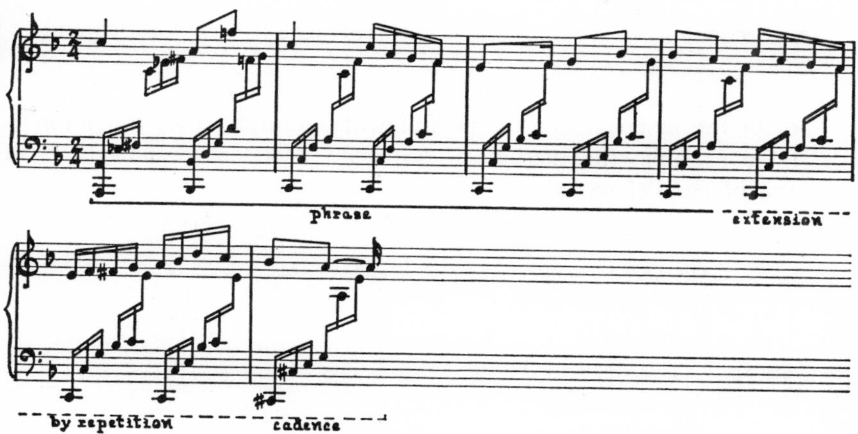

The next example illustrates the use of the sequence to extend the phrase.

Ex. 204. Mendelssohn: *Songs Without Words,* No. 8, Op. 30, No. 2

The Double Period

This consists of two periods divided in measure 8 by a strong half cadence. In the usual double period, phrases 1 and 3 are alike (parallel) while 2 and 4 are similar (contrasting). The cadences are generally used as follows:

Double Period

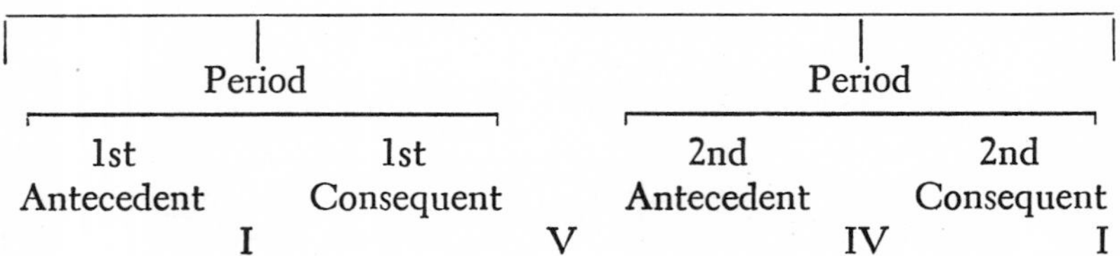

Though the first cadence in the following example is an exception to the stated formula, the example is primarily intended to show the construction of parallel periods.

Ex. 205. Schumann, Robert: *Album for the Young,* Op. 68, No. 20

In the contrasting double period shown next, it will be observed that phrases 1 and 3 are completely different as are phrases 2 and 4. Though the accent, here, is on variety, there is ample evidence of forces which unify the contrasting material.

Ex. 206. Mendelssohn: *Songs Without Words*, No. 2, Op. 19, No. 2

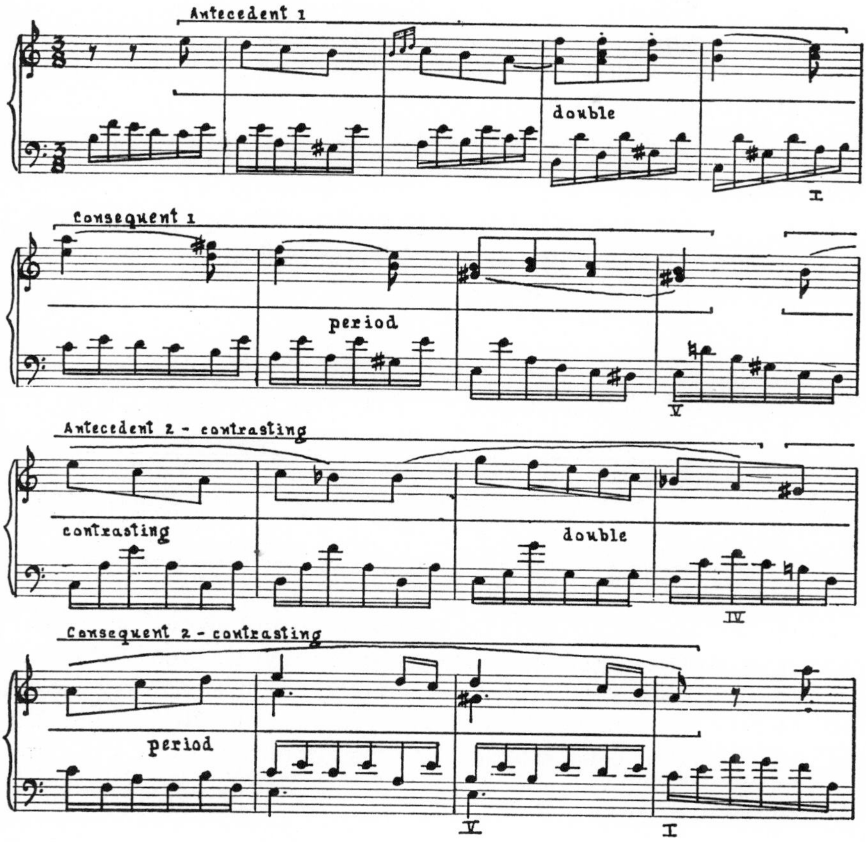
Antecedent 1
double
I
Consequent 1
period
V
Antecedent 2 - contrasting
contrasting
double
IV
Consequent 2 - contrasting
period
V
I

The Phrase Group

Sometimes this device is used in place of the period form. The phrase group usually consists of three phrases (parallel or contrasting) strung together with incomplete cadences (generally the half cadence), the last cadence being a full close.

Ex. 207. Gruber, Franz: *Silent Night*

phrase 1
I
phrase 2
I
phrase 3
V7
I

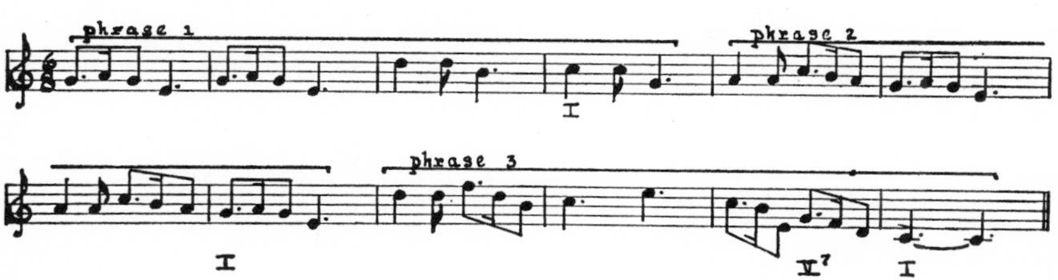

SIMPLE PART FORMS

Taken by themselves the *phrase*, the *period*, the *double period*, and the *phrase group* are called *one-part forms*. Taken in combination the result is a *two-*, a *three-*, or a *five-part* form. Since folk song literature abounds in such combinations, music theorists have come to use the term *song forms* for these classifications.

Two-Part Song Form

To see how the element of contrast plays its part in the construction of music, let us look at these one-part forms in combination. The simplest is the two-part form, also called the *binary form*.

Ex. 208. Brahms: *Cradle Song*, Op. 49, No. 4

Using the letters A and B to identify the first and second periods respectively, the form of this melody may be shown as AB. Notice how the two sections contrast each other; also, that each section ends with a full cadence. Frequently the two parts end similarly. Notice, also, that the sections are of equal length. The binary form is a continuous form.

Three-Part Song Form

The next largest part form is the three-part (ternary) form and may be designated by the letters ABA. Here is an extension of the idea of contrast and is one which has gained widest use. In the three-part song form, repetition is the dominant force. In the two-part song form there was no need for repetition, since each part ended with a perfect cadence. In the three-part form, Part III is a repetition of Part I at least to the extent that the ending and the beginning of Part III are the same. In a three-part form, Part II may consist of a phrase group of two phrases when both phrases end on the dominant chord. In the following example we see the principle of deviation and return at work.

Ex. 209. French Folk Song

Using the letter designations for the parts, the resultant form is AABA or simply ABA. It should be noted also that Part II may end with a half cadence in the tonic key, or with a full close in the new key. Part II in the example has modulated to the dominant key of F major. While the material in Part II may be new, it is *usually* derived from that of Part I.

In the ternary form the middle section may be in the dominant, relative, or parallel key; each section being harmonically closed.

Five-Part Song Form

We have seen in Ex. 209 that Part III is an exact repetition of Part I. The three-part form may be expanded into a five-part form by repetitions of Parts II and III, though mere repetitions do not constitute a five-part form. The content of Part IV is the key to the problem. The symbols for the most common types of this expanded form are as follows:

I	II	III	IV	V
		(I)	(II)	(III or I)
A	B	A	B	A

with Part IV being an exact or a modified transposition of Part II. Part V may be an exact or a modified version of Part III or I.

I	II	III	IV	V
may be repeated		(I)	new material	I or III repeated exactly, or modified
A	B	A	C	A

Illustrated in Ex. 210 is a typical realization of five-part form, since Part IV is obviously new material with only faint traces of Part II. (See also Beethoven's *Sonata*, Op. 13, Adagio, in which Part IV is entirely new.)

Ex. 210. Schumann: *Nachtstück,* Op. 23, No. 4

Codetta. This device is used with short compositions and actually is a brief extension of the composition after the complete cadence—a little coda. Used to emphasize the end of a composition, it occurs after a perfect authentic cadence. In larger compositions, the codetta is sometimes used in order to give the feeling of completeness to a section.

Sometimes a *Prelude*—a substitute for an Introduction—begins and a *Postlude* –a substitute for a codetta—ends a composition. If so, they are identical and each ends in a perfect authentic cadence. Also, an *Interlude* may be used between parts, and it may be a repetition of the Prelude.

Coda. The idea of repetition and contrast may be carried still further by the use of a coda, which is an extension of the composition after the complete cadence. The coda may consist of either old or new material, and it may be divided into sections or may be two or more codettas strung together.

HEARING SIMPLE PART FORMS

Let us test, now, what we have learned about repetition and contrast by listening to a recording of the "Dance of the Flutes" from the *Nutcracker Suite,* Op. 71a by Tschaikowsky. The differences which are inherent in this composition are best grasped as a whole even if repeated hearings are necessary. Critical listening will reveal the following: (1) a motive with subsequent repetitions; the first statement is in a major key and is played by the flutes:

Ex. 211.

(2) that in the first repetition of the statement—symbolized by the letter A—there is little change so that the repetitions will look like this—A–A′ (played by the flutes and the strings)–A; (3) that the first appearance of contrast is a typical expansion of the dominant harmony in a prevailing tonality of D major and is played by the English horn:

Ex. 212.

(4) that the contrasting material—B—after the statement begins to give the composition further shape; (5) that new contrasting material—symbolized by the letter C, played by the bass—is then modified as C′ which is presented by the brass, the strings, and the woodwinds (except flutes); (6) that after this new material, A returns, played again by the flutes and strings; and finally (7) that a five-part form emerges as the result of the interplay of repetition and contrast as: A B A′ C C′ A.

After this experience the listener should feel that the music has taken on new meaning. He needs now to test his new-found knowledge by listening and analyzing the recordings listed in Appendix V, before proceeding to the larger forms which follow.

LARGER FORMS

The larger forms are the end result of extensive experimentation with the principle of deviation and return which we found at work in the simple part forms. In these larger part forms the ideas contained in the simple part forms are compounded and refined, becoming, at one and the same time, somewhat more complex.* The forms which follow are included here because of their frequent recurrence in music literature.

Song Form with Trio

This part form has its roots in the dances of the eighteenth century and represents the combining of two different, though related, song forms. Applying the principle of deviation and return to this song form—sometimes called the *Menuet Form*—we find that this larger form consists of a *Principal Song* in either a two-part or three-part song form, more often the latter, and is complete in itself. This is followed by a deviating division called the *Trio* or *Subordinate Song*. This second song form is called the *Trio* because it was originally written for three instruments. Today we generally speak of the Trio as being the Subordinate Song, and it will be in either two or three-part form. After the Trio there is a return to the

* A definitive discussion of all the larger forms is beyond the scope of this text. The listener is therefore referred to a course in Form and Analysis or to books on forms of music.

Principal Song. If the Principal Song is to be repeated exactly, the designation "Da Capo" is used. A codetta or coda may be added. Thus we see that the Song Form with Trio is basically an extension of the ABA pattern. Expressed in symbols this expanded form is as follows:

A	B	A	
Principal Song	Subordinate Song (Trio)	Principal Song (Da Capo)	Coda optional
a–b or a–b–a	a–b or a–b–a	a–b or a–b–a	

It should be noted by the listener that the parts of the Song Form with Trio are complete entities and embody an almost distinct separation from each other.

In addition to the dance suite, the Song Form with Trio may be found in the Minuet (see p. 59) or Scherzo of the *Sonata* form, the dances of the nineteenth century, the March (see p. 66 ff.) as well as other instrumental and choral compositions.

Let us see how the principle of deviation and return is at work in this enlarged form by analyzing the third movement of a well-known composition. In listening to this movement we discover that it consists mainly of three themes:

Ex. 213. Haydn: *Symphony No. 6 in G Major,* B.H. No. 94 (Surprise), Third Movement, "Minuet"

Theme 1 is an extended double period:

followed by the contrasting second period, Theme 1a:

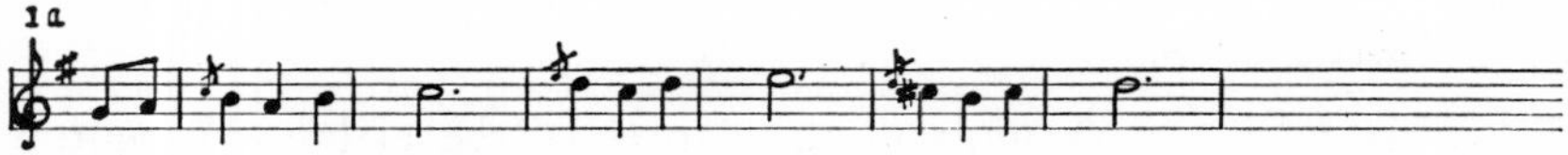

Theme 2 is an extended phrase:

Trio: Theme 3 is an inversion of Theme 2:

Principal Song (Da Capo).

By observing carefully, the listener will discover that Haydn has applied the principle of deviation and return in expanded form in the following manner:

Song Form with Trio

A	B	A
Principal Song	Trio	Prin. Song (Da Capo)
Parts	Parts	Parts
‖:a:‖ ‖:b a:‖	‖:a:‖ ‖:b a:‖	‖:a:‖ ‖:b a:‖
Themes	Theme	Themes
‖:1–1a:‖ ‖:2–1:‖	‖:3:‖ ‖:3 (modified)–3:‖	‖:1–1a:‖ ‖:2–1:‖

It should be noted that in performance today the repeats in the Da Capo are rarely taken, principally to save time and perhaps to avoid boredom.

The Rondo Form

The *Rondo* is an outgrowth of the three-part form and is derived from the French *Rondeau,* which means circle or *round.* Hence, in a Rondo, you expect that with each deviation from the principal theme or *refrain* there will be a return to it, thus completing the circle. So, in the Rondo, its distinguishing feature is the alternation of a principal theme with one or more *subordinate* themes. The principal theme must be distinctive as to melody, harmony, and particularly its rhythmic qualities. It rarely comprises less than a period or double period, often being of two-part and sometimes three-part song form. The subordinate theme is in a contrasting style, generally shorter in length than the principal theme and always in a different key. Unity is achieved through the return to the principal theme, while variety and contrast are achieved through the subordinate themes. A coda of some length is usually added for the sake of balance and interest.

Though there are many rondo forms, there are three which have been widely used. These rondo forms are the end result of the constant use and organic growth of the earlier rondo and have become the complex, idealized forms which we now call the *Classical Rondo.*

A	B	A
Principal Theme	Subordinate Theme	Principal Theme
Parts	Parts	Parts
	a period, double period	Same, perhaps with some embellishment or modification
a–b or	a–b or	
a–b–a	a–b–a	
Perhaps some transitional material	New key, maybe a codetta, some retransition	

The distinguishing feature of the example that follows is the one digression from and the inevitable return to the Principal Theme.

Ex. 214. Mozart: *Sonata No. 6*, K. 284, "Rondeau in Polonaise"

The form of this example is somewhat abbreviated in the third part (A), and the coda is quite short.

A	B	A	Coda
Parts (large) a–b–a	Parts a–b′	Parts shortened a	
Meas. 1–46	Meas. 47–69	Meas. 70–85	Meas. 86–92
Key A	Key F♯ minor	Key A	Key A

The Second Rondo Form

This is distinguished from the First Rondo Form by two digressions from and the subsequent return to the principal theme. The themes are usually shorter than those of the First Rondo Form.

A Principal Theme	B 1st Subordinate Theme	A Principal Theme
Parts Usually a–b. Sometimes a–b–a. Transitional material.	Parts Usually brief. New keys. Maybe a codetta and retransition.	Parts Somewhat shortened, embellished or modified.

C 2nd Subordinate Theme	A Principal Theme	Coda
Parts Distinctively different from either the principal theme or the 1st subordinate theme. New key retransition.	Parts Quite short, leading into	

Ex. 215. Beethoven: *Sonata,* Op. 49, No. 2, Second Movement

Note the increasing complexity of the Second Rondo form. The plan of this rondo is as follows:

A	B	A
Principal Theme	1st Subordinate Theme	Principal Theme
Parts a–b–a Meas. 1–20. Transition meas. 21–27.	Parts period Meas. 28–36. Codetta meas. 37–42. Retransition meas. 43–47.	Parts a–b–a Meas. 48–67.
Key G	Key D	Key G

C	A	
2nd Subordinate Theme	Principal Theme	Coda
Parts Double period meas. 68–83. Retransition meas. 84–87.	Parts a–b–a Meas. 88–107.	Period— consequent repeated meas. 108–120.
Key C	Key G	

The Third Rondo Form

As you would suspect, the Third Rondo form is more complex. It involves three deviations from the principal theme. To preserve unity and to avoid excess variety, the third deviation is a return to the first. It will be seen that the Third Rondo form is but a further enlargement of the three-part form, each section of which has been expanded to larger proportions.

I–1st division Exposition	II–2nd division Middle	III–3rd division Recapitulation	Coda
A–B–A Parts	C Parts	A–B–A Parts	Sectional
A complete 1st rondo form in itself: a–b–a c a–b–a / key change	a–b or a–b–a Strong key contrast. Retransition. Generally lengthy and embellished. Generally last phrase of the theme is used.	a–b–a c a–b–a No key change. Last announcement of principal theme is generally incomplete with only a motive or phrase of the 1st theme being used and absorbed in the coda. Principal theme may also be omitted.	

Since, as we said earlier, the Third Rondo form is the most complex of the three, let us analyze one such form in order to clarify for the listener what may be, on first hearing, rather vague and frustrating. Listen to the total effect first before trying to unravel the parts. For an example of the Third Rondo form, let us use one by a master craftsman of the rondo form.

Ex. 216. Beethoven: *Sonata*, Op. 2, No. 2, Fourth Movement

Pr. Th.

(1) Meas. 1–8—Period form—a

(2) Phrase—meas. 9–12—b

Transition

(3) Period form—meas. 17–26—to new key

1st sub. th.
(4) Period—antecedent phrase—meas. 27–32, consequent—meas. 33–39

(5) Retransition—meas. 40

Pr. Th.—meas. 41–56—as before, ending the Exposition
2nd sub. th.
(6) Period-form—meas. 57–66—a

(7) Period form—meas. 67–75—b

a—Exact repetition—meas. 76–80
b and a repeated—meas. 81–90
(8) Retransition—meas. 91–99

Recapitulation
Pr. Th.—meas. 100–115
Transition as before but abbreviated—meas. 116–123
1st sub. th. as before but in original key of A major and modified—meas. 124–135
Pr. Th.—meas. 135–140—dissolved into
Coda
Sec. 1—meas. 140–148, Sec. 2—meas. 149–160, Sec. 3—meas. 161–172, Sec. 4—meas. 173–180, Sec. 5 to end

Now let us see how these themes fit into the Third Rondo form, the architectural plan of which we have already described.

I–1st division Exposition	II–2nd division Middle
A–B–A	C
Parts	Parts
a–b–a c a–b–a	a–b–a

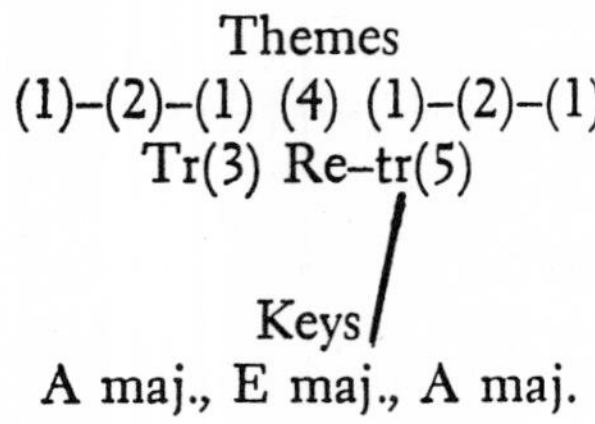

Themes
:(6): –(7)–(6)
Re–tr (8)
Key
A min.

III–3rd division
Recapitulation
A–B–A
Parts
a–b–a c a–b–a
Themes
(1)–(2)–(1) (4) (1)–(2)–(1)
Tr (3)
Keys
A maj., A maj., A maj.

Coda
Sectional
1–2–3–4–5

Rondo-Sonata

There is another type of Rondo called the Rondo-Sonata form which combines features of both the Rondo and the Sonata-Allegro form (to be discussed later). The Rondo-Sonata form substitutes a development section for the second subordinate theme of the Third Rondo form thus:

A	B	A	Development	A	B	A	Coda
a–b–a	c	a–b–a	generally sectional and based on Pr. Th. and/or 1st sub. th.	a–b–a	c	a–b–a	Sectional

In closing this discussion of Rondo form, it should be pointed out to the listener that these forms have provided the composer with a convenient and adequate vehicle for the writing of program music.

Theme and Variation Form

Let us digress for a moment from deviation and return as a device and a form to a discussion of unity and variety as found in varied repetition of one theme, called *monothematic form.* This device is almost as old as music itself but became very popular with composers of the Classic and Romantic periods. In the Classic period the form was strict, while in the Romantic and contemporary periods the form is freer. By evolution, the variation as a device in musical composition has resulted in forms in which the methods of variation may be either melodic, harmonic, or rhythmic. There are two main types of variation: (1) those motivated by a constantly recurring melodic fragment of four or five measures in the bass—*ground bass, basso ostinato, Passacaglia, Chaconne* (harmonic) (see p. 47 f.) and (2) those motivated by the variation of a complete melody usually in binary form. The number of variations ranges arbitrarily from four to thirty or more. This more familiar form of variation principle is the one we shall consider here.

Erroneously called "The Harmonious Blacksmith," the example that follows illustrates the strictly classic (small) type of the theme and variation form. This composition consists of a theme and five variations and the plan is predominantly rhythmic. The theme itself is two-part (binary) form with each part repeated. The melody is in the upper part.

Ex. 217. Handel: *Suite No. 5 in E Major*, Fourth Movement

Variation I employs the plan of a repeating design, harmony, and modulations. There is a rhythmic change of two notes to one.

Var. I.

Variation II shifts the rhythmic pattern of Variation I to the left hand, but otherwise complements it. Though the notes are not the same, the spirit remains.

In Variation III there is a repetition of design, harmony, and modulations, but the rhythmic pattern, now in the upper voice (right hand), again becomes three to one.

Var. III.

Variation IV corresponds to Variation III in that the rhythmic pattern, now in the lower part again, is three to one. The right hand now corresponds to the right hand of Variation II.

Variation V consists of complete scale passages which cascade from the right hand to the left and back in a rhythmic pattern of four to one. The harmonic framework is barren and the melodic line is obscured. The plan remains intact.

Var. V.

You probably observed while listening to this composition that the small variation is a simple form to follow since it consists of only one theme, which is repeated with regularity with unobtrusive melodic and rhythmic changes.

The large variation form gained its greatest impetus through the master craftsmanship of Beethoven. He it was who introduced *free* treatment of the theme, a diversified key system, and the use of a second theme in a variation form. The movement we are about to describe, an innovation in itself, was made to carry a load the likes of which the variation form had never experienced before. In addition to the ten variations, the form is enlarged to contain an introduction, a second theme, a codetta, and a grand coda. The movement begins with an eleven-measure introduction.

Ex. 218. Beethoven: *Symphony No.* 3 (Eroica), Op. 55, Fourth Movement

Theme I: Two-part form, each part 8 meas. repeated

Part I: Harmonic in character, meas. 1–43

Part II.

Var. I: Observe the imitation in both parts
Part I: Augmentation of theme, rhythm two to one

Part II.

Var. II: Follows the classic tradition of three notes to one
Part I.

Part II follows the same plan.

Variation III contains what may be considered to be the real theme, since it is thoroughly melodic and since it is used in addition to the first theme to unify the movement. Notice how the new theme is superimposed on the two rhythmic versions of the first theme, also the four to one rhythmic pattern.

Part I.

Part II follows the same plan. A transition to the key of C minor follows by means of old material, lifting the form from the dead level of the same key.

Variation IV is a *fugato*—a passage in fugal style as a part of a nonfugal composition—in the key of C minor.

Motives of Variation I are used as embellishment. In this variation the form breaks down—freedom is the essence.

Variation V is in the key of B minor. The melody of Variation III is heard. Part II appears in a rhythmic pattern of three to one and modulates to the new key.

Variation VI, in the key of G minor, presents a new militant melody which is heard over an augmentation of the first theme.

Var. VI.

Variation VII begins in C major and moves to C minor and E-flat major and serves as a transition. The plan is similar to Variation IV, utilizing the first and second themes.

Variation VIII, in E-flat major, presents a second fugato with the countersubject in a rhythmic pattern of four to one.

A big climax is reached through the gradual entrance of all of the orchestral instruments. At measure 329 there begins a long pedal point on the dominant of E-flat.

Variation IX in E-flat major modifies the theme of Variation III, and is in contrast to Variation VIII. Here the heroic manner is cast off and the mood is quiet and tender.

Variation X enters without benefit of a previous cadence and utilizes the theme of Variation III, Parts I and II of which are somewhat modified. The variation mounts to another climax; the codetta, at first thinly orchestrated, mounts to another climax.

The Grand Coda (Presto) in E-flat major, continues the climax and utilizes material from the several counterthemes previously heard.

It should be obvious after listening to this fourth movement of the *Eroica* that it is a great piece of music. Its psychological and aesthetic appeal will be enhanced by analysis, but the music is great because of its quality, not its structure. Here Beethoven gave full rein to his creative powers and in so doing came up with a prophetic work—freeing the theme and variation form of classical formalism.

Fugue

Though more of a style than a form, the fugue nevertheless does have certain characteristics. The fugue (derived from *fuga,* meaning flight) is dependent for its construction on the polyphonic elaboration (see counterpoint, Unit IV, p. 81 ff.) of a phrase called a *subject* which is imitated (repeated) by a fixed number of voices, generally three or four. Although two- and five-voice fugues appear in the literature, they become the exceptions rather than the rule. Written for instruments or voices, the term "voices" is always used when referring to the several parts. For example, the respective parts of a four-voiced fugue would be called soprano, alto, tenor, and bass.

Simple in plan, the fugue is based on the principle of having each voice announce the subject in succession, usually in relationship of tonic to dominant, the other voices continuing with a free counterpoint. If, on the second entrance of the subject—called the answer—the continuing counterpoint is given some degree of prominence, it is called the *countersubject*. The fugue consists of an *Exposition*—the first statement of the subject by all voices—followed by a section called an *Episode*—either new material or rhythmic and melodic motives from the subject and/or the countersubject—subsequently followed by a *Middle Entry*—reappearance of the subject in an order different from that of the Exposition. In this section there are a number of alternations of episodes and middle entries at the discretion of the composer. A *stretto*—the piling up or overlapping of the subject and answer at a closer time interval than occasioned their first announcement in the exposition—usually follows near the end for climactic and emotional effect. A pedal point (see p. 108 f.) on the tonic or the dominant, or both, often accompanies the final statement of the subject for added emotional impact which leads to a strong punctuating cadence at the end. Psychologically speaking, the subject and its repetitions supply the tension while the episode material supplies the relaxation.

Fugues are *sectional* in form, the sections being marked off by cadences, new material, or stylistic changes.

Certain other fugal devices may be utilized and applied simultaneously: If the answer is an *exact* repetition of the subject, it is called *real;* the answer is *tonal* when, for harmonic reasons, certain steps are modified—the interval g–d being answered by the interval d–g. A *double fugue* occurs when the same countersubject is sounded with the subject. Inversion occurs when the subject is turned upside down—upward movement of the subject becoming downward, and vice versa; *augmentation* (see p. 182)—note values usually increased by twice their normal length; *diminution* (see p. 182)—the opposite of augmentation; and, finally, *retrogression* (also known as *crab*)—the reading of a fugue subject backward from the right, last note, to left, first note.

The following example, called the *"Great" Fugue in G Minor* in contrast to the "Little" Fugue in the same key, is part of a composite work for organ. As seen by the title, the fugue is preceded by a fantasy—a piece, highly improvisational in character. We shall, of course, confine ourselves to the fugue, a masterpiece of structural perfection by a master craftsman of "The Art of Fugue."

Ex. 219. Bach: *Fantasy and Fugue in G Minor*

This is a four-voice fugue with the voices entering in the order shown in the following diagram.

I

EXPOSITION

MINOR

Measure 1 2 3 4 5 6 7 8 9 10 11 12 13 14 15 16 17 18 19

Soprano — Subject (mm. 1–4); Episode (mm. 8–9); Episode (mm. 12–14)

Alto — Answer (mm. 5–7)

Tenor — Subject (mm. 10–12)

Bass — Subject (mm. 15–18)

The fugue is in five sections. Section I—the Exposition (just shown); Section II—the Counterexposition—has only three statements of the subject (SAB) instead of four as in the Exposition; Section III—the Middle Entry—develops the subject in whole or in part with the emphasis on major keys; Section IV has just three statements of the subject (TSA) with a return to the basic key of G minor; in Section V the subject is stated four times (STAB). In all sections the statement of the subject is interspersed with episodes. The work builds to a triumphant climax with the last statement of the subject in the pedals, finally ending on a G major chord, called *Tierce de Picardie,* the use of a major third for a final chord of a composition in a minor key.

The fugue as a procedure reached its zenith in the Baroque period in the persons of Bach and Handel. Although the fugue as such was eclipsed in the succeeding periods, composers continued to employ imitative passages (fugato) in nonfugal choral and instrumental works.

Sonata-Allegro Form

The term Sonata-Allegro form refers to the design of a single movement, generally the first, of a sonata, a symphony, or a concerto; though it may occasionally be the form of the second or the last movement. The sonata-allegro form embodies the familiar three-part (ternary) pattern, though more complex. Its three divisions and their subdivisions are as follows:

A Exposition		
Pr. th.— tonic key	Sub. th.—	Closing sect. nearly related key
a–b or a–b–a (Transitional material, imperfect cadence)	Equal or nearly equal in length to Pr. th., hence, ending in perf. or imperf. cadence.	Sectional with one or more codettas. Generally ends Exposition with definite perf. cadence.

B Development	A Recapitulation		Optional Coda
Pr. th. or sub. th. or new material, various keys.	Pr. th.—Sub. th.—Cl. sect.— Tonic key		
Characterized by the manipulation of motives, phrases, or parts of the exposition. Sectional, ending in imperf. cadence.	Repetition exact or modified. (Transitional material)	One or more codettas. Generally ending in definite perf. cad.	Sectional, ending in complete cadence.

The classic example which follows illustrates the preceding material.
Ex. 220. Beethoven: *Sonata,* Op. 14, No. 2, First Movement

The following architectural plan illustrates the organic growth of the themes of Ex. 220:

	A Exposition		B Development
Pr. th.	Sub. th.	Cl. sec.	Pr. th.
Parts	Parts		Sectional
a–b	a–b	Codetta	I–II–III–IV
meas. 1–20.	meas. 26–40.	meas. 46–62.	meas. 63–123.
Transition	Extension		Various keys.
meas. 21–25.	meas. 41–45.		
Key	Key	Key	
G	D	D	

A Recapitulation			Coda
Pr. th.—Sub. th.—Cl. sec.			
As before, meas. 124–186			Meas. 187–199
Key	Key	Key	Key
G	G	G	G

This Unit has shown us that a great piece of music, like all great art, is a combination of many details. Though the whole composition is the sum of its parts, the whole is greater than its parts, for the whole alone can convey a complete aesthetic experience. We have explained and analyzed the many facets of unity and variety, from the structural unit in music (the motive) to the simple and larger part forms of musical composition. Unity presupposes repetition and variety presupposes contrasting material. Form is given to music through a combination of motives, phrases, periods, cadences, and parts to form larger units. The whole composition is a form, its component details are specific form which only repeated listening will provide.

UNIT X

The Final Outcome: Style

Style is omnipresent. Everywhere we are confronted with certain aspects of style in the realm of the arts, or with style in the mundane aspects of life. All of us are aware of style in some degree. But what is style?

STYLE IN MUSIC

Obviously, style is easier to recognize than to define. Style in any art is a composite of those things which make it distinctive. Detail is the essence of style. In music the details which make it distinctive are rhythm, melody, harmony, color, and form, the artful blending of which—hence, the composer's style—is dependent on his nationality, the period in which he lives, his taste, and his musical vocabulary. Style, then, is the result of a composer's instinctive adaptation of material in relation to his life and times. Obviously, Bach could not write music in the style of Schoenberg because our present ideas of rhythm, melody, harmony, color, and form were not yet available. Bach's style, then, is his distinctive use of the then known materials.

Do not confuse style with technique. Hindemith distinguishes clearly between the two when he says that "style is not wholly identical with technique. It is the peculiar manner in which a composer adds further component parts—parts, however, that are not essential to the structure's functional mechanism; parts that are added after the main decisions of construction have been made, after the technical part of the composition is virtually completed."[1] Style is the frosting on the cake. Style is an elaboration of a basic idea or ideas, not vice versa. New styles are built on seemingly outmoded ideas.

In music, the word style may be applied in many different ways. We may mean the composer's coloristic style—the use of instruments or voices; melodic, rhythmic, or harmonic style; the style of a period such as that of the Classic period; the style of a composer compared with that of another; the style of a nation compared to another—French, German, Italian, et al., or Western with Oriental style; operatic or instrumental style; homophonic or contrapuntal style, and so on. Style and form should not be confused. Compositions may differ in style but have the same form. For example, a string quartet of Haydn and Mozart may be cast in the same form but the style of Mozart will vary from that of Haydn.

The manner in which a composer combines harmony and melody is called *texture*. Monophonic and polyphonic styles create a *horizontal* texture, while homophonic style creates *vertical* texture. A certain texture results, then, from a given style. In listening to the texture of a composition, we can determine its style.

Consistency is the hallmark of a composer's style, or even of a period of music history. The composer's style is determined from the way he handles his materials and details most of the time. Thus, from his practice he establishes a certain set of principles. For example, if in the 371 Chorales which Bach wrote, he avoided the use of consecutive fifths ninety-nine per cent of the time, we could rightfully say that consecutive fifths are not in the Bach style of chorale harmonization, and the few times they are found represent an exception and should be classed as stylistic impurities. Thus, consistency—faithfulness to a principle—determines a style. Likewise, the style of a given period, or that of a given country, represents the combined principles of the outstanding composers of that period or country. Thus, in the Classic period adherence to form became an established principle because most of the composers most of the time were practicing formalism. Therefore, if one wishes to write in the Classic style, he must adhere to the formalism, in addition to other facets of the style, of the Classic period. If one does not adhere to the principle of form, even though his music may contain the other principles of the period, we say that the piece is not in the style, and the composer's knowledge and sincerity is questioned. "The perfect adaptation to conditions entails perfect unity of style, and it may be inferred conversely that complete perfection of style is to be found in perfect and relevant consistency."[2]

The style of a composer and, hence, of his period, always to be viewed in relation to the architecture, sculpture, painting, and literature of the era, is the product of his environment—religion, politics, economics, philosophy, and art in general. Viewed in their proper perspective, we can identify works of art as belonging to antiquity, the Renaissance, or the twentieth century.

Style does not remain constant; it is ever changing so that the style of a given period is not the style of the preceding one. For example, in Unit IV we discussed the textural aspects of monophony, polyphony, and homophony, in which we not only saw a shift in texture from monophony to polyphony to homophony, but also a shifting in ideas of tonality. This shift in style may be shown in a chart as follows:

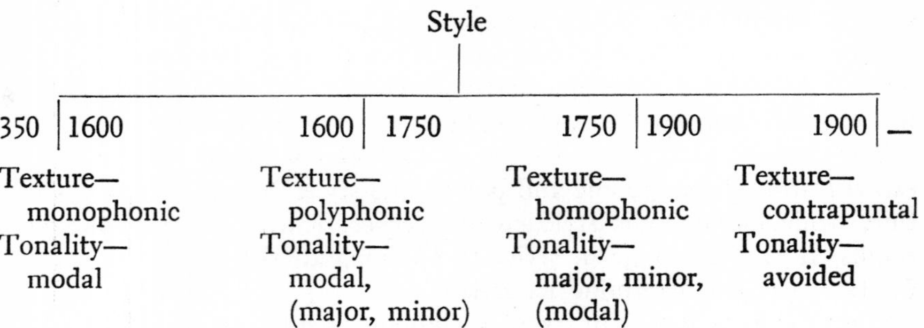

The dates given here are somewhat arbitrary, but convenient, and the listener should remember that there is an overlapping of one era on another, so that there is never a clean-cut break or dividing line. Any style is anticipated in one period and refined in the next.

STYLISTIC CONCEPTS BY PERIODS

On p. 213 ff. is a chart which is intended to show in generalities what principles may be expected in a given period of music history. It should be remembered that there is no clearly defined borderline where one device or style ends and another begins. Rather, they overlap. So, in order to show such overlapping, all lines between periods, styles, and harmonic devices are dotted lines. Also included in the charts are the forms in which the harmonic devices were cast, as well as the names of composers who had the greatest influence on the progress of music.

STYLISTIC CHART I—GENERAL

Antiquity	Middle Ages		Gothic	
350–850	850–1050	1050–1200	1200–1350	1350–1450
Monophonic Texture—Horizontal		Polyphonic Texture—Horizontal		
No Harmonic Structure		Pre-Tertian Harmony—Modal		
Plainchant. Single melodic line.	Organum. Two parts in parallel motion—fourths and fifths.	Organa. Two-part settings of plainchant in fourths, fifths, octaves in parallel and contrary motion. Thirds and sixths used but considered dissonances. Seconds and sevenths used as non-harmonic tones. Cantus firmus.	Motet and Polyphonic Mass. Cantus Firmus. Three-part writing. Open triads. Dissonance readily admitted as non-harmonic tones. Full triads of root, third, fifth sometimes occur.	Motet and Madrigals. Cantus Firmus. Open triads in first inversions. Chord progressions based on parallel sixths. Landini cadence—the use of the sixth degree between the leading tone and its final.
	St. Martial School.	Guido d'Arezzo, Notre Dame School—Leoninus, Perotinus.	Franco of Cologne. Petrus de Cruce.	Landini, Machault.

Stylistic Chart I—General (*Continued*)

Renaissance	Baroque	Classic
1400–1600	1600–1750	1750–1825
Polyphonic Texture—Horizontal		Homophonic Texture—
Tertian Harmony—Major, Minor		Tertian Harmony—
Mass, Motet, Madrigal, Anthem, Chorale. Three and four parts. First inversions of complete triads. Chromatic tones added to the harmonic structure. Antiphonal style developed. Tierce de Picardie introduced. Cantus Firmus elaborated. Diatonic melodies in major and minor or modal. No feeling of real tonality. Passing tones and suspensions used.	Mass, Motet, Madrigal, Cantata, Oratorio, Catch, Chorale, Opera, Aria, Recitative. Four-part writing with seventh chords, all inversions. Thorough bass. Wider use of I–IV–V chords creating a feeling of tonality. Modulations to closely related keys. Altered chords. Enharmonic changes. Some chromatic movement. Wider use of passing tones, suspensions. Two, three, or four simultaneous melodies. Tierce de Picardie.	Opera, Oratorios, German Lied, Glee, Ballet. Basic harmonies of I, IV, V. Bass figures of broken chords called Alberti Bass. Fairly distant modulations sometimes without pivot chords. Seventh and ninth chords widely used. Strict adherence to form. Simple melodies.
Instrumental Music Begins: Toccata, Canzona, Variation, Fugue-like style, Dances, some program music.	Instrumental Music gains equal footing with vocal. Concerto grosso, Sonata, Concerto added to other instrumental forms. Program music.	Instrumental Forms: Symphony, Classic Concerto, Classic Sonata, Variation, String Quartet, Overture, Program music.
Palestrina, A. Gabrieli, G. Gabrieli, Goudimel, Jannequin, Hasler, M. Praetorius, Dufay, Okeghem, Isaak, Des Pres, Lassus, Morales, Victoria, Byrd, Dowland, Gibbons.	Bach, Handel, Monteverdi, Frescobaldi, Corelli, A. Scarlatti, Vivaldi, D. Scarlatti, Lully, Couperin, Rameau, Schütz, Buxtehude, Kuhnau, Tartini, Telemann, Purcell.	Haydn, Mozart, Beethoven, Boccherini, Grétry, W. F. Bach, C. P. E. Bach, J. C. Bach.

Stylistic Chart I—General (*Continued*)

Romantic	Modern
1825–1900	1900–
Vertical	Contrapuntal—Horizontal
Major, Minor (modal)	Post-Tertian—Tonality Avoided
Opera, Oratorio, Anthem, Lied, English and French Art Songs. Wide use of chords with superimposed thirds, especially ninth chords. Some use of eleventh and thirteenth chords. Harmonic and melodic chromaticism used profusely, typified by altered and unresolved chords. Remote modulations. Fusion of major and minor keys. Extended phrases by avoidance of strong cadences. Reversion to church modes late in century to avoid major-minor tonality.	Opera, Oratorio, Art Songs, Lied. Harmonic principles of tertian harmony abandoned by use of parallel chords, polytonality, atonality, pan-diatonicism. Much use of dissonance. Ostinato revived by serious composers. Ostinato also used in jazz as the "riff" and "boogie-woogie." Harmonic and melodic structure based on church modes to avoid tonality.
Instrumental Forms: Symphonic Poem, String Quartet, Symphony, Sonata, Overture, Ballet.	Instrumental Forms: Sonata, Program music, Symphonic Poem, String Quartet, Concerto grosso, Overture, Fugue, Ballet-suites.
Schubert, Wagner, Franck, Tschaikowsky, Brahms, Rossini, Puccini, Verdi, Berlioz, Bizet, Saint-Saens, Fauré, Weber, Schumann, Mendelssohn, Chopin, Bruchner, Mahler, R. Strauss, Liszt, Dvořák, Moussourgsky, Grieg, Albéniz, Sibelius, MacDowell.	Debussy, Scriabin, Schoenberg, Hindemith, Ravel, Satie, Milhaud, Stravinsky, Bartók, Prokofieff, Vaughan Williams, Bloch, Gershwin, Copland, Harris, Piston, Hanson, Britten, Menotti, Griffes, Berg, Webern, Křenek.

RECOGNIZING STYLISTIC TRAITS OF TYPICAL COMPOSERS

First, let it be said that the information given in Chart II is not definitive for all known composers, or even for the specific composers we have chosen to summarize for recognizable stylistic traits. To make such a definitive study would require an almost endless amount of research. Such a study is not within the scope of these Units. We shall have to content ourselves, then, with some generalizations which are possible to make that will be indicative of some of the greater composers who seem to have dominated the period in which they lived, and who had a great deal of influence on the periods of music history which followed them.

Just as it is possible for us to spot a new Cadillac or Ford by looking for certain stylistic features, we can, by listening to the harmonic structure of a composition, determine the composer, or at least be able to identify the period. Poets, painters, sculptors, architects, writers, all have stylistic traits which identify them.

As stated earlier (Scope), "the music literature of the Units is concentrated in the Baroque, Classic, Romantic, and the Modern periods of music history." We propose in Chart II to start with the Renaissance so that we may show the connection between the "golden era" of polyphony and its culmination in the succeeding period in the crowning contrapuntal style of Bach.

Stylistic Chart II—Fifteen Representative Composers

Renaissance	Baroque	Classic		
1450–1600	1600–1750		1750–1825	
Polyphonic Texture—Horizontal			Homophonic Texture—Vertical	
Tertian Harmony, Tonality—Modal	Major, Minor	Tertian Harmony, Tonality—Major, Minor		
Palestrina, 1524?–1594	Bach, 1685–1750	Haydn, 1732–1809	Mozart, 1756–1791	Beethoven, 1770–1827
Style: Vocal–a cappella. Both simple and complex structure. Chords: Primarily major and minor triads. Tierce de Picardie. Nonharmonic tones: Prepared suspensions, passing tones, cambiata figure. Melody: Diatonic and modal. Few accidentals. Tonality: Strong mode feeling, no definite major or minor feeling. Modulation: Free passage from tone centers due to voice leading in contrapuntal style.	Style: Instrumental. Fugue, sonata, concerto. Vocal: Chorale. Complex structure. Chords: All kinds of major, minor, diminished triads, dominant seventh chords and other sevenths. Tierce de Picardie at cadences. Nonharmonic tones: A profusion of passing tones and suspensions, pedal point, anticipations, neighboring tones. Escape tones also used. Melody: Generally diatonic. Chromatic infrequent. Tonality: Definite. Modulation: To related keys.	Style: Instrumental. Symphony. (Vocal). Simple structure. Classic forms. Chords: Triads and seventh chords. Rarely used seventh of dominant in cadence. Nonharmonic tones: Few used and usually on weak beats. Melody: Diatonic, simple, with melodic line outlining harmony. Tonality: Definite. Modulation: To related keys as a rule.	Style: Instrumental. (Vocal). Simple structure. Strict adherence to classic forms. Chords: Triads and sevenths. Distinct preference for tonic and dominant. Nonharmonic tones: Suspensions and other dissonance used on weak beats. Melody: Diatonic. Melodic lines outline harmony. Tonality: Definite. Modulation: To closely related keys.	Style: Instrumental. Symphonies. (Vocal). Structure more complex. More freedom in use of form. Chords: Triads, sevenths, ninths. Altered and borrowed chords. Preference for tonic and dominant. Deceptive cadence. Nonharmonic tones: Frequent suspensions and passing tones on weak beats. Appoggiaturas. Melody: Diatonic. Line clear-cut and outlines harmony. More chromaticism. Tonality: Definite. Modulation: Generally to related keys though freer than Haydn or Mozart.

Stylistic Chart II—Fifteen Representative Composers (*Continued*)

Romantic				
1825–1900				
Homophonic Texture—Vertical				
Tertian Harmony, Tonality—Major, Minor, (Modal)				
Schubert, 1797–1828	Wagner, 1813–1883	Franck, 1822–1890	Tschaikowsky, 1840–1893	Brahms, 1833–1897
Style: Vocal-Lied. (Instrumental). Complex structure. Chords: Tonic and dominant sevenths. Borrowed altered chords. Nonharmonic tones: Passing tones, neighboring tones, suspensions. Melody: Diatonic. Melodic line outlines the harmony. More chromaticism. Tonality: Definite. Modulation: Some unexpected, to remote keys.	Style: Vocal-Instrumental. Use of Leitmotiv. Complex structure. Chords: Triads, sevenths, ninths, altered and borrowed chords, augmented triads, diminished seventh chords. Nonharmonic tones: Profusion of unprepared suspensions, passing tones, pedal points. Sharper dissonances unprepared. Melody: Chromatic and diatonic, some leaps of fourth, sixth, octave. Tonality: Obscure but it exists. Modulation: Constant, to remote keys.	Style: Instrumental–Cyclic symphony. Complex structure. Chords: Chromaticism, dominant sevenths and ninths. Triads borrowed and altered. Nonharmonic tones: Foreign tones, unprepared suspensions and passing tones, pedal points. Melody: Diatonic and chromatic. Tonality: Shifting. Modulation: Constant and to remote keys.	Style: Instrumental–Cyclic form. Chords: Sevenths, altered chords, especially tonic and subdominant. Nonharmonic tones: Frequent suspensions on strong beats. Melody: Diatonic, with chromaticism in inner parts. Preference for second, sixth, seventh, and eighth degrees of scale. Tonality: Definite and generally diatonic. Modulation: Usually conservative.	Style: Instrumental, Vocal-Lied. Complex structure and rhythm. Chords: Triads, plain and diminished sevenths. Some use of altered chords. Full chords in bass. Nonharmonic tones: Few suspensions. Melody: Melodic line outlines harmony, usually diatonic. Borrowed from folksongs. Tonality: Definite, usually diatonic. Modulation: By false dominants.

Modern				
		1900		
		Polyphonic Texture—Horizontal		
		Post-Tertian Harmony—Tonality Avoided		
Debussy, 1862–1918	Scriabin, 1872–1915	Schoenberg, 1874–1951	Stravinsky, 1882–	Hindemith, 1895–
Style: Instrumental, Vocal. Reminiscent of organum. Chords: No sequential movement. Triads sevenths, ninths used. Much use of augmented triads. Nonharmonic tones: Not important feature because of modes, whole-tone scale and dissonance. Unprepared and unresolved foreign tones. Melody: Part of harmony underneath. Modal melodies sometimes used. Tonality: Vague and shifting, sometimes avoided. Modes and whole-tone scale. Modulation: To unrelated keys by parallel motion.	Style: Instrumental. Rarely contrapuntal. Used forms from Romantic era. Chords: "Mystic (fourth) chord." Altered chords and arbitrary scales. Successive sevenths and ninths. Arbitrary chords in cadence. Nonharmonic tones: Not important feature. Dissonance for its own sake. Melody: Usually four measure phrases. Chromatic. Tonality: Early music had tonal centers. Later tonal patterns outside of key or mode. Modulation: To unrelated keys.	Style: Instrumental, Vocal. Classic forms. Chords: All types, including chords of fourths and fifths. In 12-tone system, no doubling of parts in chords. Any interval may be used in chord. Nonharmonic tones: Nonexistent in traditional sense because there is no tonality. Melody: Tone row. Ragged, with awkward skips. Dissonant and contrapuntal. Tonality: Atonal. 12-tone. Modulation: In 12-tone system it is not needed.	Style: Instrumental. Use of classical forms. Complex structures. Chords: Polyharmony, polyrhythmic, and polymetric. Parallel use of all types of chords. Some chords constructed from 12-tone scale. Nonharmonic tones: Not used in traditional sense. Melody: Two or three melodies in different keys independent of each other. Each melody may be diatonic. Tonality: Key center present but obscured by polytonality and pan-diatonicism. Modulation: Not in traditional sense.	Style: Instrumental–Atonal. Complex structure. Use of classic forms. Chords: Fourth chords. Use of tonal bridges. Chords unrelated. Use of augmented fourth and diminished fifth. All tone combinations possible. Nonharmonic tones: None, absorbed by the chords. Melody: Freed from harmonic structure. Dissonant counterpoint. Tonality: May be achieved through cadences. May begin and end on a tonic chord. Modulation: Not in traditional sense.

Appendices

Appendix I—*Quotations*

PART I

(For reference abbreviations see Appendix II.)

UNIT I—AESTHETIC PRINCIPLES OF MUSIC AND THE ALLIED ARTS

1. "Music began with singing." (SachsRMAW 21)
2. "Song did not grow out of impassioned speech, but arose coeval [of the same age] with speech, when men found—perhaps by accident—that they could make with their voices pure and pleasing tones and intervals of tones, and express something of their inner souls in so doing." (Parker-PAE 141)
3. "With the Chukchi in Northeastern Siberia, 'the shaman uses his drum for modifying his voice, now placing it directly before his mouth, now turning it at an oblique angle.' " (SachsHMI 34)
4. "He ventriloquizes, sings through the nose, cries, yodels, yells and squawks, but is never what modern singers strive to be: at liberty and natural." (SachsRMAW 23)
5. The dictionary gives the following definition of aesthetics: "The branch of philosophy dealing with the beautiful, chiefly with respect to theories of its essential character, tests by which it may be judged, and its relation to the human mind; also, the branch of psychology treating of the sensations and emotions evoked by the fine arts and belles-lettres."
6. ApelHD 17
7. Athenaeus says, "Pythagoras of Samos, with all his just fame as a philosopher, is one of many conspicuous for having taken up music as no mere hobby; on the contrary, he explains the very being of the universe as bound together by musical principles." (AthenDE 411)
8. Plato says in his *Republic*: ". . . because omissions and the failure of beauty in things badly made or grown would be most quickly perceived by one who was properly educated in music, and so, feeling distaste rightly, he would praise beautiful things and take delight in them and receive them into his soul, to foster its growth and become himself beautiful and good." (PlatoRE 259)

   ". . . surely the end and consummation of culture is the love of the beautiful." (PlatoRE 265)
9. In his *Politics* Aristotle says: "A task and also an art or a science must be deemed vulgar if it renders the body or soul or mind of free men useless for the employment and actions of virtue. Hence we entitle vulgar all such arts as deteriorate the conditions of the body, and also the industries that earn wages; for they make the mind preoccupied and degraded." (AristPOL 639)

   Further he says: "And since we accept the classification of melodies made by some philosophers, as ethical melodies, melodies of action, and passionate melodies, distributing the various harmonies among these classes being in nature akin to one or the other, and as we say that music ought to be employed not for the purpose of one benefit that it confers but on account of several (for it serves the purpose both of education and purgation— . . . —and thirdly it serves for amusement, serving to relax our tension and to give rest from it), it is clear that we should employ all harmonies yet not employ them in the same way, but use the ethical ones for education, and the active and passionate kinds for listening to when others are performing." (AristPOL 669f)

10. Boethius says: "The third is that which assumes the skill of judging, so that it weighs rhythms and melodies and the whole song. And seeing that the whole is founded in reason and speculation, this class is rightly reckoned as musical, and that man as a musician who possesses the faculty of judging, according to speculation or reason, appropriate and suitable to music, of modes, and rhythms, . . ." (StrunkSRMH 86)
11. "Professing to be more interested in the formulation of basic principles than in laying-down of rules to govern particular cases, he [Zarlino] looks on music as an imitation of nature and endeavors to derive his teachings from natural law. Starting from ratios for the primary consonances, he succeeds in arriving at many of the conclusions that modern theory draws from the harmonic series [see p. 136] a phenomenon unknown to Zarlino and his time. . . . [He was] the first to deal with harmony in terms of the triad rather than the interval, the first to recognize the importance of the fundamental antithesis of major and minor, the first to attempt a rational evaluation of the old rule forbidding the use of parallel fifths and octaves, the first to isolate and to describe the effects of the false relation; . . ." (StrunkSRMH 228)
12. "The spirit of the Renaissance eschewed medieval longing for the beyond and reinstated love of life as cherished by the ancients. Man and his natural circumstances became the center of interest. The baroque contributed to this new conception a keener sense for the comprehension of characters, passions, and 'affection.'" (LangMWC 435)

    "Rationalism sought in music as in other arts the 'imitation of nature,' the cherished dogma and foundation of its musical thought. We should not, however, expect this to mean tone-painting or program music, or the imitation of sounds that can be found in nature, such as the rippling of a stream, the buzzing of insects, or the chirping of birds. While such things sometimes occupied composers, literal imitations form a very small part of the musical aesthetics of the baroque, the musical thought of which was first and foremost concerned with the temper, disposition or frame of mind, passions, and mental reactions characteristic of man." (LangMWC 436)
13. Quantz in his method for the flute gives us a good idea of the music of this period. "The Italian way of singing is profound and artful, at once moving and astonishing; it engages the musical understanding and is pleasing, charming, expressive, rich in taste and stylish in delivery; it transports the listener in an agreeable way from one passion to another. The French way of singing, exaggerated rather than natural in expressing the passions and in voice, wanting in taste and stylish in delivery, and always the same; it is more for amateurs than for musical experts, better suited to drinking songs than to serious arias, and, while it amuses

the senses, it leaves the musical understanding wholly disengaged. The Italian way of playing is arbitrary, extravagant, artificial, obscure, likewise frequently audacious and bizarre, difficult in performance; it permits a considerable addition of embellishments and requires a fair knowledge of harmony; in the uninstructed it arouses less pleasure than astonishment. The French way of playing is servile but modest, clear, neat and pure in delivery, easy to imitate, neither profound nor obscure, but intelligible to every man and suited to the amateur; it requires little knowledge of harmony, for the embellishments are for the most part prescribed by the composer; at the same time, it is, for the musical expert, little conducive to reflection." (StrunkSRMH 594)

14. "In taste consisting, like the German taste, in a mixture of the tastes of various peoples, each nation finds something similar to its own—something, then, with which it cannot be displeased. Considering everything said up to this point about divergence in taste, the purely Italian must have the preference over the purely French; yet, since the former is not as thorough as it was, having become audacious and bizarre, and since the latter has remained all too simple, everyone will concede that a mixed taste, composed of what is good in both, must be unfailingly more general and more pleasing. For music that is accepted and pronounced good, not by a single country or by a single province or by this or that nation alone, but by many peoples—that is pronounced good, nay, that, for reasons offered, cannot be pronounced other than good—must be, if based in other respects on reason and sound feeling, beyond all dispute the best." (StrunkSRMH 597f)
15. StrunkSRMH 746.
16. StrunkSRMH 777.
17. StrunkSRMH 788f.
18. HanBM 66.
19. ApelHD 378f.

UNIT II—THE ART OF LISTENING

1. HanBM 20
2. "While listening to the musical structure, as it unfolds before his ears, he [the recipient] is mentally constructing parallel to it and simultaneously with it a mirrored image. Registering the composition's components as they reach him he tries to match them with their corresponding parts of his mental construction. Or he merely surmises the composition's presumable course and compares it with the image of a musical structure which after a former experience he had stored away in his memory. In both cases the more closely the external musical impression approaches a perfect coincidence with his mental expectation of the composition, the greater will be his aesthetic satisfaction." (HindCW 16)
3. "The reactions music evokes are not feelings, but they are the images, memories of feelings." (HindCW 38)
4. "Intellectually we build up structures parallel to actual musical ones, and these mental structures receive weight and moral meaning through the attitude we assume towards their audible or imaginary originals; either we consciously allow music to impress us with its ethic power, or we transpose it into moral strength. Emotionally we simply are slaves of musical

impressions and react to their stimulus, inevitably and independent of our own will power, with memories of former actual feelings." (HindCW 41f)

5. "[This] is the way of all experience, whether commonplace or creative, for every experience begins as a vague impression which grows in definiteness and in meaningfulness with repetition. But there is a difference between commonplace and aesthetic familiarity. Commonplace familiarity is *habituation,* and habituation is decline and not growth of interest and significance of what is experienced." (SchoenUM 149)
6. "Every form has a structure, but where the purpose is to understand the whole for what it is in its wholeness, the dissections of it into parts can result only in an intellectual understanding, not on its esthetic appreciation. There is, of course, an intellectual phase in art, but this is a means to an end." (SchoenUM 155)
7. "The way of interpretation consists in baiting the music to catch the attention of the listener. The bait used is either a story about the selection, what the composer intended to express through it, anecdotes about the composer, or its historical setting and importance." (SchoenUM 161)
8. "The psychological fact that must serve as a guide for the formulation of an educational procedure for the musical hearing of music is that expression is a function of the degree of experience, and this is in turn conditioned by the degree of one's sensitivity to the source of experience." (SchoenUM 169)
9. "The seed of esthetic experience is thus implanted in the soil of inborn sensory equipment. It is not of the same quality in all persons, but in all it needs the same cultivation in order to reach its full fruition. For music this means the cultivation through exercise, of the individual's auditory endowment for the perception of the melodic and harmonic elements of musical form." (SchoenUM 176)
10. "Unlike current methods, it concentrates upon *experience with tone in place of talk about tone,* and thereby contains the promise of building the habit of listening to music which will have no room for extra-musical intrusions. . . . The cultivation of the attitude of paying close attention to the tonal material that is being directly presented is a more urgent need of our day than ever before, because at no previous period has there been so much talk, and so much of it irresponsible, as is now pouring into the ears of millions of music listeners." (SchoenUM 179f)
11. "Schoen's theory is only a modification of the older theory of Hanslick. The aesthetic response is described as a detached, subjective experience, complete within the individual. He has tried to demonstrate how much form-mindedness is inherent, a natural power, by relating it to the more simple discriminatory reactions to pitch, loudness, etc. This may follow if one accepts the inheritance of such sensory capacities. However, the foregoing chapters [of Lundin's *An Objective Psychology of Music*] have demonstrated that such discriminatory responses are not inherent but acquired, so it follows that the aesthetic response as Schoen has tried to describe exists can only be examined in terms of verbalizations. Certainly, it is not subject to any objective analysis or investigation. Finally, I [Lundin] know of no evidence to support the contention that the individual who depends on his associations, feelings, and imaginative reactions for part of the aesthetic enjoyment is the less musical or that

such reactions are necessarily outside of the aesthetic experience. I [Lundin] believe they are just as much a part of the aesthetic response as is the perception of form in the object." (LundinOPM 168)

12. Lundin OPM 171.
13. "The aesthetic response equipment of the organism is directed wholeheartedly toward the stimulus object. Such an intense attention reaction is going to require much of the organism's equipment. It is an active type of reaction involving muscular tension. The habits of attention which allow us to maintain this activity are a matter of practice and skill." (LundinOPM 171)
14. "The aesthetic response is also a *perceptual* reaction. Without this developed perceptual ability, the beauties of the objective world may be completely lost. It involves a keen perception of the qualities of the object. At one moment we may perceive the rhythmic progressions, the harmony, the melody, or all the elements combined. Acquiring such perceptive ability means finding enough detail in the stimulus to engage all the organism's response equipment. Such perceptual habits are usually directed toward the formal aspect of the stimulus—the patterns, rhythms, melodic construction, etc." (LundinOPM 171f)
15. "It is an attentive state, with musculature and all the senses alert and active, following every detail of the stimulus and making the experiencing of it a forceful and vivid awareness. With so much bodily activity in the perception of the stimulus, meaning is crowded into it richly, and these meanings are the unusual, impersonal, and abstract in contrast to the concrete and practical meanings of ordinary day-to-day activity. All of these activities are made more poignant because they occur on a background of widespread and unlocalized bodily sensations, especially from the involuntary muscles and viscera which give the experience affective and emotional qualities." (HevnerPR 257)
16. "If we take any piece of popular music, whether the popularity be ephemeral or more lasting, like that of popular classics, and study its predominant traits, we find that it is either tuneful, exciting, sentimental, picturesque, dramatic, or astonishing. All these traits go back to the childhood of music and are characteristic responses that children make to music before they attain the aesthetic stage of mental growth." (SchoenUM 127)
17. "Popular music tends to reach the maximum of pleasantness at an early repetition, whereas classical selections reach their affective height with later performances. . . . Popular music reaches a peak in affective value followed by a rapid decline in pleasantness with continued repetition." (LundinOPM 152)
18. "Classical selections tend to gain more in pleasant affective value with repetition than do popular ones. . . . With repetition, compositions considered by experts to be the greatest in musical aesthetic value show the greatest gain in affective reaction with repetition." (LundinOPM 152)
19. "Great music is music that is beautiful, music that one not only likes but lives. The difference is between commonplace and creative experience, between ordinary pleasure and aesthetic enjoyment." (SchoenUM 121f)

    "Great music is that which rises above what is commonly familiar and is presented in an uncommon way." (SchoenUM 125)

"We do not designate it [music] as an object of art until many individuals find it beautiful. Thus the beautiful characteristic of the object has a cultural stimulus function. It is not typically idiosyncratic, to be enjoyed by only one person. Rather, it has the same significance for more than one person." (LundinOPM 170)

PART II

UNIT III—THE PULSE OF MUSIC: RHYTHM

1. "It is a well-known fact, cited in most discussions of this subject, that the motor mechanism of the body is somewhat attuned to rhythm. When we hear rhythmical sounds, we not only follow them with the attention, we follow them also with our muscles. With hand and foot and head and heart and respiratory apparatus. Even where we do not visibly move in unison with the rhythm—as we usually do—we tend to do so, which proves that in any case the motor mechanism of the body is stimulated and brought into play by the sounds. There is a direct psychological connection between the hearing of rhythmic sounds and the tendency to execute certain movements." (ParkerPAE 138f)
2. ". . . There is an equally direct relation between emotions and tendencies to movements, through which the former find expression and are given effect in the outer world. To every kind of emotion—love and hate, and fear and sorrow and joy—there corresponds a specific mode of motor manifestation. The connection between rhythmic sound and emotion is therefore plain. The link is a common motor scheme. Rhythms arouse into direct and immediate activity the motor 'sets' that are the physical basis of the emotions, and hence arouse the corresponding emotions themselves without any ground for them outside of the organism. And these emotions, since they are aroused by the sounds and not by any object to which they might be directed and upon which they might work themselves off in a meaningful reaction, are interwoven into the sounds,—they and the sounds come to us as a single indissoluble whole of experience. The emotions become the content of the sounds. And hence the strangeness of the musical experience—the fact that we feel so deeply over nothing." (ParkerPAE 139)

UNIT IV—THE LINEAR ASPECTS OF MUSIC: MELODY AND COUNTERPOINT

1. "*Propinquity* . . . A tonal progression proceeding from one note to another by small intervals gives a greater unity and coherence to a series of tones than large skips do. That is, the closeness of the tones gives them organization, so that we are able to call the result a melody. An analysis of melodies shows that skips of sevenths are rarer than skips of seconds and thirds. When large skips do occur, they are usually followed by smaller changes in the interval of progression." (LundinOPM 69)
2. "*Repetition*. Another attribute of melody is the repetition of its elements. . . . The point to be remembered is that melodies frequently involve the repetition of the same notes, and this attribute helps us characterize a particular tonal configuration as a melody." (LundinOPM 69f)

3. "*Finality.* A third attribute of melody is *finality* or what is often called *cadence.* The feeling of ending expressed by a falling movement of tones or a certain sequence of tones may give the feeling of conclusion, and that it is a proper ending.
   "We have emphasized that the ending preference in a melody is a result of what we are used to hearing. Certain endings are preferred because they appear more often that way, thus showing the cultural evolution of our music. However, all musicians and psychologists do not follow this interpretation." (LundinOPM 70f)
4. "Psychologically, any tonal succession becomes a melody if it gives an impression of being a sequence, and not merely a haphazard collection of tones of different pitch. There are then tonal successions that never constitute a melody and others that invariably do so." (SchoenPM 32)
5. "It seems as though these characteristics of the melodic line—the single appearance of the climax, and its location near the end, between a long ascending and a short descending branch—would have their roots outside of music or art altogether in physical and psychical provinces.
   "In the progress of many natural phenomena similar conditions prevail. There are thunderstorms with a marked tendency to rise to a mounting fury by comparatively slow degrees and to abate quickly after their most vehement outbursts. It is the pattern of many illnesses to develop slowly towards a 'crisis' after which recession and reaction set in quickly. It is also the trend of slowly developing anxieties, fears and hopes to be quickly released after the materialization of their objective. Finally, the phenomenon touches upon the physical-psychical borderland of our love-life.
   "These natural tendencies lie, metaphorically speaking, hidden in the work of art. The artist, in the process of creating his work is not conscious of them. But his work is a pulsation and manifestation of nature. Imbuing him, the man, nature imbues his work with her own features." (TochSFM 82)
6. ParryEAM 20.

UNIT V—THE VERTICAL ASPECTS OF MUSIC: HARMONY

1. BudgeSCF 61.
2. Op. cit.

UNIT VI—NEW TONAL CONCEPTS

1. TochSFM 10ff.
2. MeyerAMI 73
3. MeyerAMI 123
4. MeyerAMI 157
5. MeyerAMI 161
6. LuddenMC 6f.
7. MusAM 13
8. BoisIX 12
9. BoisIX 3
10. BoisIX 34f.
11. BoisIX 36

UNIT VII—THE ACOUSTICAL ASPECTS OF MUSIC: TONE COLOR

1. "There are two theories of tone quality, both of which are necessary to explain the tone qualities of musical instruments. Neither tells the whole story alone. The *harmonic theory* states that the characteristic tone quality of an instrument is due entirely to the relationship among fundamental and upper partials, which relationship is supposed to remain unchanged no matter what the fundamental is. . . . The *formant theory* states that the characteristic tone quality of an instrument is due to the relative strengthening of whatever partial lies within a *fixed or relatively fixed* region of the musical scale. . . . Thus, according to the harmonic theory, if the instrument plays a different pitch, the vibration form will be similar, since, although the particular harmonic series will be shifted, its members will still retain the same intensity relation to each other. But according to the formant theory, whatever partial lies within or close to the formant range will be strengthened. If the pitch of the fundamental changes, so that some other partial comes into the formant range, this partial will be strengthened. Thus, although the formant range is fixed, the vibration form will change as the fundamental changes." (BarthAM 15ff)
2. SeaPM 33.
3. SeaISBM 62.
4. In general, the following areas are covered in the good voice studio: (FieldTSV 10f)
   "Breathing—the activation and control of the respiratory organs in singing.
   "Phonation—the inception of vibratory activity in the glottis to produce voice.
   "Range—extent of the musical scale covered between the lowest and highest pitches of the voice.
   "Dynamics—the variation and control of loudness and varying power of tone.
   "Ear Training—developing hearing acuity for vocal sounds.
   "Diction—enunciation and verbal intelligibility in vocal expression [English, French, German, Italian if the singer has professional intentions].
   "Interpretation—the communication of mood and thought values in singing."
   These skills can be accomplished through exercise and appropriate song material.
5. CopWLM 80ff.

PART III

UNIT VIII—JUXTAPOSITION OF MUSICAL ELEMENTS UNIT IX—THE ARCHITECTURAL ASPECTS OF MUSIC: FORM

1. SchoenUM 18.
2. SchoenUM 12.

3. "Every combination of a few tones is apt to become a motif and, as such, to pervade and feed the cellular tissue of a composition, emerging and submerging alternately, giving and receiving support and significance by turns. It revives and animates, and is revived and animated, in a continuous cycle of give and take. It lives on repetition and yet on constant metamorphic [transformation], polymorphic [assuming various forms, character or styles], opalescent [reflecting colors] in itself, it takes on the hue, the flavor, the very mood of the environment in which it is imbedded. It smoothes and ruffles, it soothes and arouses; it bridges and reconciles, glues and splices, planes and levels, polishes and varnishes. But above all it creates and feeds movement, movement, movement, *the very essence of life,* and fends off the arch-enemy, stagnation, the very essence of death. *"It, the little motif, becomes the motive, the motive power, the MOTOR."* (TochSFM 200f)

UNIT X—THE FINAL OUTCOME: STYLE

1. HindCW 114.
2. ParrySMA 24.

Appendix II—*Specific Bibliography*

Though the following lists of references constitute the bibliography of the several Units, they are also intended as a broad overview of the material of the text, and as a means of listener orientation for each Unit. The complete titles with their abbreviations are given. Thereafter only the abbreviations are listed for each specific reference to subject matter.

AbraTMS — Abraham, Gerald. *This Modern Stuff*. Hoddeston, Herts, England: The Clock House Press, 1933.

ApelHD — Apel, Willi. *Harvard Dictionary of Music*. Cambridge, Mass.: Harvard University Press, 1944.

ApelMK — ———. *Masters of the Keyboard*. Cambridge, Mass.: Harvard University Press, 1947.

AristPOL — Aristotle. *The Politics* (tr. H. Rackham for The Loeb Classical Library). London: William Heinemann, Ltd. Cambridge, Mass.: Harvard University Press, 1932.

ArveyCM — Arvey, Verna. *Choreographic Music*. New York: E. P. Dutton & Co., Inc., 1941.

AthenDE — Athenaeus. *The Deipnosophists*, VI (tr. Charles Burton Gulick for The Loeb Classical Library). London: William Heinemann, Ltd. Cambridge, Mass.: Harvard University Press, 1937.

BabbHF — Babbitt, Milton. High Fidelity. Vol. VIII (February 1958), *Who Cares if You Listen?*

BabbJMT — ———. The Journal of Music Theory. Vol. VIII (Winter 1964), *An Introduction to the R.C.A. Synthesizer.*

BarthAM — Bartholomew, Wilmer T. *Acoustics of Music*. Englewood Cliffs, N. J.: Prentice-Hall, Inc., 1942.

BauerTCM — Bauer, Marion. *Twentieth Century Music*. New York: G. P. Putnam's Sons, 1947 (1933).

BoisIX — Bois, Mario. *Iannis Xenakis: The Man and His Music.* London: Boosey and Hawkes, Ltd., 1967.

BudgeSCF — Budge, Helen. A *Study of Chord Frequencies*. New York: Teachers College, Columbia University, Bureau of Publications, 1943.

BukMBE — Bukofzer, Manfred F. *Music in the Baroque Era*. New York: W. W. Norton & Company, Inc., 1947.

CageS — Cage, John. *Silence*. Middletown, Conn.: Wesleyan University Press, 1966.

ChuDE — Chujoy, Anatol. *The Dance Encyclopedia*. New York: A. S. Barnes & Co., 1949.

CopONM — Copland, Aaron. *Our New Music*. New York: Whittlesey House, 1941.

CopWLM — ———. *What to Listen for in Music*. New York: McGraw-Hill Book Company, Inc., rev. ed., 1957 (1939).

CoweHMH — Cowell, Henry. Hi-Fi Music at Home. Vol. II (January–February 1956), *Composing with Tape*.

CroceAE — Croce, Benedetto. *Aesthetic* (tr. Douglas Anislie); 2nd ed. London: Macmillan & Co., Ltd., 1922.

DockEMR — Dockstader, Tod. Electronic Music Review. No. 5 (January 1968), *Inside-Out: Electronic Rock*.

DorianHMP — Dorian, Frederick. *The History of Music in Performance*. New York: W. W. Norton & Company, Inc., 1942.

DouglasEMIM — Douglas, Alan. *The Electronic Musical Instrument Manual*. New York: Pitman Publishing Corp., 1954.

EimeEM — Eimert, Herbert. Die Reihe. Vol. I, *Electronic Music*. Bryn Mawr, Pa.: Theodore Presser, 1958.

EinstMRE — Einstein, Alfred. *Music in the Romantic Era*. New York: W. W. Norton & Company, Inc., 1947.

EricksonSM — Erickson, Robert. *The Structure of Music*. New York: The Noonday Press, 1955.

EwenWTCM — Ewen, David. *The World of Twentieth Century Music*. Englewood Cliffs, New Jersey: Prentice-Hall, Inc., 1968.

FieldsTSV — Fields, Victor A. *Training the Singing Voice*. New York: King's Crown Press, 1947.

FinnHM — Finney, Theodore. *A History of Music*. New York: Harcourt, Brace & Co., 1947.

GardOH — Gardner, Maurice. *The Orchestrator's Handbook*. Great Neck, N. Y.: Staff Music Publishing Co., 1948.

Gilbert–KuhnHA — Gilbert, Katherine E., and Kuhn, Helmut. *A History of Aesthetics*. New York: The Macmillan Company, 1939.

GleasonMMAR — Gleason, Harold. *Music Literature Outlines, Series I.* "Music in the Middle Ages and Renaissance." Rochester, N. Y.: Levis Music Stores.

GoetschLMF — Goetschius, Percy. *Lessons in Music Form*. Boston: Oliver Ditson & Co. (1904).

HanBM — Hanslick, Eduard. *On the Beautiful in Music* (tr. Gustave Cohen); 7th ed. New York: H. W. Gray & Co., Inc., 1891.

HaydonIM — Haydon, Glen. *Introduction to Musicology*. New York: Prentice-Hall, Inc., 1941.

HevnerPR — Psychological Review. *The Aesthetic Experience: A Psychological Description*. K. Hevner, Vol. 44, 1937.

HindCW — Hindemith, Paul. *A Composer's World*. Cambridge, Mass.: Harvard University Press, 1952.

HorstPCDF — Horst, Louis. *Pre-Classic Dance Forms*. New York: The Dance Observer, 1937 (1940).

HowOAM — Howard, John Tasker. *Our American Music*. New York: Thomas Y. Crowell Company, 1946.

HullHS — Hull, A. Eaglefield. *Harmony for Students*. London: Augener, Ltd., 1918.

HullMH — ———. *Modern Harmony*. New York: Edwin F. Kalmus, 1934.

JuddARR — Judd, Frederick Charles. Audio and Record Review. Vol. I (November 1961), *The Composition of Electronic Music*.

JuddEMMC ———. *Electronic Music and Musique Concrète.* London: Neville Spearman, 1961.

LangMWC Lang, Paul Henry. *Music in Western Civilization.* New York: W. W. Norton & Company, Inc., 1941.

LeichMF Leichtentritt, Hugo. *Musical Form.* Cambridge, Mass.: Harvard University Press, 1951.

LeichMHI ———. *Music, History, and Ideas.* Cambridge, Mass.: Harvard University Press, 1947.

LenSTCH Lenormand, René. A *Study of Twentieth Century Harmony.* London: Joseph Williams, Ltd., 1940.

LuddenMC Musical Courier. *Composing by the Yard.* Bennet Ludden, January 1943, Vol. CXLIX, No. 1.

LuenJR Luening, Otto. Juilliard Review. Vol. VI (Winter 1958-59), *Karlheinz Stockhausen.*

LundinOPM Lundin, Robert William. *An Objective Psychology of Music.* New York: The Ronald Press Company, 1953.

MachICM Machlis, Joseph. *Introduction to Contemporary Music.* New York: W. W. Norton and Company, Inc., 1961.

McHoseCHT McHose, Allen Irvine. *The Contrapuntal Harmonic Technique of the Eighteenth Century.* New York: F. S. Crofts & Co., 1947.

McKin–AndCL McKinney, Howard D., and Anderson, W. R. *The Challenge of Listening.* New Brunswick, N. J.: Rutgers University Press, 1943.

McKin–AndMH McKinney, Howard D., and Anderson, W. R. *Music in History.* New York: American Book Company, 1940.

MEJ Music Educators Journal. *Electronic Music.* November 1968, Vol. 55, No. 3.

MeyerAMI Meyer, Leonard B. *Music, The Arts and Ideas.* Chicago: University of Chicago Press, 1967.

MeyerH ———. Horizon. Vol. III (September 1960), *Art by Accident.*

MillerNHD Miller, Horace Alden. *New Harmonic Devices.* Boston: Oliver Ditson Company, 1930.

MorrisSM Morris, R. O. *The Structure of Music.* London: Oxford University Press, 1935 (1947).

MusAm Musical America. *By the Numbers.* September 1956, Vol. LXXVI, No. 11.

NettlSDM Nettl, Paul. *The Story of Dance Music.* New York: Philosophical Library, Inc., 1947.

NewlinBMS Newlin, Dika. *Bruckner—Mahler—Schoenberg.* New York: Columbia University Press, 1947.

NYT *New York Times.* Ed. Dec. 25, 1949. The New York Times Publishing Co.

Ogden–RichMM Ogden, C. K., and Richards, I. A. *The Meaning of Meaning.* New York: Harcourt, Brace & Co., 1936.

ParkerPAE Parker, DeWitt H. *The Principles of Aesthetics.* 2nd ed. New York: F. S. Crofts & Co., Inc., 1946.

ParryEAM Parry, Charles Hubert. *Evolution of the Art of Music.* New York: D. Appleton & Co., 1930.

ParrySMA ———. *Style in Musical Art.* London: Oxford University Press, 1900.

PlatoRE Plato. *The Republic,* I (tr. Paul Shorey for The Loeb Classical Library). William Heinemann, Ltd. Cambridge, Mass.: Harvard University Press, 1930 (1943).

PoussEMR Pousseur, Henri. Electronic Music Review. Vol. V (January 1968), *Calculation and Imagination in Electronic Music.*

RaderMBA Rader, Melvin M. A *Modern Book of Aesthetics.* New York: Henry Holt & Co., Inc., 1935.

ReadTOD Read, Gardner. *Thesaurus of Orchestral Devices.* New York: Pitman Publishing Corp., 1953.

ReeseMMA Reese, Gustave. *Music in the Middle Ages.* New York: W. W. Norton & Company, Inc., 1940.

SachsHMI Sachs, Curt. *The History of Musical Instruments.* New York: W. W. Norton & Company, Inc., 1940.

SachsOMH ———. *Our Musical Heritage.* New York: Prentice-Hall, Inc., 1948.

SachsRMAW ———. *The Rise of Music in the Ancient World, East and West.* New York: W. W. Norton & Company, Inc., 1943.

SachsRT ———. *Rhythm and Tempo.* New York: W. W. Norton & Company, Inc., 1953.

SachsWHD ———. *World History of the Dance* (tr. Bessie Schoenberg). New York: W. W. Norton & Company, Inc., 1937.

SchoenPM Schoen, Max. *The Psychology of Music.* New York: The Ronald Press Company, 1940.

SchoenUM ———. *The Understanding of Music.* New York: Harper & Brothers, 1945.

SchoenbSI Schoenberg, Arnold. *Style and Idea.* New York: Philosophical Library, Inc., 1950.

SeaISBM Seashore, Carl E. *In Search of Beauty in Music.* New York: The Ronald Press Company, 1947.

SeaPM Seashore, Carl E. *Psychology of Music.* New York: McGraw-Hill Book Co., 1938.

SeawRE Seawright, James. Radio-Electronics. Vol. XXXVI (June 1965), *What Is Electronic Music?*

SlonMS1900 Slonimsky, Nicolas. *Music Since 1900;* 3rd rev. ed. New York: Coleman-Ross Company, Inc., 1949.

StockDR Stockhausen, Karlheinz. Die Reihe. Vol. V (1961), *Electronic and Instrumental Music.*

StrunkSRMH Strunk, Oliver. *Source Readings in Music History* (Selected and Annotated). New York: W. W. Norton & Company, Inc., 1950.

TochSFM Toch, Ernst. *The Shaping Forces in Music.* New York: Criterion Music Corp., 1948.

WallPM Wallescheck, Richard. *Primitive Music.* London: Longmans, Green & Co., Inc., 1893.

WeinMA Weinstock, Herbert. *Music as an Art.* New York: Harcourt, Brace & Co., 1953.

Wen-ChungCMS Wen-Chung, Wen. College Music Symposium. Vol. VI (1966), *Writings on the Use of Computers in Music.*

Wen-ChungMQ ———. Musical Quarterly. Vol. L (April 1966), *Varèse: A Sketch of the Man and His Music.*

PART I—GENERAL PRINCIPLES

UNIT I—AESTHETIC PRINCIPLES OF MUSIC AND THE ALLIED ARTS

From Primitive to Aesthetic Art

ParkerPAE	154ff
ParryEAM	61ff
SachsRMAW	19ff

Definition of Art

Gilbert–KuhnHA	550ff
Ogden–RichMM	139ff
ParkerPAE	16ff
RaderMBA	xi–xxxv *et passim*
SchoenUM	1ff

Definition of Musical Aesthetics

HanBM	66ff
HaydonIM	113ff
ParkerPAE	153ff
SchoenUM	74ff
SealSBM	17ff
	378ff

Antiquity

ApelHD	17ff
FinnHM	12ff
LangMWC	16ff
LeichMHI	8ff
McKin–AndMH	88ff
ReeseMMA	20ff
SachsOMH	16ff

Middle Ages

ApelHD	249
LangMWC	17
ReeseMMA	44ff
SachsOMH	29ff
SachsRMAW	253ff

Gothic

HaydonIM	5f
HindCW	1ff
LangMWC	59ff
LeichMHI	51ff
McKin–AndMH	123
ReeseMMA	118f
SachsOMH	66
StrunkSRMH	87ff

Renaissance

DorianHMP	35ff
FinnHM	125ff
LangMWC	292ff
LeichMHI	74ff
	94ff
McKin–AndMH	221ff
SachsHMI	297ff
StrunkSRMH	229ff

Baroque

ApelHD	76f
BukMBE	1ff
	370ff
	394ff
DorianHMP	58ff
FinnHM	290ff

Baroque—(Cont.)

LeichMHI	113ff
	134ff
McKin–AndMH	307ff
SachsOMH	206ff
	224ff
	240ff
	262ff
SachsHMI	351ff

Rococo

ApelHD	240
	289f
	647
DorianHMP	87ff
	647
LangMWC	530ff
McKin–AndMH	368ff
SachsOMH	273f

Classic

ApelHD	336f
FinnHM	368ff
	384ff
	407ff
LangMWC	567ff
	618ff
LeichMHI	161ff
McKin–AndMH	449ff
SachsOMH	285ff
	307ff
StrunkSRMH	577ff
	599ff

Romantic

ApelHD	649f
CopWLM	207ff
	216ff
DorianHMP	217ff
EinMRE	75ff
	293ff
	337ff
FinnHM	422
	427ff
	485ff
LangMWC	734ff
	801ff
	843ff
LeichMHI	196ff
	222ff

Romantic—(Cont.)

McKin–AndMH	512ff
	545ff
SachsHMI	383ff
SachsOMH	307ff
	326ff
	340ff
StrunkSRMH	743ff
	750ff
	764ff
	808ff
	846ff
	874ff

Modern

ApelHD	289
	350f
	451
	452
	489ff
	550f
	552f
	815
DorianHMP	324
FinnHM	556ff
LangMWC	990ff
LeichMHI	243ff
McKin–AndMH	649ff
SachsOMH	358ff
ApelHD	478ff
DorianHMP	355f
FinnHM	479f
	523f
	528
	543f
	550ff
	644ff
HowOAM	226ff
	326ff
LangMWC	938ff
LeichMHI	215f
McKin–AndMH	699ff
SachsOMH	369f
ApelHD	59f
	253f
	775ff
FinnHM	551f
LangMWC	1024ff
McKin–AndMH	816ff
SachsOMH	336ff

PART II–MUSICAL ELEMENTS

UNIT II–ART OF LISTENING

UNIT III–THE PULSE OF MUSIC: RHYTHM

Temporal Aspects

ApelHD	6
	442
	593f
	639ff
	726f
CopWLM	33ff
LeichMF	222
LundinOPM	97ff

Tempo

ApelHD	442f
	736f
LundinOPM	100
SeaPM	90ff

Habañera

ApelHD	315
ChuDE	221
NettlSDM	309
SachsWHD	446

Tango

ApelHD	732
ChuDE	464
NettlSDM	309
SachsOMH	369
SachsWHD	446f

Polka

ApelHD	591
ChuDE	376ff
NettlSDM	280f
SachsWHD	434ff

Pavane

ApelHD	561
	716ff
ArveyCM	137
ChuDE	354f
HorstPCDF	9ff
McKin–AndMH	354
SachsWHD	355ff

Gavotte

ApelHD	291
ArveyCM	139
ChuDE	202
HorstPCDF	89ff
NettlSDM	115f
SachsWHD	388f

Galop

ApelHD	290
ArveyCM	178
ChuDE	201
NettlSDM	264

Trepak

ApelHD	760
ArveyCM	174
ChuDE	483

Chaconne

ApelHD	126f
ArveyCM	139f
ChuDE	89
HorstPCDF	127ff
NettlSDM	179f
SachsWHD	371ff

Passacaglia

ApelHD	126f
	546f
ArveyCM	212
ChuDE	354
HorstPCDF	127ff
NettlSDM	180
	338
SachsWHD	373

Courante

ApelHD	193f
ArveyCM	136f
ChuDE	112
HorstPCDF	43ff
NettlSDM	103f
SachsWHD	361ff

Galliard

ApelHD	290
ArveyCM	137
ChuDE	200f
HorstPCDF	23ff
NettlSDM	100ff
SachsWHD	358ff

Polonaise

ApelHD	592
ArveyCM	197f
	201ff
ChuDE	385

Polonaise—(*Cont.*)

NettlSDM 276ff
SachsWHD 424ff

Sarabande

ApelHD 660f
ArveyCM 137
ChuDE 420
HorstPCDF 57ff
NettlSDM 173ff
SachsWHD 376ff

Fandango

ApelHD 256f
ArveyCM 336f
ChuDE 183
NettlSDM 307f
SachsWHD 98f

Waltz

ApelHD 813
ArveyCM 222ff
ChuDE 497ff
NettlSDM 252ff
SachsWHD 427ff

Seguidilla

ApelHD 671
ArveyCM 206
ChuDE 424
NettlSDM 311
SachsWHD 161

Minuet

ApelHD 449
664f
ArveyCM 138f
ChuDE 305
CopWLM 131ff
HorstPCDF 79ff
NettlSDM 164ff
SachsWHD 405ff

Bolero

ApelHD 90
ArveyCM 210
ChuDE 74
446f
NettlSDM 308f
SachsWHD 99

Mazurka

ApelHD 430f
ArveyCM 199ff
ChuDE 305
NettlSDM 291ff
SachsWHD 440

Bourrée

ApelHD 92
ArveyCM 139
ChuDE 78
HorstPCDF 99ff
NettlSDM 171f
SachsWHD 408ff

Allemande

ApelHD 22f
ArveyCM 136
ChuDE 6
HorstPCDF 35ff
NettlSDM 200ff
SachsWHD 413f

Fox Trot

ApelHD 280
374ff
593f
ArveyCM 276ff
ChuDE 197
NettlSDM 336ff
SachsWHD 445

Tarantella

ApelHD 733
ArveyCM 208
ChuDE 468
NettlSDM 188ff
SachsWHD 254f

Gigue

ApelHD 297
ArveyCM 99f
ChuDE 204
319ff
HorstPCDF 69ff
NettlSDM 180ff
SachsWHD 410f

Early vs. the Suite of Bach

ApelHD 716ff
DorianHMP 112ff

Early vs. the Suite of Bach—(Cont.)

FinnHM	218ff
	295ff
	332
LangMWC	246f
	247f
	291
	386f
	486
McKin–AndMH	353f
	354f
	430f
	434
SachsOMH	222f
	223f
	249f

Minuet

DorianHMP	123ff
	125ff
	127ff
LangMWC	598
	613f
SachsOMH	248

Sonata da Camera

ApelHD	692
	718
FinnHM	300
	304
	361
LangMWC	366ff
	482
SachsOMH	251f

French Overture

ApelHD	548f
	718
FinnHM	264
	273f
McKin–AndMH	342f
SachsOMH	247

Modern Suite

ApelHD	716

"Apotheosis of the Dance"

DorianHMP	111
	129f
McKin–AndMH	537f
SachsOMH	42

March

ApelHD	425
FinnHM	416ff
LangMWC	950f
SachsOMH	177

UNIT IV—THE LINEAR ASPECTS OF MUSIC: MELODY AND COUNTERPOINT

Psychological and Aesthetic Aspects

ApelHD	435ff
CopWLM	49f
HaydonIM	159ff
SchoenPM	32
	33f
SchoenUM	72

Monophonic Melody

ApelHD	145ff
	304ff
	427ff
	455
	486ff
	493ff
FinnHM	31ff
LeichMHI	22ff
ReeseMMA	114ff
	149ff
SachsOMH	56ff

Polyphonic Melody

ApelHD	117f
FinnHM	60ff
GleasonEx	24ff
LangMWC	128ff
McKin–AndMH	146ff
ReeseMMA	250ff
SachsOMH	63ff

Consonance and Dissonance

ApelHD	180ff
BarthAM	163ff
FinnHM	65f
	99f
SchoenPM	58f
	60ff

Counterpoint

ApelHD	112ff
	189ff
	349f
	417ff
	427ff
	451
	457ff
	653
	742
DorianHMP	47ff
FinnHM	107ff
	258ff
GleasonMMAR	90f
LangMWC	258ff
McKin–AndMH	166ff
ReeseMMA	311ff
	362ff
	413ff
SachsOMH	97f
	170f
TochSFM	10ff
	133ff

Homophonic Melody

ApelHD	208
	421f
BauerTCM	16
	24ff
CopWLM	52ff
FinnHM	46f

Chromatic Scale

ApelHD	144f
	465ff
BukMBE	16
LangMWC	139
	325
	655
	885f
McKin–AndMH	241

Whole-Tone Scale

ApelHD	350f
	452
	563f
	815
ApelMK	272ff
BauerTCM	98
DorianHMP	299ff
FinnHM	556ff
	560

Whole-Tone Scale—(Cont.)

LangMWC	1020
LeichMHI	250ff
McKin–AndMH	736ff
	777ff
	785ff
	795
	797ff
	802ff
SachsOMH	363ff

UNIT V—THE VERTICAL ASPECTS OF MUSIC: HARMONY

Psychological and Aesthetic Aspects

ApelHD	17ff
	180ff
HaydonIM	90ff
	149f
LundinOPM	12ff
	32ff
	45ff
	76ff
	82ff
ParkerPAE	126ff
	161ff
SchoenPM	47ff
SchoenUM	72f
SeaISBM	121ff
TochSFM	1ff

Consonance and Dissonance

ApelHD	13f
BarthAM	3ff

Structure of Harmony

ApelHD	144f
	208
	317f
	322ff
	388f
	453f
	492f
	677
	742f
	760
EricksonSM	71ff
HullHS	171ff
	178ff
	182ff

Structure of Harmony—(Cont.)

LenSTCH	105ff
McHoseCHT	105ff
	118ff
	131ff
	137f
	138f
	139
	139f
MillerNHD	58ff
TochSFM	1ff
	23ff

UNIT VI—NEW TONAL CONCEPTS

"Mystic Chord"

ApelHD	476
ApelMK	281ff
BauerTCM	169ff
CopONM	36ff
HullMH	72ff
McKin–AndMH	723
MillerNHD	61ff
	75f
SachsOMH	366
WeinMA	299f

Atonality

AbraTMS	55ff
ApelHD	59f
	253f
	452
	752f
	775ff
ApelMK	287ff
BauerTCM	207ff
DorianHMP	329ff
LangMWC	1024f
McKin–AndMH	839
SachsOMH	366ff
SchoenbSI	102ff

Polytonality

AbraTMS	52ff
ApelHD	594f
ApelMK	300ff
CopWLM	75f
DorianHMP	324ff
McKin–AndMH	829f
SachsOMH	368ff

Polytonality—(Cont.)

WeinMA	288f

Pan-diatonicism

ApelHD	484
	550f
ApelMK	298f
BauerTCM	204
	245f
CopONM	100ff
	106ff
SachsOMH	370ff
SlonMS1900	743

New Tonal Horizons

ApelHD	445
	619
SlonMS1900	726
	745

Hindemith Theory

ApelHD	291f
BauerTCM	255ff
CopONM	108ff

Schillinger System

SlonMS1900	531

Music from Electronic Instruments

ApelHD	235ff
DouglasEMIM	127ff
	133ff
	139f
	157ff
	165ff
	172ff

Scientism in Music

BabbHF	38
BabbJMT	251
BoisIX	5ff
	25ff
CageS	10
CoweHMH	23
DockEMR	15
EimeEM	1ff
EwenWTCM	viiff
	915ff
JuddARR	27
JuddEMMC	1ff
LuenJR	10
MachICM	425ff
MeyerAMI	72f
	156f

Scientism in Music—(Cont.)

UNIT VII—THE ACOUSTICAL ASPECTS OF MUSIC: TONE COLOR

Physical Aspects of Tone Color

Vocal Tone Color

Vocal Tone Color—(Cont.)

Classification of Vocal Tone Color

Woodwinds

Brasses

Brasses—(Cont.)

	45
	46
HaydonIM	43ff
ReadTOD	90ff
SachsHMI	417ff
	424f
	425ff
	428ff
	432ff
	504

Percussion

ApelHD	135
	198
	220f
	299
	355
	425
	564ff
	777
	819f
BarthAM	129ff
	160
GardOH	48ff
HaydonIM	51ff
ReadTOD	22ff
SachsHMI	492f
	434ff

Organ

ApelHD	523ff
BarthAM	106f
	107ff
	110f
	116ff
	123f
	124ff
	128f
SachsHMI	499

Piano

ApelHD	386ff
	388
	574ff
	576ff
	579ff
	637
	638
BarthAM	89f
	90f
	94f

Piano—(Cont.)

	95f
	192ff
LundinOPM	240ff
ReadTOD	237
SachsHMI	381ff
SeaPM	225ff
SeaISBM	136ff

Harp

ApelHD	325ff
BarthAM	37ff
	94f
GardOH	20ff
ReadTOD	250ff
SachsHMI	495

Strings

ApelHD	93f
	80
	218
	711f
ApelHD	791
	794ff
	797
	798ff
	802f
	803f
	804f
BarthAM	85ff
GardOH	7
	9
	10ff
	16ff
	17f
HaydonIM	40ff
LundinOPM	247
ReadTOD	26ff
	278ff
SachsHMI	361f
	362
	363f
	504f
SeaPM	199ff
SeaISBM	150ff

Orchestra—Growth

ApelHD	519ff
DorianHMP	174
ReadTOD	29ff

PART III—SYNTHESIS OF MUSICAL ELEMENTS

UNIT VIII—JUXTAPOSITION OF MUSICAL ELEMENTS

UNIT IX—THE ARCHITECTURAL ASPECTS OF MUSIC

UNIT X—FINAL OUTCOME

Appendix III—*General Bibliography*

PART I

The books listed in this bibliography are intended to serve three purposes: (1) general reading, (2) reference, or (3) as source material to help the listener with program notes if such are required. The books having to do with specific composers and their works are listed only once and are correlated with the first appearance of the respective composer in the record lists of Appendix V.

UNIT I—AESTHETIC PRINCIPLES OF MUSIC AND THE ALLIED ARTS

Abraham, Gerald. *Tschaikovsky*. New York: A. A. Wyn, Inc., Publishers, 1949.

Anderson, W. R. *Introduction to the Music of Brahms*. London: Dennis Dobson, Ltd., 1949.

Baker, Theodore. *Biographical Dictionary of Musicians;* 4th ed. New York: G. Schirmer, Inc., 1940.

———. Slonimsky, Nicolas, ed. *Supplement*. New York: G. Schirmer, Inc., 1949.

Barlow, Harold, and Morgenstern, Sam. *A Dictionary of Musical Themes*. New York: Crown Publishers, Inc., 1950.

———. *A Dictionary of Vocal Themes*. New York: Crown Publishers, Inc., 1950.

Barzun, Jacques. *Romanticism and the Modern Ego*. New York: Little, Brown & Co., 1943.

Berlioz, Hector. *A Critical Study of Beethoven's Nine Symphonies*. London: William Reeves, Ltd. (1913?).

Biancolli, Louis. *Tschaikowsky and His Orchestral Music*. New York: Grosset & Dunlap, Inc., 1950.

Blom, Eric. *Tschaikowsky: Orchestral Works*. London: Oxford University Press, 1927.

Browne, Phillip Austin. *Brahms: The Symphonies*. London: Oxford University Press, 1933.

Burk, John H. *The Life and Works of Beethoven*. New York: Modern Music Library, Inc., 1946.

Burrows, Raymond, and Redmond, Bessie Carroll. *Symphony Themes*. New York: Simon and Schuster, Inc., 1942.

Cooper, Martin. *French Music: From the Death of Berlioz to the Death of Fauré*. New York: Oxford University Press, 1951.

Davison, Archibald, and Apel, Willi. *Historical Anthology of Music*, Vol. 2 Cambridge, Mass.: Harvard University Press, 1950.

DeLong, Patrick, Egner, Robert, and Thomas; Robert. *Art and Music in the Humanities*. Englewood Cliffs, New Jersey: Prentice-Hall, Inc., 1965.

Dudley, Louise, and Fericy, Austin. *The Humanities*. New York: McGraw-Hill Book Co., 1967.

Evans, Edwin, Sr. *Beethoven's Nine Symphonies*. London: William Reeves, Ltd. (1923/4?)

Evans, Edwin, Sr. *Handbook to the Chamber and Orchestral Music of Brahms*. Vols. 2, 3. London: William Reeves, Ltd., 1933/35 (1950/49).

Ewen, David. *The Book of Modern Composers*. New York: Alfred A. Knopf, Inc., 1950.

Foss, Hubert James. *Ralph Vaughan Williams*. New York: Oxford University Press, 1950.

Gardner, Helen. *Art Through the Ages*; Ed. Sumner McK. Crosby, by the Department of the History of Art, Yale University. New York: Harcourt, Brace and World, Inc., 1959.

Geiringer, Karl. *Brahms: His Life and Work*. London: Oxford University Press, 1947.

Grove, Sir George. *Dictionary of Music and Musicians*; 3rd ed., 5 vols., edited by H. C. Colles. New York: The Macmillan Company, 1927–28. *American Supplement*, edited by Waldo S. Pratt and Charles N. Boyd, 1928. Suppl. Vol., 1940.

Hale, Phillip. *Boston Symphony Program Notes*; Ed. John N. Burk. New York: Garden City Publishing Co., 1939.

Hall, David. *Records*; rev. ed. New York: Alfred A. Knopf, Inc., 1950.

Horton, John. *César Franck*. London: Oxford University Press, 1948.

Hurt, Peyton. *Bibliography and Footnotes*. Berkeley, Calif.: University of California Press, 1949.

Karel, Leon. *Avenues to the Arts*. Kirksville, Mo.: Simpson Publishing Co., 1966.

Kolodin, Irving. *The New Guide to Recorded Music*. New York: Garden City Publishing Co., 1950.

Lawrence, Robert. *The Victor Book of Ballets and Ballet Music*. New York: Simon and Schuster, Inc., 1950.

Munro, Thomas. *The Arts and Their Inter-relations*. New York: The Liberal Arts Press, Inc., 1949.

Niecks, Friedrich. *Programme Music*. London: Novello & Co., Ltd., 1907.

Niemann, Walter. *Brahms*. New York: Alfred A. Knopf, Inc., 1929 (1947).

O'Connell, Charles. *The Victor Book of the Symphony*. New York: Simon and Schuster, Inc., 1948.

Santayana, George. *The Sense of Beauty*. New York: Charles Scribner's Sons, 1896.

Scholes, Percy A. *The Listener's History of Music*; Vol. 3, 4th ed. New York: Oxford University Press, 1950.

———. *The Oxford Companion to Music*; 9th ed. New York: Oxford University Press, 1955.

Seaman, Julian (ed.). *Great Orchestral Music*. New York: Rinehart & Company, Inc., 1950.

Sessions, Roger. *The Musical Experience*. Princeton, N. J.: Princeton University Press, 1950.

Thayer, Alexander W. *The Life of Ludwig van Beethoven*. New York: The Beethoven Association, 1921.

Thompson, Oscar. *International Cyclopedia of Music and Musicians*. New York: Dodd, Mead & Co., 1939.

Tovey, Donald. *Essays in Musical Analysis;* 6 vols. New York: Oxford University Press, 1935/39.

Vuillermoz, Emile. *Gabriel Fauré.* Tr. by Kenneth Schapin. Philadelphia: Chilton Book Co., 1968.

Weinstock, Herbert. *Chopin: The Man and His Music.* New York: Alfred A. Knopf, Inc., 1949.

———. *Tschaikovsky.* New York: Alfred A. Knopf, Inc., 1943 (1946)

White, Eric. *Stravinsky.* New York: Philosophical Library, Inc., 1948.

UNIT II—THE ART OF LISTENING

Andriessen, Henrik. *César Franck.* Stockholm, Sweden: Continental Book Publications Distributing Co., 1947.

Blesh, Rudi, and Janis, Harriet. *They All Played Ragtime.* New York: Alfred A. Knopf, Inc., 1950.

Chase, Gilbert. *America's Music.* New York: McGraw-Hill Book Company, Inc., 1955.

Delaunay, C. *Hot Discography.* New York: Commodore Record Co., 1943

Demuth, Norman. *César Franck.* London: Dennis Dobson, Ltd., 1949.

Deutsch, Maury. *Musical Psychology.* New York: Author, 1948.

Dewey, John. *Art as Experience.* New York: Minton, Balch and Co., 1934.

Dieserens, Charles M. *The Influence of Music on Behavior.* Princeton: Princeton University Press, 1926.

——— and Fine, Harry. *A Psychology of Music:* The Influence of Music on Behavior. Cincinnati: The Authors for the College of Music, 1939.

Goodman, Benny, and Kolodin, Irving. *The Kingdom of Swing.* Harrisburg, Pa.: The Stackpole Co., 1939.

Gurney, Edmund. *The Power of Sound.* London: Smith, Elder & Co., 1880.

Hobson, Wilder. *American Jazz Music.* New York: W. W. Norton & Company, Inc., 1939.

Hughes, Charles W. *The Human Side of Music.* New York: Philosophical Library, Inc., 1948.

Mursell, James. *The Psychology of Music.* New York: W. W. Norton & Company, Inc., 1937.

Panassié, H. *Hot Jazz.* New York: M. Witmark & Sons, 1936.

———. *The Real Jazz.* New York: Smith & Durrell, 1942.

Pratt, Carroll. *The Meaning of Music.* New York: McGraw-Hill Book Co., 1931.

Puffer, Ethel D. *The Psychology of Beauty.* Boston: Houghton Mifflin Co., 1905.

Sargeant, Winthrop. *Jazz Hot and Hybrid.* New York: Arrow Press, 1938.

Schuller, Gunther. *Early Jazz: Its Roots and Musical Development.* New York: Oxford University Press, 1968.

Slonimsky, Nicolas. *Music of Latin America.* New York: Thomas Y. Crowell Company (1945) 1946.

Ulanov, Barry. *A History of Jazz in America.* New York: The Viking Press, Inc., 1953.

PART II

UNIT III—THE PULSE OF MUSIC: RHYTHM

Abraham, Gerald (ed.). *Grieg*. Norman, Okla.: University of Oklahoma Press, 1950.

———. *The Music of Schubert*. New York: W. W. Norton & Company, Inc., 1947.

———. *Rimsky-Korsakov*. New York: A. A. Wyn, Inc., Publishers, 1949.

Anderson, W. R. *Introduction to the Music of Elgar*. London: Dennis Dobson, Ltd., 1949.

Arbeau, Thoinot. *Orchesography* (1588). New York: Kamin Dance Publications, 1948.

Armstrong, Thomas. *Strauss's Tone Poems*. London: Oxford University Press, 1931 (1948).

Barzun, Jacques. *Berlioz and the Romantic Century*. New York: Little, Brown & Co., 1950.

Berlioz, Hector. *Gluck and His Operas*. London: William Reeves, Ltd., 1914

Blom, Eric. *Mozart*. New York: Pellegrini and Cudahy, Inc., 1949.

Broder, Nathan. *Samuel Barber*. New York: G. Schirmer, Inc., 1954.

Burrows, Raymond, and Redmond, Bessie Carroll. *Concerto Themes*. New York: Simon and Schuster, Inc., 1951.

Calvocoresi, M. D., and Abraham, G. *Mussorgsky*. London: J. M. Dent and Sons, Ltd., 1946.

Chissell, Joan. *Schumann*. London: J. M. Dent and Sons, Ltd., 1948.

Cobbett, Walter Wilson. *Cyclopedic Survey of Chamber Music*. 2 vols. London: Oxford University Press, 1929/30.

Colson, Percy. *Massenet: Manon*. London: Boosey and Hawkes, Ltd., 1947.

Cooper, Martin. *Bizet: Carmen*. London: Boosey and Hawkes, Ltd., 1947.

———. *Georges Bizet*. London: Oxford University Press, 1938.

Culshaw, John. *Rachmaninoff: The Man and His Music*. London: Oxford University Press, 1950.

Cummings, William H. *Purcell*. London: William Reeves, Ltd. [n.d.]

Davenport, Marcia. *Mozart*. New York: Charles Scribner's Sons, 1947.

Davison, Archibald. *Bach and Handel*. Cambridge, Mass.: Harvard University Press, 1951.

Dean, Winton. *Bizet*. London: J. M. Dent and Sons, Ltd., 1948.

———. *Introduction to the Music of Bizet*. London: Dennis Dobson, Ltd., 1950.

Del Mar, Norman. *Richard Strauss: A Critical Commentary on His Life and Works*. Philadelphia: Chilton Book Co., 1968.

Demarquez, Suzanne. *Manuel de Falla*. Tr. by Salvator Attanasio. Philadelphia: Chilton Book Co., 1968.

Demuth, Norman. *Introduction to the Music of Gounod*. London: Dennis Dobson, Ltd., 1950.

Dent, Edward J. *Eugene Onegin*. London: Oxford University Press, 1946.

Deutsch, Otto Erich. *The Schubert Reader*. New York: W. W. Norton & Company, Inc., 1947.

Dickinson, A. E. F. *The Art of J. S. Bach*. London: Hinrichsen, 1950.

———. *A Study of Mozart's Last Three Symphonies*. London: Oxford University Press, 1947.

Einstein, Alfred. *Mozart*. London: Oxford University Press, 1945.
———. *Schubert: A Musical Portrait*. New York: Oxford University Press, 1951.
Elliot, J. H. *Berlioz*. London: J. M. Dent and Sons, Ltd., 1938 (1946).
Fisher, Trevor. *Verdi: La Traviata*. London: Boosey and Hawkes, Ltd., 1948.
Flower, Newman. *George Frederic Handel*. New York: Charles Scribner's Sons, 1948.
Geiringer, Karl. *Haydn: A Creative Life in Music*. New York: W. W. Norton & Company, Inc., 1946.
Grout, Donald. *Short History of the Opera*. 2 vols. New York: Columbia University Press, 1947.
Grove, George. *Beethoven and His Nine Symphonies*. London: Oxford University Press, and Novello & Co., Ltd., 1948.
Handy, William Christopher. *Father of the Blues: An Autobiography*. New York: The Macmillan Company, 1941 (1947).
Hill, Ralph. *Liszt*. New York: A. A. Wyn, Inc., Publishers, 1950.
Holland, A. K. *Henry Purcell*. Harmondshire, Middlesex, Eng.: Penguin Books, 1948.
Howes, Frank. *The Dramatic Works of Ralph Vaughan Williams*. London: Oxford University Press, 1937.
———. *The Later Works of Ralph Vaughan Williams*. London: Oxford University Press, 1937 (1945).
———. *The Music of William Walton*. London: Oxford University Press, 1943.
———. *The Music of Ralph Vaughan Williams*. London: Oxford University Press, 1954.
Hughes, Rosemary. *Haydn*. New York: J. M. Dent and Sons, Ltd., and Pellegrini and Cudahy, 1950.
Hussey, Dyneley. *Introduction to the Music of Haydn*. London: Dennis Dobson, Ltd., 1950.
Jacob, H. E. *Johann Strauss, Father and Son*. New York: Halcyon House, 1948.
———. *Joseph Haydn: His Art, Times, and Glory*. New York: Rinehart and Company, Inc., 1950.
Johansen, David Monrad. *Edward Grieg*. New York: Tudor Publishing Co., 1945.
Jonson, G. C. Ashton. *A Handbook to Chopin's Works*. London: William Reeves, Ltd., 1905.
Kobbé, Gustav. *The Complete Opera Book*. New York: G. P. Putnam's Sons, 1950.
Lederman, Minna. *Stravinsky in the Theatre*. New York: Pellegrini and Cudahy, 1949.
Leibowitz, René. *Schoenberg and His School*. New York: Philosophical Library, Inc., 1949.
Leyda, Jay, and Bertenson, S. *The Musorgsky Reader*. New York: W. W. Norton & Company, Inc., 1947.
Lockspeiser, Edward. *Debussy*. New York: Pellegrini and Cudahy, Inc., 1949.
MacDowell, Marian. *Random Notes on Edward MacDowell and His Music*. Boston: Arthur P. Schmidt, 1950.
Magriel, Paul. *A Bibliography of Dancing*. New York: H. W. Wilson Co., 1936.

———. *4th Cumulated Supplement, 1936–1940*. New York: H. W. Wilson Co., 1941.

Manuel, Roland. *Maurice Ravel*. London: Dennis Dobson, Ltd., 1947.

Marek, George. *Puccini: A Biography*. New York: Simon and Schuster, Inc., 1951.

Martin, John. *The Dance: The Story of the Dance Told in Pictures and Text*. New York: Tudor Publishing Co., 1946.

Martynov, Ivan. *Shostakovich*. New York: Philosophical Library, Inc., 1947.

Mellers, Wilfred. *Studies in Contemporary Music*. London: Dennis Dobson, Ltd., 1947.

Milne, A. Forbes. *Beethoven's Pianoforte Sonatas*. 2 vols. London: Oxford University Press, 1925/28.

Mitchell, Donald, and Keller, Hans (eds.). *Benjamin Britten*. New York: The Ronald Press Company, 1953.

Myers, Rollo H. *Erik Satie*. London: Dennis Dobson, Ltd., 1948.

Nestyev, Israel V. *Sergei Prokofiev*. New York: Alfred A. Knopf, Inc., 1946.

Newman, Ernest. *The Life of Richard Wagner*. 4 vols. New York: Alfred A. Knopf, Inc., 1933/46.

O'Connell, Charles. *The Victor Book of Overtures, Tone Poems and Other Orchestral Works*. New York: Simon and Schuster, Inc., 1950.

Posner, Sandy. *Coppélia*. London: A. and C. Black, Ltd., 1947.

Pryce-Jones, Alan. *Richard Strauss: Der Rosenkavalier*. London: Boosey and Hawkes, Ltd., 1947.

Reed, William Henry. *Elgar*. New York: Pellegrini and Cudahy, 1949.

Reinecke, Karl. *The Beethoven Pianoforte Sonatas*. London: Augener and Co., Ltd. (1897).

Robertson, Alec. *Dvořák*. New York: Pellegrini and Cudahy, 1949.

Robertson, Marion. *La Boutique Fantasque*. London: Newman Wolsey, 1947.

Saint-Foix, Georges de. *The Symphonies of Mozart*. New York: Alfred A. Knopf, Inc., 1949.

Schattmann, Alfred. *Richard Strauss' Der Rosenkavalier: A Guide to the Work*. New York: G. Schirmer, Inc., 1911.

Schauffler, Robert Haven. *Florestan, The Life and Work of Robert Schumann*. New York: Henry Holt & Co., Inc., 1945.

Schmitz, E. Robert. *The Piano Works of Claude Debussy*. New York: Duell, Sloan & Pearce, Inc., 1950.

Seroff, Victor Ilyich. *Dimitri Shostakovich*. New York: Alfred A. Knopf, Inc., 1943.

Schweitzer, Albert. *J. S. Bach*. London: A. and C. Black, Ltd., 1935.

Smith, William C. *Concerning Handel*. London: Cassell and Co., Ltd., 1948.

Sourek, Otakar. *Antonin Dvořák*. New York: Philosophical Library, Inc., 1955.

Stebbins, Lucy Poate, and Poate, Richard. *Enchanted Wanderer: The Life of Carl Maria von Weber*. New York: G. P. Putnam's Sons, 1940.

Stuckenschmidt, Hans H. *Maurice Ravel: Variations on his Life and Work*. Tr. Samuel R. Rosenbaum. Philadelphia: Chilton Book Co., 1968.

Suerdmondt, R. P. *Smetana and Dvořák*. Stockholm, Sweden: Continental Book and Publications Distributing Co., n.d. (1948/9?).

Terry, Charles Sanford. *The Music of Bach*. London: Oxford University Press, 1933.

Trend, J. B. *Manuel de Falla and Spanish Music*. New York: Alfred A. Knopf, Inc. (1929), 1934.

Tovey, Donald Francis. A *Companion to Beethoven's Pianoforte Sonatas*. London: Royal Schools of Music, 1931.
Ulrich, Homer. *Chamber Music*. New York: Columbia University Press, 1948.
Vallas, Léon. *The Theories of Claude Debussy*. London: Oxford University Press, 1929.
———. *Claude Debussy*. New York: Oxford University Press, 1933.
Veinus, Abraham. *Victor Book of Concertos*. New York: Simon and Schuster, Inc., 1948.
Wellecz, Egon. *Introduction to the Music of Wagner*. London: Dennis Dobson, Ltd., 1950.
Westerby, Herbert. *Beethoven and his Piano Works*. London: William Reeves, Ltd. (1931).
———. *Liszt, Composer, and His Piano Works*. London: William Reeves, Ltd., n.d. (1936).
Westrup, J. A. *Purcell*. New York: Pellegrini and Cudahy, 1949.
White, Eric Walter. *Benjamin Britten: A Sketch of His Life and Work*. London: Boosey and Hawkes, Ltd., 1948.
Winn, Cyril. *Mendelssohn*. London: Oxford University Press, 1927.
Young, Percy. *Introduction to the Music of Mendelssohn*. London: Dennis Dobson, Ltd., 1949.
———. *The Oratorios of Handel*. New York: Roy Publishers, 1950.

UNIT IV—THE LINEAR ASPECTS OF MUSIC: MELODY AND COUNTERPOINT

Apel, Willi. *The Notation of Polyphonic Music, 900–1600*. Cambridge, Mass.: The Mediaeval Academy of America (1942), 1949.
Benedictines of Solesmes (ed.). *The Liber Usualis*. Tournai, Belgium: Desclée et Cie. (Agent, J. Fischer and Bro., N. Y.) (1934), 1947.
Busoni, Ferruccio. *A New Aesthetic of Music*. New York: G. Schirmer, Inc., 1911.
Clokey, Joseph W. *Plainsong*. Boston: C. C. Birchard Co., 1934.
Cooper, Martin. *Opera Comique*. New York: Chanticleer Press, Inc., 1949.
Darlington, W. A. *The World of Gilbert and Sullivan*. New York: Thomas Y. Crowell Company, 1950.
Dickinson, Edward. *Music in the History of the Western Church*. New York: Charles Scribner's Sons, 1925.
Downes, Olin. *Ten Operatic Masterpieces*. New York: Charles Scribner's Sons, 1953.
Dyson, George. *The Progress of Music*. London: Oxford University Press, 1932.
Edwards, Arthur C. *The Art of Melody*. New York: Philosophical Library, Inc., 1956.
Fellowes, Edmund H. *The English Madrigal*. London: Oxford University Press (1921), 1949.
Gray, Cecil. *The Forty-eight Preludes and Fugues of J. S. Bach*. London: Oxford University Press (1938), 1948.
Hill, Edward Burlingame. *Modern French Music*. New York: Houghton Mifflin Co., 1924.
Holst, Imogene. *The Music of Gustave Holst*. London: Oxford University Press, 1951.

Howard, John Tasker. *Our Contemporary Composers*. New York: Thomas Y. Crowell Company (1941), 1948.

Jeppesen, Knud. *Counterpoint, The Polyphonic Vocal Style of the Sixteenth Century*. New York: Prentice-Hall, Inc. (1939), 1949.

Johner, (Dom) P. Dominicus. *A New School of Gregorian Chant*. Cincinnati: Frederick Putset Co., 1925.

Leichtentritt, Hugo. *History of the Motet*. New York: Musurgia Book and Music Publishers, 1951.

LeMassena, C. F. *The Songs of Schubert*. New York: G. Schirmer, Inc., 1928.

Myers, Robert Manson. *Handel's Messiah*. New York: The Macmillan Company, 1948.

Parrish, Carl, and Ohl, John F. *Masterpieces of Music Before 1750*. New York: W. W. Norton & Company, Inc., 1951.

Reiss, Claire. *Composer in America*. New York: The Macmillan Company (1930), 1947.

Richardson, A. Madeley. *Mediaeval Modes*. New York: H. W. Gray Company, Inc., 1933.

Saminsky, Lazare. *Music of Our Day*. New York: Thomas Y. Crowell Company, 1932.

Schering, Arnold. *History of Music in Examples*. New York: Broude Bros. (1931), 1950.

Schreiber, Flora Rheta, and Persichetti, Vincent. *William Schuman*. New York: G. Schirmer, Inc., 1955.

Schumann, Elizabeth. *German Song*. New York: Chanticleer Press, Inc., 1948.

Scott, Charles Kennedy. *Madrigal Singing*. London: Oxford University Press (1907), 1931.

Slonimsky, Nicolas. *Thesaurus of Scales and Melodic Patterns*. New York: Coleman-Ross Co., 1947.

Suñol, (Dom) Gregorio M. *Textbook of Gregorian Chant*. Tournai, Belgium: Desclée et Cie. (Agent, J. Fischer and Bro., N. Y.), 1930.

Terry, Charles Sanford. *Bach: The Cantatas and Oratorios*. London: Oxford University Press, 1928.

———. *Bach: The B Minor Mass*. London: Oxford University Press (1931), 1949.

White, Newman Ivey. *American Negro Folk-Songs*. Cambridge, Mass.: Harvard University Press, 1928.

UNIT V—THE VERTICAL ASPECTS OF MUSIC: HARMONY

Abraham, Gerald. *On Russian Music*. New York: Charles Scribner's Sons, 1939.

Calvocoressi, M. D. *A Survey of Russian Music*. Harmondshire, Middlesex, England: Penguin Books, 1944.

Culver, Charles Aaron. *Musical Acoustics*. Philadelphia: The Blakiston Company, rev. and ed., 1947.

Ewen, David. *Twentieth Century Music*. New York: Prentice-Hall, Inc., 1953.

Harrison, Sidney. *Music for the Multitudes*. New York: The Macmillan Company (1940), rev. ed., 1948.

Hindemith, Paul. *A Concentrated Course in Traditional Harmony*. New York: Associated Music Publishers, Inc., 1944.

Jeans, (Sir) James. *Science and Music*. London: Cambridge University Press, 1937 (1947).
Kitson, C. H. *The Evolution of Harmony*. London: Oxford University Press (1914); 2nd ed., 1924 (1945).
Montagu-Nathan, M. *A History of Russian Music*. London: William Reeves, Ltd., rev. ed., 1918 (1950).
Piston, Walter. *Harmony*. New York: W. W. Norton & Company, Inc., 1948.
———. *Principles of Harmonic Analysis*. Boston: E. C. Schirmer Music Co., 1933.
Redfield, John. *Music: A Science and an Art*. New York: Alfred A. Knopf, Inc., 1928 (1949).
Schoenberg, Arnold. *Theory of Harmony* (*Harmonielehre*). New York: Philosophical Library, Inc., 1948.
Sessions, Roger. *Harmonic Practice*. New York: Harcourt, Brace & Co., 1951.
Stevenson, Robert. *Music in Mexico*. New York: Thomas Y. Crowell Company, 1953.
Stravinsky, Igor. *An Autobiography*. New York: Simon and Schuster, Inc., 1936.
Tansman, Alexander. *Stravinsky*. New York: G. P. Putnam's Sons, 1949.
Tenschert, Roland (tr. Emily Anderson). *Wolfgang Amadeus Mozart*. New York: The Macmillan Company, 1953.

UNIT VI—NEW TONAL CONCEPTS

Bassart, Ann Phillips. *Serial Music: A Classified Bibliography of Writings on Twelve-Tone and Electronic Music*. Berkeley, Calif.: University of California Press, 1961.
Begun, S. J. *Magnetic Recording*. New York: Rinehart & Company, Inc., 1949.
Cross, Lowell M., ed. *A Bibliography of Electronic Music*. Toronto, Canada: University of Toronto Press, 1967/68.
Davies, Hugh, ed. *International Electronic Music Catalog*. Cambridge, Mass.: The M.I.T. Press, 1968.
Dyson, George. *The New Music*. New York: Oxford University Press, 1948.
Eschmann, Karl. *Changing Forms in Modern Music*. Boston: E. C. Schirmer Music Co., 1945.
Graf, Max. *Modern Music: Composers and Music of Our Time*. New York: Philosophical Library, Inc., 1946.
Gray, Cecil. *A Survey of Contemporary Music*. New York: Oxford University Press, 1924.
Hiller, Lejaren A., and Isaacson, Leonard M. *Experimental Music*. New York: McGraw-Hill Book Co., 1959.
Hindemith, Paul. *The Craft of Musical Composition*. New York: Associated Music Publishers, Inc. (1934), 1945.
Howard, John Tasker. *This Modern Music*. New York: Thomas Y. Crowell Company, 1946 (1942).
Katz, Adele T. *Challenge to Musical Tradition*. New York: Alfred A. Knopf, Inc., 1945.
Křenek, Ernst. *Music Here and Now*. New York: W. W. Norton & Company, Inc., 1939.
Mellers, Wilfred. *Studies in Contemporary Music*. London: Dennis Dobson, Ltd., 1947.

Mills, John. A *Fugue in Cycles and Bels*. New York: D. Van Nostrand Co., Inc., 1935.

Reich, Willi. *Alban Berg*. London: Dennis Dobson, Ltd., 1937.

Ruffer, Joseph. *Composition with Twelve Tones*. New York: The Macmillan Company, 1955.

Salazar, Adolfo. *Music in Our Time*. New York: W. W. Norton & Company, Inc., 1946.

Salzer, Felix. *Structural Hearing*. New York: Charles Boni, 1952.

Saminsky, Lazare. *Living Music of the Americas*. New York: Crown Publishers, Inc., 1949.

Schenker, Heinrich. *Harmony*. Tr. by Elizabeth Mann Borgese. Chicago: University of Chicago Press, 1954.

Schillinger, Joseph. *The Schillinger System of Musical Composition*. New York: Carl Fischer, Inc., 1946.

Thompson, Oscar. *Great Modern Composers*. New York: Dodd, Mead & Co., 1941.

Tremaine, Howard M. *The Audio Cyclopedia*. Indianapolis, Indiana: Howard W. Sams. Distributed by Bobbs-Merrill, Indianapolis.

Weismann, Adolf. *Problems of Modern Music*. New York: E. P. Dutton & Co., Inc., 1925.

Wellesz, Egon. *Arnold Schönberg*. New York: E. P. Dutton & Co., Inc., 1925.

Wilhelm, Richard, Tr. *The I—Ching, or Book of Changes*. Tr. into English by Cary F. Baynes. Bollingen Series XIX. Princeton, New Jersey: Princeton University Press, 1968.

UNIT VII—THE ACOUSTICAL ASPECTS OF MUSIC: TONE COLOR

Apel, Willi. *Early History of the Organ*. Cambridge, Mass.: The Mediaeval Academy of America, 1946.

Barnes, William H. *The Contemporary American Organ*. New York: J. Fischer and Bro. (1930), 1948.

Bessaraboff, Nicholas. *Ancient European Musical Instruments*. Cambridge, Mass.: Harvard University Press, 1941.

Berlioz, Hector (and Strauss, Richard). *Treatise on Instrumentation*. New York: Edwin F. Kalmus (1905), 1948.

Carse, Adam. *The Orchestra from Beethoven to Berlioz*. Cambridge, England: W. Heffer and Sons, Ltd., 1948. Broude Bros., 1950.

———. *Musical Wind Instruments*. New York: The Macmillan Company, 1939.

Closson, Ernest. *History of the Piano*. London: Paul Elek, 1947.

Cowell, Henry and Cowell, Sidney. *Charles Ives and His Music*. London: Oxford University Press, 1955.

Drinker, Henry S. *The Chamber Music of Johannes Brahms*. Philadelphia: Elkan-Vogel Co., Inc., 1932.

Forsyth, Cecil. *Orchestration*. New York: The Macmillan Company, 1935 (1948).

Galpin, Francis W. A *Textbook of European Musical Instruments*. New York: E. P. Dutton & Co., Inc., 1937.

Geiringer, Karl. *Musical Instruments*. London: Oxford University Press, 1945.

Jacob, Gordon. *How to Read a Score*. London: Boosey and Hawkes, Ltd., 1944.
Johnstone, A. E. *Instruments of the Modern Symphony Orchestra and Band.* New York: Carl Fischer (1917), 1948.
Klein, Adrian Bernard. *Coloured Light*. New York: Anglo-books (1937), 1950.
Lange, Arthur. *Arthur Lange's Spectrotone System of Orchestration*. Hollywood: Co-Art, 1943.
Lewer, S. K. *Electronic Musical Instruments*. London: Electronic Engineering Office, 1948.
Mason, Daniel Gregory. *The Chamber Music of Brahms*. New York: (The Macmillan Company, 1933), J. W. Edwards, Ann Arbor, Mich., 1950.
Miller, Dayton C. *The Science of Musical Sounds*. New York: The Macmillan Company, 1937.
Panum, Hortense. *The Stringed Instruments of the Middle Ages*. London: William Reeves, Ltd. (1941).
Rensch, Roslyn. *The Harp*. New York: Philosophical Library, Inc., 1950.
Stanley, Douglas. *The Science of Voice*. New York: Carl Fischer (1929), 1948.
———. *Your Voice*. New York: Pitman Publishing Corp. (1945), 1950.

PART III

UNIT VIII—JUXTAPOSITION OF MUSICAL ELEMENTS

Adequate source material may be obtained from the general bibliography listed for each Unit. In addition, the listener is directed to the many references listed in Appendix II.

UNIT IX—THE ARCHITECTURAL ASPECTS OF MUSIC: FORM

Abraham, Gerald. *Design in Music*. London: Oxford University Press, 1949.
Doty, E. W. *The Analysis of Form in Music*. New York: F. S. Crofts & Co., 1947.
Goetschius, Percy. *The Homophonic Forms of Musical Composition*. New York: G. Schirmer, Inc. (1926).
———. *The Larger Forms of Musical Composition*. New York: G. Schirmer, Inc. (1943).
Harris, Cuthbert. *The Student's Short Course in Musical Forms*. Boston: Arthur P. Schmidt, 1945.

UNIT X—THE FINAL OUTCOME: STYLE

Abraham, Gerald. *Chopin's Musical Style*. London: Oxford University Press, 1939.
Bekker, Paul. *The Story of Music: An Historical Sketch of Changes in Musical Form*. New York: W. W. Norton & Company, Inc., 1927.
Goetschius, Percy. *The Material Used in Musical Composition*. New York: G. Schirmer, Inc., 1913.

Jeppesen, Knud. *The Style of Palestrina and the Dissonance*. Copenhagen: E. Munksgaard, 1946.

Moore, Douglas. *From Madrigal to Modern Music*. New York: W. W. Norton & Company, Inc., 1942.

Rothschild, Fritz. *The Lost Tradition in Music: Rhythm and Tempo in J. S. Bach's Time*. New York: Oxford University Press, 1953.

Sachs, Curt. *The Commonwealth of Art*. New York: W. W. Norton & Company, Inc., 1946.

Spencer, Herbert. *Literary Style and Music*. New York: Philosophical Library, Inc., 1951.

Appendix IV—*Supplementary Material*

UNIT VII–THE ACOUSTICAL ASPECTS OF MUSIC:

Classification of Vocal Tone Color

In addition to acting, opera requires that a singer reflect the part in the character and tone color of his voice. This means, of course, that voices are used in opera to portray specific character types. Opera, therefore, demands a high degree of specialization—the cantata and oratorio are less exacting—on the part of the singer. The voices are shown below from the highest to the lowest in each classification.

OPERATIC VOICES—WOMEN:

Coloratura Soprano. This voice is the highest of the sopranos and is exceedingly flexible, taking scale passages and trills in stride. Its tone color is clear and brilliant, being likened to that of the flute, with which it sometimes does duets. If it were not for the vibrato, this voice would sound cold because it contains few overtones. Some coloraturas can sing the F above high C—f^3.

Lyric Soprano. Here is a voice which is flexible and capable of expressing personal feeling rather than incidents or events. The tone color is light but heavier than the coloratura. A pleasant singing (*cantabile*) style is required.

Dramatic Soprano. The dramatic soprano is possessed of a powerful voice which is capable of great emotion, dramatic characterization, and declamatory ability. This voice is heavier and darker than the lyric soprano. Mezzo-sopranos and contraltos may develop into dramatic sopranos.

Mezzo-Soprano. This voice is, literally, half soprano and half contralto in that its tone color is heavier than the dramatic soprano and lighter than the contralto. Its range usually lies between these two voices.

Contralto. The contralto voice is quite dark, heavy, rich, and mellow, even somber in color. It is the lowest of women's voices. The real contralto is rare.

OPERATIC VOICES—MEN:

Lyric Tenor. The description of this voice corresponds to that of the lyric soprano, and is the highest of men's voices. Some lyric tenors are able to sing the C above middle C.

Dramatic Tenor. The dramatic tenor is a robust voice and is darker in tone color than the lyric tenor. It is capable of the same dramatic and histrionic qualities as the dramatic soprano. The voice of the *Heldentenor* is agile, brilliant in tone color, and expressive. Sometimes a high baritone will develop into a Heldentenor. This type of voice is required of the hero in Wagnerian operas.

Baritone. This is the middle voice between tenor and bass. Its color is darker than the lyric tenor but lighter than the bass. The *bass-baritone's* tone color is darker than the baritone but lighter than a real bass.

Bass. The bass voice may be of three types: the *basso cantante*—singing bass; the *basso profundo*—deep, heavy, powerful voice of solemn stately character; and the *basso buffo*—an agile bass voice suited to comic roles in operas.

Classification of Instrumental Tone Color

WOODWIND—REEDS:

Piccolo (in C).

Ex. 1. Range

The piccolo in C, sometimes called the octave flute, is the one generally used in the orchestra, while the D-flat piccolo is usually employed in bands. The D-flat piccolo sounds a minor ninth higher than the written note. The tone color of the piccolo may be described as brilliant, bright, vivid, hard, and in the upper register, penetrating, and even piercing. Therefore, the composer uses the extreme upper notes sparingly and with care, usually for climactic effects. The piccolo represents the highest soprano voice in the woodwind section. Being a cylindrical, open pipe, the piccolo overblows at the octave.

Flute.

Ex. 2. Range

The flute, twice the size of the piccolo, is the next highest of the soprano voices and, like the piccolo, is quite agile. It is capable of fast scalewise passages, arpeggios, grace notes, trills; double, triple, and flutter tonguing. The fingering is similar to that of the piccolo and, like it, is played in a horizontal position. The tone color of the flute in the lowest register may be described as soft, cool, fluid, feathery, velvety, and breathy, but in its higher registers it is clear, pure, and bright, largely because of the fewness of overtones. The *alto flute* is self-descriptive. It is pitched in G and is therefore a transposing instrument. The alto flute sounds a fourth lower than the written note—reads C, sounds G. Its best range corresponds to the lowest tones of the flute. There are usually three flutes in the orchestra, one of which doubles on the piccolo.

Oboe.
Ex. 3. Range

The oboe is a double-reed instrument of conical bore, which means that it overblows at the octave. The column of air in the instrument is vibrated by a double reed which is inserted in the upper end. All the double-reed instruments are held perpendicularly to the body. The double reed is made with two pieces of cane bound together. Dating back to early history, the oboe remains one of the most difficult instruments to play because, surprisingly, it takes so little air to play it. Therefore, the player's ability to control the air pressure is the very secret of playing the instrument. The oboe does not speak as fast as the flute and therefore adapts better to a singing style. Its tone color may be described as nasal and reedy, due to the presence of a large quantity of overtones. The middle register may be described as sweet, and its upper register as penetrating. The tone color of the oboe may be further described as pastoral or plaintive. There are usually three oboes in the orchestra, with one of them doubling on the *English horn*, which we learn about next.

English Horn.
Ex. 4. Range

The English horn—a transposing instrument—belonging to the oboe family of double-reed instruments, is considered an alto oboe and, of course, corresponds to the alto voice in the choir. It is longer than the oboe, and in order to facilitate its playing, a small metal tube is attached to the upper end. This tube is bent back toward the player and the double reed is then attached to it. The English horn is further distinguished from the oboe by the pear-shaped bulb at the lower end. It is this bell which largely accounts for the tone color of the English horn.

Its tone color is soft and rather melancholy, and the sound in its lower register is thick and heavy. It speaks more slowly than the oboe, but the tone is not quite as difficult to control as the oboe. Being of conical bore also, it overblows at the octave. Though the English horn is not of English origin, it is thought that it derived its name from a poor translation of the French *cor anglé* (bent horn) which was later corrupted to *cor anglaise*.

E-Flat Clarinet.
Ex. 5. Range

The E-flat clarinet, a small instrument, is one of the members of the clarinet family and is the high soprano of a group characterized by the use of a single reed. Being a transposing instrument, it sounds a minor third higher than the written note. The tone color of the instrument is rather crude and very piercing in its highest register. The low and high registers are its best; the middle one is weak. It is sometimes used to produce burlesque or comedy effects. Having the acoustical properties of a stopped cylindrical pipe, it overblows at the twelfth.

Clarinet in B-Flat.
Ex. 6. Range

The *clarinet in B-flat*—a transposing instrument—is by far the most important of the single-reed instruments. The clarinet has a more recent history than the oboe, coming into wider use since the time of Mozart, who is perhaps responsible for giving it its impetus through his later symphonies. Since that time, there are not less than two or more than four clarinets in the orchestra, the average number being three. Unless one is at close range, the oboe and the clarinet may be confused. At close inspection it will be seen that the mouthpieces differ greatly. The clarinet's mouthpiece is tapered to a smooth edge with a flat reed attached to its back. The clarinet is quite versatile and has a wide range of usable tones and tone color. Its tone color may be described by the following terms: smooth, clear, rich, warm, velvety, full, brilliant, silvery, and creamy. It may be likened to the prima donna soprano and is capable of singing of love or anger. The instrument is capable of a wide range of dynamics. In the clarinet's lowest register—the *chalumeau*—it is rich, dark, and sonorous, while its top range is bright and penetrating. The clarinet is cylindrical and overblows at the twelfth and thus acts as a stopped pipe. The *clarinet in A* has most of the characteristics of the one in B-flat, but is used in symphony orchestras because of the ease in playing in sharp keys. The clarinetist in the dance or radio band uses only the B-flat instrument. All the clarinets are fingered similarly and are held perpendicularly to the body in playing position.

The *alto clarinet in E-flat* has most of the characteristics of the B-flat instrument. It is fingered similarly, but its tone color is somewhat more "reedy," and its playing range is lower. The alto clarinet is a transposing instrument sounding a major sixth lower than it reads and, of course, sings an alto part in the clarinet choir.

Bass Clarinet in B-Flat.
Ex. 7. Range

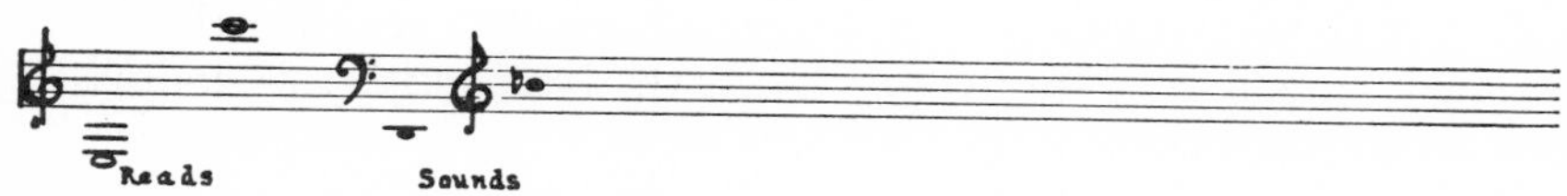

Sounding a major ninth lower than the written note, the bass clarinet is both played and written like the B-flat clarinet. The instrument is larger, of course, and is not as flexible in playing and speed as the B-flat clarinet. The tone color is darker and heavier, especially in its lower register. The bass clarinet is used more extensively in the symphony, opera, radio orchestra, and the band, because of its expressive—grave to humorous—and utilitarian capabilities as well as its wide dynamic range. The bass clarinet might easily be mistaken for a saxophone were it not for its wooden barrel.

Saxophones.
Ex. 8. Range

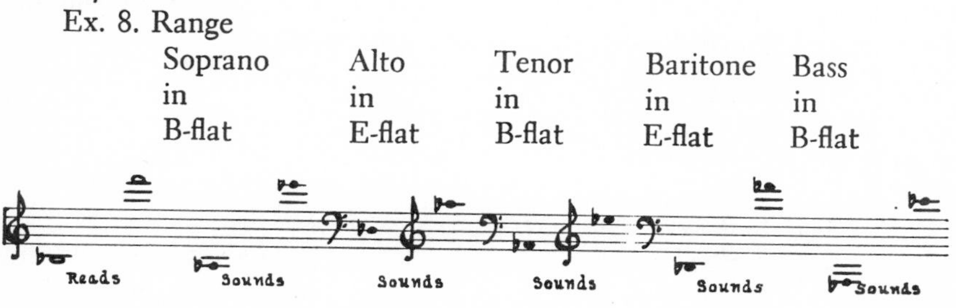

All saxophones are single-reed instruments. They are of conical bore and overblow at the octave. The body of all saxophones is made of metal (some are now made of plastic). The tone color is between that of the woodwind and the brass; as a result, these instruments have been classed as hybrid instruments, being neither woodwind nor brass. To date, saxophones have been used but rarely in symphony orchestras. There are a number of reasons for this, but the principal one is that their ranges duplicate those of other reed instruments. The fingerings and the written ranges for all of them are similar. The alto saxophone in E-flat is perhaps the most widely used instrument of the saxophone family. It is quite flexible and versatile, and its tone color generally smooth and mellow.

Bassoon.

Ex. 9. Range

The *bassoon* is a double-reed, nontransposing instrument serving as the bass voice for the woodwind section. Its long cylindrical tube is bent back on itself for ease in handling. Though much larger than the oboe, it is much more flexible. In its low register the bassoon is reedy and nasal, while at high range it is mellow and delicate, even pale. It is quite capable in solo passages, being particularly good at depicting humor in its low register. It has a wide dynamic range. The tenor clef (see p. 85) is often used so as to limit the reading of so many ledger lines above the staff.

The *contra bassoon,* or double bassoon, is the low bass voice of the woodwind choir. It is actually sixteen feet in length, but is doubled back on itself four times for ease in handling. The bell, unlike that of the bassoon, points downward. The contra bassoon sounds an octave lower than the bassoon. Its lowest and highest tones are rarely used. It speaks slowly, and the tone color and intonation are inferior to that of the bassoon and therefore is used mostly as a harmonic instrument. The fingering is the same as for the bassoon. There are usually three bassoons in the orchestra, one of which doubles on the contra bassoon.

Brass Instruments—Wind:

Horn in F (French Horn)

Ex. 10. Range

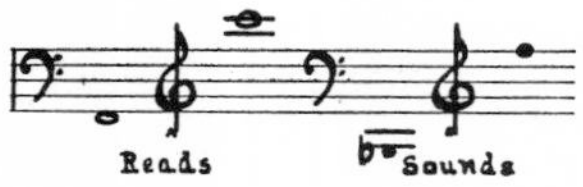

Having its origin in the hunting horn, the French horn was not introduced into the orchestra until the late seventeenth century, having materially reduced its size from the parent instrument. The modern French horn, so-called to distinguish it from the English horn—is a far cry from the hunting horn which could produce only the natural (open) tones of only one harmonic series. Horns of different sizes were therefore necessary to play in different keys. Later, by using different crooks—additional pieces of pipe which were inserted in the body of the instrument—the horn player could play in different keys by changing the crooks. Today the French horn is capable of producing a chromatic scale through the use of rotary valves whose invention has revolutionized horn technique.

Although the French horn does not play the highest part in the brass section of the orchestra, its place in the score following the woodwinds is the result of seniority within the brass section and also to the fact that the French horn is often used with the woodwind section. In this capacity it performs a valuable function in the orchestra because it serves as a bridge of tonal color between the woodwinds and the other members of the brass family. The part played by the French horn corresponds to the alto of a choral group.

The French horn is an instrument of conical bore wound into a spiral which flares out at the lower end into a large bell. It has three or four rotary valves and its mouthpiece is funnel-shaped. The tone color of the French horn may be described as soft, mellow, full, and warm because it is so rich in overtones. By placing the hand in the bell, called *muting,* the horn player can not only soften the tone but change its color and pitch. Played loudly, the tonal color is somewhat brassy. In the hands of an experienced player, the horn is expressive and beautiful, though quite difficult to play. As can be seen from Ex. 10, it is an instrument of wide range. It is a slow-speaking instrument and for this reason does quite well as a solo instrument. Though any number of horns may be called for in an orchestral score, the usual number is four.

Trumpet in B-Flat.
Ex. 11. Range

Being the highest of the brass voices and also a transposing instrument, the trumpet is of cylindrical bore which flares out into a bell of considerably smaller proportions than the French horn. Using a cupped mouthpiece, the player produces the natural (open) harmonic overtones by changes of embouchure. The modern trumpet, introduced in 1813, is provided with three piston or rotary valves which make it possible for the player to produce a complete chromatic scale. Like the French horn, the trumpet went through the natural and crook stage before the valve system was introduced, the latter giving the trumpet great flexibility and brilliant colors. Capable of a wide range of dynamics, it is also quite expressive and, with the aid of a *mute*—a hand or a pear-shaped cardboard device—the player can soften the tone and, at the same time, change its color and pitch. Three standard mutes provide a variety of tone colors and effects. The trumpet is often used as a melody instrument, but is equally at home in fast scale and rhythmic passages. Standard practice in the modern orchestra is to use three trumpets.

Though more mellow, but similar in tone production, the *cornet in B-flat* is fingered the same as the trumpet. Its use is usually confined to the brass band.

Tenor Trombone.
Ex. 12. Range

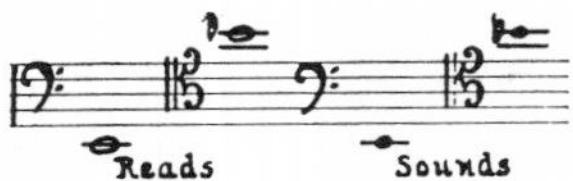

Using a cupped mouthpiece coupled to a long piece of metal tubing of cylindrical bore for two thirds of its length, the trombone flares out into a bell somewhat larger than that of the trumpet. The instrument is actually in two pieces, the second part being a slide which, when attached to the bell and the mouthpiece portion, permits the player, by moving the slide to and away from himself, to fill in the half steps between the natural tones, thus creating a complete chromatic scale. The trombone is pitched in B-flat. As its name indicates, the tenor trombone sings a tenor part in the brass section. Its tone color is rich, smooth, and less brilliant than the trumpet. The mutes used are of the same variety as those for the trumpet. The trombone is capable of a wide range of dynamics from very soft to very loud. It can be bold, powerful, and majestic, or quite lyrical. It is also capable of humorous caricature. Standard practice calls for three trombones in the orchestra.

Bass Trombone.
Ex. 13. Range

The *bass trombone*, pitched in F, is similar to the tenor trombone, but its compass ranges from a fourth below the latter and, obviously, is used to supply a bass part for the brass section. The bass trombone player may double as one of the three tenor trombones previously mentioned.

Tuba.

Ex. 14. Range

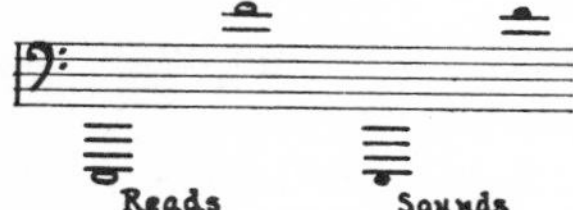

Pitched in BB-flat or E-flat, but treated as a C instrument, the tuba is the double bass of the brass family. It consists of a huge spiral of brass tubing of conical bore ending in an enormous bell. The instrument is supplied with a cupped mouthpiece. There are four or five valves to help supply the chromatic scale. Used largely as a harmonic instrument, it may also be treated melodically. It is sometimes used to portray grotesque or ominous characters. Usually there is one tuba in the orchestra.

PERCUSSION INSTRUMENTS OF DEFINITE PITCH:

Timpani.

Ex. 15. Range

The chief instrument of this group is the *timpani,* or *kettledrum.* The timpani, used in pairs, threes, or fours, consists of a metal hemisphere, generally of copper, covered with a "head" usually made of calfskin, which may be tightened or loosened for tuning purposes either by screws around the rim which are turned by hand or, as in the case of modern timpani, by a pedal device. The head can be stretched so tightly that definite pitch can be recognized when struck. Two sticks or mallets are used for striking the "head"; one end of each stick is usually covered with felt. The timpani are tuned to the tonic and dominant (fifths) of the key of the composition as follows:

Ex. 16. Tuning the Timpani

Besides being useful as rhythm instruments, the timpani are indispensible in regulating the dynamic effects of the orchestra. The timpani player must be a skilled musician, for he must possess what we normally call absolute pitch, be able to make quick pitch changes—here the pedal timpani are of decided advantage—while the rest of the orchestra is playing. While all of this is going on, he must be counting the correct number of beats rest he may have before playing the right note at the precise instant.

Although the pedal timpani is not as resonant as the hand-tuned type, their use has become widespread in radio, dance, and symphony orchestras because of the ease and speed in changing their pitch.

The following percussion instruments of definite pitch will be described briefly due to their infrequent use.

Glockenspiel.
Ex. 17. Range

The glockenspiel is an instrument consisting of two rows of rectangular metal bars of varying lengths arranged similarly to a piano keyboard. It is played with one or two hard or soft hammers. Its music is written two octaves below its actual sound. The tone color is bright, piercing, and bell-like.

Xylophone.
Ex. 18. Range

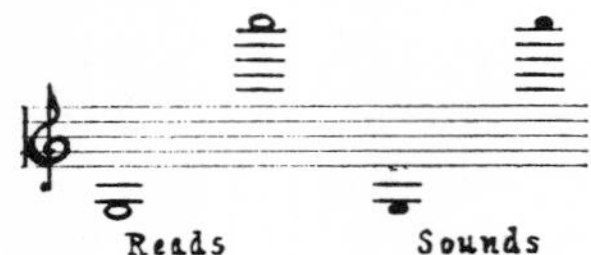

Similar to the glockenspiel in general construction, the bars of the xylophone are made of wood. Played with hard or soft mallets, the xylophone produces a hard, "wooden" clatter of sound. A very close relative of the xylophone is the *Marimba* which may be distinguished from the former by metal tubes which are suspended beneath the wooden bars, which gives a softness and mellowness to the tone. These instruments are pitched an octave below the glockenspiel.

Chimes.
Ex. 19. Range

Sometimes called *tubular bells,* the chimes are used primarily to give an effect of church bells. The chimes consist of a series of about eighteen long metal tubes arranged like a piano keyboard and suspended from a metal frame. The chimes are struck by a wooden hammer. Generally speaking, the chimes are said to sound an octave higher than written.

Vibraphone.

Ex. 20. Range

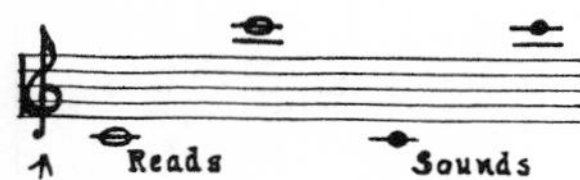

Built similarly to the Xylophone and the marimba, the bars of the vibraphone are made of metal, with large resonating tubes suspended below. These tubes contain an electric mechanism which gives the tone a vibrato effect. There is a foot pedal connected to a damping mechanism to sustain or stop the tone similar to the right-hand pedal on the piano. The vibraphone is played with from two to four hard or soft mallets. The instrument is used primarily in radio and dance orchestras.

Celesta.

Ex. 21. Range

The celesta resembles a small upright piano. It consists of a keyboard whose soft hammers strike a series of metal bars which give off clear, tinkling, bell-like tones. The action of the keyboard is slower than that of the piano. The celesta sounds an octave above the written pitch. It is grouped on the score page with the percussion instruments, along with the pipe organ, the piano, and the harp.

Percussion Instruments of Indefinite Pitch:

The quantity of instruments represented by this classification makes it prohibitive for all of them to be described in detail. We will confine ourselves to the more important ones of this group.

Snare Drum. Sometimes called the *Side Drum,* this instrument consists of two "heads" stretched over a cylindrical metal shell. The upper head

—called the batter head—is struck by means of wooden sticks. Across the lower head wires or cords, called snares, are tightly stretched. Although its tone color is brilliant, the snares may be released for a tom-tom or muffled effect.

Bass Drum. Although there are different sizes of bass drums, they may be described in general as being much larger in diameter and depth than the snare drum. The bass drum is without snares. Played with a large, soft-headed stick, it produces a low, heavy sound. Because of its slow response, it is at its best in slower passages.

Tambourine. This instrument is a small, single-headed drum. Its head is stretched over a round wooden frame which is slit at intervals, into which slits pairs of thin metal disks are inserted. The tambourine may be played by hitting the head with the hand, by shaking to give a "jingling" effect, or by rubbing the thumb on the head causing a tremolo of the metal disks.

Triangle. The triangle is simply constructed from a metal rod bent in the shape of a triangle which is open at the upper end. It is struck with a beater of the same material. The triangle produces very high partials of indefinite pitch; thus the sound is quite penetrating and it is used sparingly for this reason.

Cymbals. The cymbals are made of two large saucer-like plates of equal size so constructed that the rims of the plates touch when struck together. The cymbals produce a crashing, clashing sound when struck together. They may also be played singly or in pairs by striking them with drum or timpani sticks.

Gong. Sometimes referred to as a tam-tam, the gong is a huge metal disk-shaped, shallow saucer with upturned sides which gives off an ominous, sometimes terrifying sound. It is struck with a heavy bass-drum beater.

Other percussion instruments of indefinite pitch are: *tenor* or *street drum, castanets, wood-blocks, cowbells, chains, anvil, claves, maracas, rattle, siren, slapstick, thunder-machine, wind-machine, bongos, autohorn,* etc.

Organ (*Pipe*).
Ex. 22. Range

Although a keyboard, wind instrument, the *pipe organ* is grouped with the percussion section as far as its place in the score page is concerned and is discussed here, briefly, for this reason.

Though one of the oldest musical instruments, the organ, by comparison, is rarely used with the orchestra largely because of the duplication of tonal color. Its greatest use is in the church service, where it is a valuable partner in the singing of the liturgy, the hymns, and the anthem.

Musical sound is created by the pipe organ through the medium of a keyboard of five complete octaves—sixty-one notes installed in a console which comprises two or more keyboards for hands—called *manuals,* a *pedal* keyboard for the feet, and a wind chest on which a series of pipes of varying sizes and shapes are placed. The wind chest contains a valve for each pipe which may be opened or closed by means of a mechanical, pneumatic, or electrical impulse which is initiated by the keyboard or the foot pedals. The compressed air which is supplied to the wind chest by means of an electric blower is kept at a steady pressure by means of a bellows placed between the blower and the wind chest. The console contains, besides manuals, all other controls which the performer must know how to operate such as the stops which control the different tone colors, mixtures, and tremolo (vibrato). Skill at choosing and varying these stops is called the art of *registration.*

Pipe organs vary in size and, consequently, in cost, depending on the number and ranks of pipes specified. An organ of considerable size would contain the following manuals which divide it into a *Swell organ, Great organ, Positive organ, Choir organ,* and *Pedal organ,* each of which can be used singly or in combination by means of *couplers.* The couplers make it possible for the stops of one manual to be sounded with those of another. Thus, in coupling the Swell organ to the Great, stops of the Swell are made available on the manual for the Great. Further, any manual may be (1) coupled to the Pedal, and (2) the Pedal may be coupled to any or all manuals.

Mutation stops are those which provide one of the harmonics of a given unison and are not to be used alone but in combination with a unison of considerably greater power to change the tone color of the unison stop. *Mixtures* are those stops which combine selected unisons with the mutation stops and must be used in combination with a strong unison stop. With the present interest in the Baroque organ, mutations and mixtures have again become important to the organist.

Loudness is controlled by means of "shutters" on the swell box. Expertly played and acoustically well placed in a hall or a church, the organ becomes the king among instruments.

Pianoforte (abbr. piano).
Ex. 23. Range

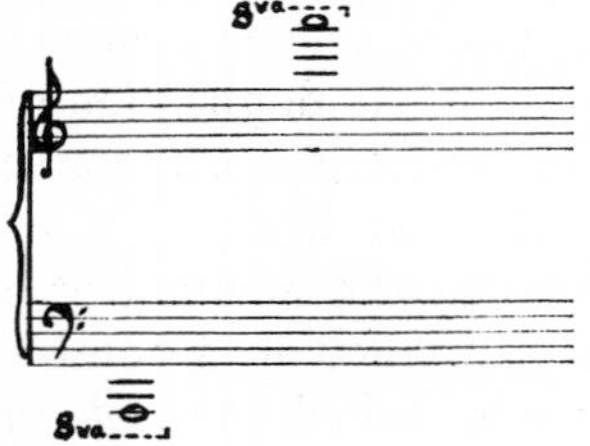

The piano—successor to the clavichord and the harpsichord—was invented by Bartolomeo Cristofori of Florence, Italy, in 1709. Since it could be played either loud or soft, it was called the pianoforte. By the late eighteenth century, the piano had become the dominant keyboard instrument. Mozart, who was noted for the quantity and quality of compositions in addition to his virtuosity on the instrument, became, in the Classic period, the fountainhead of a long line of composers and virtuosi—Beethoven, Schumann, Chopin, Liszt, Brahms, to name but a few.

The piano is here treated by itself because it is at one and the same time a percussive instrument of definite pitch, and a stringed instrument, since the strings are set in motion by means of a hammer mechanism which is activated by keys—eighty-eight. The connecting mechanism between the keys and the hammers is called *the action*. This mechanism limits the control that the performer has over his instrument. Once the string is struck by the hammer, the performer is unable to vary the tone either by the use of vibrato or swell. His touch can create only varying degrees of loudness and softness. Also, the fact that the instrument is pre-tuned prohibits him from varying the intonation.

These limitations are compensated for by the fact that the pianist can play more than one tone at a time, as is not the case with most instruments, and much easier than can be produced on most stringed instruments. He can at once become a soloist, an accompanist, or a percussionist.

In addition to the action, the piano is usually provided with a set of three pedals: (1) the damper pedal—right; (2) the soft pedal—left; and (3) the sostenuto pedal—middle. The damper pedal is a device for permitting the string to sound after the keys are released. In depressing the soft pedal, the keyboard shifts so that the hammers strike only two strings instead of their usual three, or in the case of lower registers, one instead of two. The sostenuto pedal raises the dampers from just those tones which the pianist wishes to sustain, allowing at the same time, free use of the rest of the keyboard with or without the damper pedal.

In keyboard instruments a system of tuning called *equal temperament* is used. This system divides the octave into twelve equal half steps. Actually, in equal temperament, only the octave is acoustically correct, the other intervals within the octave having been "compromised" to create the equal half steps. It is only since 1850 that equal temperament has become universal.

In recent years some composers have treated the piano as a thoroughly percussive instrument, notably Stravinsky and Cowell.

Harp.

Ex. 24. Range

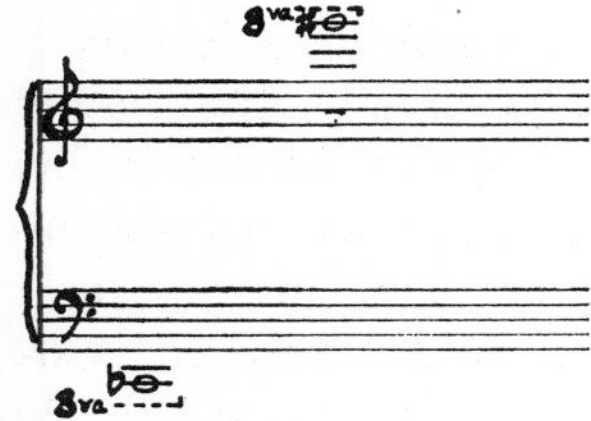

Although grouped with the percussion instruments, the harp may also be considered a stringed instrument. One of the most ancient of instruments, it remains the only plucked stringed instrument in the modern orchestra.

The harp used in symphony orchestras today—called the "double-action" harp—has seven pedals at the foot so contrived that the C pedal can raise all the C strings one half step or a whole step, the D pedal can raise all the D strings one half step or a whole step—hence the name double-action. There are, then, three positions for each pedal: the first gives the flatted note, the second the natural note, the third the sharped note, i.e., C-flat, C-natural, C-sharp.

There are forty-seven strings on the harp, arranged vertically to the soundboard which, with the aid of the seven pedals, give a range of six octaves and a fifth with seven strings to the octave. The harp is normally tuned to the key of C-flat major. The method of playing the harp is by plucking one or more strings with the four fingers of each hand. By sweeping one or more fingers over the strings a *glissando*—an overworked effect—may be produced. Struck or broken chords, scales, and diatonic passages are its stock in trade. Though used as a color instrument, the harp may be used for simple accompaniments and rhythmic effects.

Other plucked instruments used rarely in the symphony orchestra are the *banjo,* the *guitar,* and the *mandolin.* Of these the guitar is favored, especially in the modern dance band.

Violin.
Ex. 25. Range

The most important instrument of the string family is the violin. This is true because of its expressive qualities and tone color, which sometimes approximates that of the human voice. Coupled with its wide range of dynamics from ppp to fff is its ability to execute rapid passages. The first violins—numbering about eighteen—normally sing the highest soprano part, while the second violins—numbering about sixteen—usually sing a second soprano part in the orchestra. Of the string family, the violins are the most brilliant in tone color. The four strings of the violin are tuned a perfect fifth apart, i.e., G, D, A, E. The range of the instrument covers fifteen positions—various places which the left hand may occupy on the fingerboard—with the violinist utilizing the odd numbered positions—1, 3, 5, etc.—more frequently than the even numbered—2, 4, 6, etc. Though usually employed to play a single note at a time, the violin is also capable of sounding two tones simultaneously—double stops. The violin can play chords consisting of groups of three or four tones by rotating the bow across the strings from the lowest to the highest of the chord. This ability to sound tones in combination—double stops and chords—enhances the value of the instrument for the soloist and the orchestra from the standpoint of harmony and tone color. Of further value is the violin's ability to play harmonics. If the strings are plucked, it is called *pizzicato* playing. Placing a *mute* on the bridge thins the tone color, but does not necessarily soften the tone.

Viola.
Ex. 26. Range

One seventh larger than the violin and tuned a fifth lower, i.e., C, G, D, A, the viola possesses a somewhat larger and richer tone color, but more nasal and masked. Although recently some excellent music has been written for the solo viola, it is considered primarily an ensemble instrument. In the orchestra it plays an alto part, and the player reads from the alto clef and G clef. The positions and the bowing, harmonics, and dynamic capabilities are similar to those of the violin. There are usually fourteen violas in a symphony orchestra.

Violoncello (abbr. cello).
Ex. 27. Range

Tuned an octave below the viola and an octave and a fourth below the violin, i.e., C, D, G, A, the cello is the tenor voice of the string family. Its articulation is as rapid as that of the violin, and possesses the other attributes as well. It is used as a solo as well as an ensemble instrument. The symphony orchestra usually has twelve cellos.

Double Bass (bass viol).
Ex. 28. Range

The double bass is the largest member of the string family and, as the name implies, is the bass voice of the string section. It is often used to double the cello part. Its four strings are tuned to E, A, D, G. The double bass is rarely used as a solo instrument and is more at home supplying a firm foundation for the upper strings. There are usually ten double basses in an orchestra.

Appendix V—*Records*

PART I–GENERAL PRINCIPLES

UNIT I–AESTHETIC PRINCIPLES OF MUSIC AND THE ALLIED ARTS

The following is a partial list of representative recordings which are illustrative of descriptive music in varying degrees. The records are paired: one descriptive with one absolute. In this way the difference between the two will appear, yet their essential similarity in being examples of good music will be evident.

With the title unannounced, play the composition as a whole. Replay, testing the autonomous theory by giving the student the opportunity to identify descriptive music for himself. Identify the composition as to period in music history, observing, at the same time, how a specific philosophy will influence the sound of the music of a given period. This is best accomplished by contrasting the music of one period with that of another.

Composer	Title	Movement
1. Kuhnau	Biblical Sonata	The Battle of David and Goliath
2. Bach, C. P. E.	Sonata in A Minor, Op. 2, No. 1	First
1. Beethoven	Symphony No. 6 in F, Op. 68 (Pastoral)	Second
2. Beethoven	Symphony No. 7 in A, Op. 92	Second or Third
1. Berlioz	Fantastic Symphony, Op. 14	Third
2. Brahms	Symphony No. 1 in C Minor, Op. 68	Fourth
1. Carpenter	Adventures in a Perambulator	Fifth
2. Hanson	Symphony No. 2 (Romantic)	First
1. Debussy	L'Après-midi d'un Faune	
2. Vaughan Williams	Fantasia on a Theme by Tallis	
1. Weber	Invitation to the Dance, Op. 65	
2. Ravel	La Valse	
1. Gershwin	An American in Paris	
2. Stravinsky	Symphony in Three Movements	

Composer	Title	Movement
1. Liszt	Les Preludes, Symphonic Poem No. 3	
2. Franck	Symphony in D Minor	
1. Milhaud	La Création du Monde	Third
2. Barber	Adagio for Strings, Op. 11	
1. Moussorgsky	Pictures at an Exhibition (for Piano)	Promenade
2. Chopin	Preludes, Op. 28	No. 20
1. Thomson	Five Portraits	
2. Bartók	Divertimento for String Orchestra	
1. Couperin	Pièces de Clavecin	Four Portraits
2. Mozart	Adagio in B Minor, K. 540	
1. Copland	Billy the Kid, Ballet	The Card Game
2. Harris	Symphony No. 3	Fifth Theme
1. Dukas	L'Apprenti Sorcier	
2. Tschaikowsky	Symphony No. 4 in F Minor, Op. 36	First

UNIT II—THE ART OF LISTENING

Many examples could be listed which would illustrate what is meant by the terms "serious" and "popular" music. However, it is believed that those listed here will be self-evident. Contrast the following:

Composer	Title	Movement
1. Sousa	Stars and Stripes Forever	
2. Berlioz	Fantastic Symphony, Op. 14	Fourth: March to the Scaffold
1. Strauss, O.	The Chocolate Soldier	My Hero
2. Brahms	Waltz, Op. 39, No. 12	
1. Verdi	La Traviata, Act I	Prelude
2. Franck	Symphony in D Minor	First
1. Handy	St. Louis Blues	
2. Gershwin	An American in Paris	Third Theme: Blues
1. Kern	The Song is You	
2. Carpenter	Gitanjali (Song Cycle)	Serenade
1. Joplin	Maple Leaf Rag	
2. Debussy	Children's Corner Suite	Golliwog's Cake Walk

Composer	Title	Movement
1. Latin America	La Comparsa (Rumba)	
2. McDonald	Symphony No. 2	Rhumba
1. Morton, "Jelly Roll"	King Porter Stomp	
2. Liebermann	Concerto for Jazz Band and Symphony Orchestra	

PART II—MUSICAL ELEMENTS

UNIT III—THE PULSE OF MUSIC: RHYTHM

The following is a partial list of idealized dance music. With the aid of the study material and the examples shown, the student should now be able to determine the basic "beat," the superimposed rhythmic pattern and, therefore, be able to identify the dance form in the following list of recordings. Bear in mind that the recordings should be played with their titles unannounced.

Composer	Title	Movement
Habañera		
Bizet	Carmen	Habañera
Sarasate	Danses Espagnoles, Op. 21, No. 2	Habañera
Yradier	La Paloma	
Aubert, Louis	Habañera	
Debussy	Preludes, Book II	No. 3: La Puerta del Vino
Ravel	Pièce en Forme de Habañera	
Ravel	Rapsodie Espagnole	Third
Tango		
Albéniz	Tango in D, Op. 165, No. 2	
Gould	Latin-American Symphonette	Tango
Milhaud	Le Boeuf sur le Toit	Sixth Theme: Tango
Stravinsky	L'Histoire du Soldat	Tango
Polka		
Field, John	Polka	
Dvořák	Suite in D, Op. 39	Polka
Smetana	The Bartered Bride	Act I, Polka
Strauss, J.	Pizzicato Polka	
Rachmaninoff	Polka de W. R.	
Shostakovitch	The Golden Age, Ballet, Op. 22	Polka
Stravinsky	Circus Polka	
Stravinsky	Suite No. 2	Third: Polka
Weinberger	Schwanda	Polka

Composer	Title	Movement
Pavane		
Byrd	The Parthenia	Pavan: The Earl of Salisbury
Dowland	M. John Langton's Pavan	
Gibbons	The Lord of Salisbury, His Pavane	
Albéniz	Pavana-Capricho, Op. 12	
Delibes	Le Roi s'Amuse	Scène du Bal: Pavane
Coates	Four Centuries Suite	Pavane
Menotti	Sebastian Ballet Suite	Pavane
Ravel	Pavane pour une Infante Défunte	
Vaughan Williams	Job	Pavane
Warlock	Capriol, Suite	Second: Pavane
Gavotte		
Bach	English Suite No. 3 in G Minor	Gavotte
Bach	French Suite No. 5 in G Minor	Gavotte
Gluck	Air de Ballet	Fifth: Gavotte
Handel	Concerto No. 11 in G Minor	Fourth: Gavotte
Handel	Suite No. 1 in G	Sixth: Gavotte
Mozart	Les Petits Riens	Nos. 6, 12: Gavotte
Beethoven	Fidelio, Op. 72	Act II, Gavotte
Grétry	Céphale et Procris, Ballet	Gavotte
Grieg	Holberg Suite, Op. 40	Third: Gavotte
Massenet	Manon	Act II, Gavotte
Thomas	Mignon	Act II, Intermezzo (Gavotte)
Prokofieff	Classical Symphony in D, Op. 25	Third: Gavotte
Stravinsky	Pulcinella Suite	Gavotte
Galop		
Delibes	Coppélia, Ballet	Act II, Galop
Liszt	Grand Galop Chromatique	
Offenbach	Orpheus in Hades	Act I, Galop
Bernstein	Fancy Free, Ballet Suite	Galop
Khachaturian	Masquerade Suite	Galop
Stravinsky	Suite No. 2	Fourth: Galop
Trepak		
Moussorgsky	Songs and Dances of Death	Death and the Peasant (Trepak)
Tschaikowsky	Nutcracker Suite, Op. 71a	Russian Dance (Trepak)
Khachaturian	Gayne, Ballet	Dance of the Young Kurds

COMPOSER	TITLE	MOVEMENT
Chaconne		
Bach	Partita No. 1 in B Minor	Sixth: Chaconne
Purcell	Chacony in G Minor (also known as Sonata No. 6)	
Handel	Second Set of Piano Suites	Chaconne No. 9 in G
Gluck	Orfeo ed Euridice	Act II, Chaconne
Brahms	Symphony No. 4 in E Minor, Op. 98	Fourth
Franck	Symphony in D Minor	Finale
Grieg	Peer Gynt, Suite No. 1, Op. 46	Fourth
Busoni	Toccata	Ciaccona
Dello Joio	Variations, Chaconne and Finale	
Křenek	Toccata und Chaconne, Op. 13	
Passacaglia		
Bach	Passacaglia in C Minor (Organ)	
Dohnányi	Marche Humoresque (basso ostinato)	
Copland	Passacaglia	
Ravel	Trio in A Minor	
Schuman, W	Symphony No. 3	Pt. I, First theme: Passacaglia
Courante		
Bach	English Suite No. 5 in E Minor	Second: Courante
Bach	French Suite No. 1 in D Minor	First: Courante
Bach	Partita No. 2 in D Minor	Second: Courante
Handel	Suite No. 5 in E	Third: Courante
Dohnányi	Suite nach altem Stil, Op. 24	Courante
Strauss, R.	Der Bürger als Edelmann, Op. 60	Courante
Galliard		
Byrd	The Parthenia	Galliard: The Earl of Salisbury
Dowland	The Earl of Essex	Galliard
Frescobaldi	Gagliarda	
Vaughan Williams	Job	Galliard
Polonaise		
Bach	French Suite No. 6 in E	Third: Polonaise
Handel	Concerto Grosso in E Minor, Op. 6, No. 3	Fourth: Polonaise
Beethoven	Polonaise in C, Op. 89	
Chopin	Polonaise, Op. 26, No. 1 in C♯ Minor	
Chopin	Polonaise, Op. 40, No. 1 in A	
Chopin	Polonaise, Op. 40, No. 2 in C	
Chopin	Polonaise, Op. 53 in A-Flat	
Glinka	A Life for the Czar	Polonaise
Liszt	Polonaise No. 1 in C Minor	

Composer	Title	Movement
Polonaise—(*Cont.*)		
Liszt	Polonaise No. 2 in E	
Tschaikowsky	Eugen Onégin, Op. 24	Act III: Polonaise
Chabrier	Le Roi malgré lui	Fête Polonaise
Sarabande		
Bach	Partita No. 1 in B-Flat	Sarabande
Bach	English Suite No. 1 in A	Sarabande
Bach	English Suite No. 5 in E Minor	Sarabande
Bach	French Suite No. 1 in D Minor	Sarabande
Handel	Rinaldo	Lascia ch'io pianga
Handel	Suite No. 4 in D Minor	Third: Sarabande
Grieg	Holberg Suite, Op. 40	Second: Sarabande
Debussy	Pour le Piano, Suite	Second: Sarabande
Piston	Suite for Oboe and Piano	Second: Sarabande
Satie	Three Sarabandes	First
Vaughan Williams	Job	Sarabande
Fandango		
Gluck	Don Juan, Ballet	Fandango
Mozart	Le Nozze di Figaro, K. 492	Act III: Finale
Albéniz	Iberia, Book II	Rondeña
Albéniz	Iberia, Book IV	Malagueña
Rimsky-Korsakov	Capriccio Espagnole, Op. 34	Fifth: Fandango
Granados	Goyescas	Fandango
Lecuona	Suite Andalucia	Malagueña
Turina	Fandanguillo	
Waltz		
———	Ach du Lieber Augustin (Example of Ländler)	
Mozart	Deutsche Tänze, K. 509, No. 1 (Example of Ländler)	
Beethoven	Variations on a Waltz of Diabelli, Op. 120 (Example of Ländler)	
Berlioz	Fantastic Symphony, Op. 14	Second: A Ball
Brahms	Liebeslieder Waltzes, Op. 52	Nos. 1, 5
Chopin	Waltz, Op. 18, in E-Flat	
Chopin	Waltz, Op. 64, No. 1, in D-Flat	
Glazunoff	Valse de Concert, Op. 47	
Gounod	Roméo et Juliette	Act I: Waltz Song
Grieg	Peer Gynt Suite No. 1, Op. 46	Third: Anitra's Dance
Liszt	Mephisto Waltz	
Puccini	La Bohème	Act II: Musetta's Waltz
Rossini	La Boutique Fantasque, Ballet	Sixth: Valse Lente
Schubert	Ländler, Op. 18	
Schubert	Ländler, Op. 171	

Composer	Title	Movement
Waltz—(*Cont.*)		
Sibelius	Kuolema, Op. 44	Valse Triste
Strauss, J.	Beautiful Blue Danube, Op. 317	
Strauss, J.	Die Fledermaus, Op. 367	Waltzes
Strauss, J.	Roses from the South, Op. 388	Waltzes
Strauss, R.	Der Rosenkavalier, Op. 59	Waltzes
Tschaikowsky	Eugen Onégin, Op. 24	Act II: Waltz
Weber	Aufforderung zum Tanz, Op. 65	
Verdi	La Traviata	Act I: Libiamo, libiamo
Hindemith	Kleine Kammermusik, Op. 24, No. 2	Second: Waltz
Khachaturian	Masquerade Suite	First: Waltz
Lehar	The Merry Widow	Act III: Waltz: Lippen schweigen
Rachmaninoff	Suite No. 2, Op. 17	Second: Valse
Ravel	L'Enfant et les Sortilèges	Waltz
Ravel	La Valse	
Thomson	Filling Station, Ballet	No. 8: Waltz
Walton	Façade, Suite No. 1	Second: Valse
Seguidilla		
Albéniz	Cantos de España, Op. 232	Seguidillas
Albéniz	Suite Española, Cadiz	Seguidillas
Bizet	Carmen	Act I: Séguidille
de Falla	Canciones Populares Españoles	Seguidilla Murciana
Minuet		
Purcell	Suite No. 1 in G	Minuet
Bach	Brandenburg Concerto No. 1 in F	Fourth: Minuetto
Bach	English Suite No. 4 in F	Minuets I–II
Bach	French Suite No. 1 in D Minor	Minuets I–II
Bach	French Suite No. 6 in E	Minuet
Gluck	Air de Ballet	Act IV: Minuet
Handel	Fireworks Music	Fifth: Minuet No. 1 Sixth: Minuet No. 2
Handel	Suite No. 3 in D Minor	Fifth: Minuet
Handel	Suite No. 8 in G	Fifth: Minuet
Handel	Water Music	Eighteenth: Minuet
Haydn	Symphony in G, No. 94	Third: Minuet
Haydn	Symphony in E Flat, No. 103	Third: Minuet
Haydn	Symphony in C	Third: Minuet
Haydn	Trio No. 2 in G Major (London)	Minuet
Mozart	Don Giovanni	Act I: Minuet
Mozart	Symphony No. 40 in G Minor, K. 550	Third

Composer	Title	Movement
Minuet—(*Cont.*)		
Mozart	Symphony No. 41 in C, K. 551	Third
Beethoven	Quartet in C Minor, Op. 18, No. 4	Third: Minuet
Beethoven	Quartet in A, Op. 18, No. 5	Second: Minuet
Beethoven	Minuet in G	
Beethoven	Trio in C Minor, Op. 1, No. 3	Third: Minuet
Beethoven	Serenade, Op. 8	Third: Minuet
Beethoven	Sonata No. 1 in F Minor, Op. 2, No. 1	Third: Minuet
Beethoven	Sonata No. 7 in D, Op. 10, No. 3	Third: Minuet
Beethoven	Symphony No. 1, Op. 21	Third: Minuet
Bizet	L'Arlesienne Suite No. 1	Minuetto
Bizet	L'Arlesienne Suite No. 2	Minuetto
Brahms	Serenade No. 1 in D, Op. 11	Fourth: Minuet I–II
Chausson	Concerto in D	Third
Paderewski	Minuet in G, Op. 14, No. 1	
Schubert	Sonata in G, Op. 78	Third: Minuet
Verdi	Rigoletto	Prologue, Menuetto
Debussy	Petite Suite	Minuet
Debussy	Suite Bergamasque	Minuet
Elgar	The Wand of Youth, Suite No. 1, Op. 1a	Minuet
Prokofieff	Romeo and Juliet, Suite No. 1, Op. 64	Fourth: Minuet
Ravel	L'Enfant et les Sortilèges	Minuet
Ravel	Le Tombeau de Couperin	Minuet
Schoenberg	Piano Suite, Op. 25	Minuet
Vaughan Williams	Job	Minuet
Bolero		
Chopin	Bolero in C, Op. 19	
Delibes	Les Filles de Cadiz	Bolero: Nous venions de voir
Moszkowski	Spanish Dances, Op. 12, No. 5	Bolero
Rossini	Soirées Musicales	Bolero
Ravel	Bolero	
Mazurka		
Chopin	Mazurka, No. 13, Op. 17, No. 4	
Delibes	Coppélia Ballet	Act I: Third Theme: Mazurka
Glinka	A Life for the Czar	Mazurka
Lalo	Namouna, Ballet Suite	Thème varié
Debussy	Mazurka	
Khachaturian	Masquerade Suite	Third: Mazurka
Scriabin	Mazurka, Op. 25, No. 3	

Composer	Title	Movement
Bourrée		
Bach	English Suite, No. 1 in A	Bourrée
Bach	French Suite, No. 5 in G	Bourrée
Bach	Partita No. 1 in B Minor	Bourrée
Bach	Suite, No. 1 in C	Bourrée
Handel	Concerto No. 7 in B-Flat, Op. 7, No. 1	Fourth
Handel	Fireworks Music	Second: Bourrée
Handel	Water Music	Ninth: Bourrée
Chabrier	Bourrée Fantasque	
Britten	Simple Symphony	First: Boisterous Bourrée
Allemande		
Bach	English Suite No. 3 in G Minor	Allemande
Bach	French Suite No. 6 in E	Allemande
Bach	Partita No. 1 in B Minor	Allemande
Handel	Suite No. 5 in E	Second: Allemande
Rameau	Suite in E Minor	First: Allemande
Beethoven	Bagatellen, Op. 119	A l'allemande (a different species from that described in the text)
Schumann	Carnaval, Op. 9	Valse allemande (this is a different species from that described in the text)
Křenek	Little Suite, Op. 13a	Allemande
Fox Trot		
Carmichael	Stardust	
Carpenter	Krazy Kat, Ballet	Fox Trot
Debussy	Children's Corner Suite	Golliwog's Cake Walk
Debussy	Preludes, Book I	No. 12: Minstrels
Ellington	Mood Indigo	
Gershwin	An American in Paris	Charleston
Gershwin	The Man I Love	
Gershwin	Rhapsody in Blue	
Gould	Chorale and Fugue in Jazz	
Handy	St. Louis Blues	
Hindemith	Suite 1922	Ragtime
Joplin	Maple Leaf Rag	
Kern	Smoke Gets in Your Eyes	
McDonald	Symphony No. 2	Rhumba
Milhaud	Création du Monde	Third
Satie	Parade Ballet	Ragtime

Composer	Title	Movement
Fox Trot—(*Cont.*)		
Stravinsky	Ebony Concerto	
Stravinsky	Ragtime	
Walton	Façade, Suite No. 2	Fox Trot
Weill	Die Dreigroschenoper	
Tarantella		
Liszt	Années de pèlerinage	Venezia e Napoli
Mendelssohn	Symphony No. 4 in A, Op. 90	First Theme
Mendelssohn	Songs without Words	No. 45 in C: Tarantella
Rossini	La Boutique Fantasque	Second: Tarantella
Rossini	Soirées Musicales	Tarantella
Sarasate	Introduction and Tarantelle, Op. 43	
Verdi	La Forza del Destino	Act III: Nella la guerra
Casella	Serenata	Sixth: Tarantella
Debussy	Danse, Tarantelle Styrienne (irregular)	
Hindemith	Sonata in E	Tarantella
Rachmaninoff	Suite No. 2, Op. 17	Fourth: Tarantelle
Stravinsky	Pulcinella	Part 4: Tarantella
Walton	Façade, Suite No. 1	Tarantella
Gigue		
Purcell	The Fairy Queen	Jig
Bach	English Suite No. 4 in F	Gigue
Bach	French Suite No. 4 in E-Flat	Gigue
Bach	Partita No. 1 in B Minor	Gigue
Corelli	Concerto Grosso in B-Flat, Op. 6, No. 11	Fifth: Giga
Handel	Suite No. 3 in D Minor	Fourth: Gigue
Handel	Suite No. 4 in E Minor	Fifth: Gigue
Grétry	Cephale et Procris, Ballet Suite	Gigue
Delibes	Coppélia Ballet	Gigue
Saint-Saens	King Henry VIII, Ballet Music	Gigue
Debussy	Images, Set III	No. 1: Gigues
Piston	Suite for Oboe	Fifth: Gigue
Ravel	L'Enfant et les Sortilèges	Gigue

Dance Influence on Non-Dance Music

Minuet-with-Trio		
Haydn	Symphony in G, B.&H. No. 94 (Surprise)	Third
Mozart	Symphony No. 40, K. 550	Third
Mozart	Symphony No. 41, K. 551	Third

COMPOSER	TITLE	MOVEMENT
Sonata da Camera		
Corelli	Sonata da Camera in B-Flat, Op. 2, No. 5	
Corelli	Sonata da Camera in G, Op. 2, No. 12	
Corelli	Sonata, Op. 5, No. 1 (Sonata da Chiesa)	
Pierné	Sonata da Camera, Op. 48	
French Overture		
Lully	Thésée	Overture
Bach	Suite No. 3 in D	Overture
Handel	The Messiah	Overture
Telemann	Suite in A Minor	Overture
Mendelssohn	Elijah, Op. 70	Overture
Modern Suite		
Bizet	L'Arlesienne Suite No. 1	
Bizet	L'Arlesienne Suite No. 2	
Grieg	Peer Gynt Suite No. 1	
Grieg	Peer Gynt Suite No. 2	
Tschaikowsky	Nutcracker Suite, Op. 71a	
Debussy	Petite Suite	
Debussy	Pour le Piano	
Grofé	Grand Canyon Suite	
Holst	The Planets, Op. 32	
MacDowell	Suite No. 2, Op. 48 (Indian)	
MacDowell	Woodland Sketches, Op. 51	
Ravel	Daphnis and Chloe Suite No. 1	
Ravel	Daphnis and Chloe Suite No. 2	
Stravinsky	Petrouchka Suite	
Walton	Façade Suite No. 1	
"**Apotheosis of the Dance**"—used broadly to include:		
Beethoven	Symphony No. 7 in A, Op. 92	
Goldmark	Symphony No. 26 (Rustic Wedding)	First, Fifth
Carpenter	Concertino for Piano and Orchestra	
Copland	Concerto for Piano and Orchestra	
Honegger	Concertino for Piano	
Ravel	Sonata for Violin and Piano	
March:		
Military		
Sousa	El Capitan	
Sousa	Stars and Stripes Forever	
Sousa	Washington Post	

Composer	Title	Movement
March—(*Cont.*)		
Processional		
Berlioz	Fantastic Symphony, Op. 14	Fourth
Mendelssohn	Athalia	War March of the Priests
Mendelssohn	Midsummer Night's Dream, Op. 61, No. 9	Wedding March
Meyerbeer	Le Prophète	Coronation March
Verdi	Aïda	Triumphal March
Wagner	Die Meistersinger	Act III, Scene 5 Procession
Wagner	Lohengrin	Act III: Bridal Chorus
Wagner	Tannhäuser	Fest March
Elgar	Pomp and Circumstance, Op. 39, No. 1	
Menotti	Amahl and the Night Visitors	Kings' March
Funeral		
Beethoven	Symphony No. 3 in E-Flat, Op. 55 (Eroica)	Second
Chopin	Sonata in B-Flat Minor, Op. 58	Third: Funeral March
Mendelssohn	Songs without Words, Op. 63, No. 3	No. 27
Wagner	Götterdämmerung	Act III: Scene 2: Siegfried's Funeral March
March as Absolute Music		
Mozart	Symphony No. 35 in D, K. 385 (Haffner)	First
Beethoven	Variations in F, Op. 34	Fifth
Chopin	Polonaise Militaire, Op. 40, No. 1	
Schubert	Marche Militaire, Op. 51, Nos. 1, 2, 3	
Schumann	Album for the Young, Op. 68	Soldiers March
Tschaikowsky	Symphony No. 6 in B Minor, Op. 74 (Pathétique)	Third
Holst	Suite No. 1 in E-Flat for Band	March
Prokofieff	March, Op. 12, No. 1	

UNIT IV—THE LINEAR ASPECTS OF MUSIC: MELODY AND COUNTERPOINT

In the following partial list of recordings illustrating the various kinds of melody, it will be noted that there is a preponderance of vocal music. This is not only due to the very history of music itself which had its origin in song—but of all the Units contained in this book, it is the only one in which so much vocal music could conveniently and logically be placed.

Large choral works, such as opera and oratorio, are indicated as *complete* only to show that the complete works are available on recordings if desired. Separate items have been indicated if a particular purpose is served.

After sufficient listening, discussion, and study, the student should be able to determine if a melody is monophonic, polyphonic, or homophonic. Monophonic music should be readily recognized because it has no accompaniment to obscure it. While the melodies are diatonic, they are based on the modal scales which in themselves create an individual atmosphere which is easily recognized. The phrases will be irregular and often florid.

The examples of organum should create no real problem in recognition. Remember, the voices move in parallel motion and the tonality is diatonic and modal. In listening to the counterpoint of the later polyphonic music, remember to listen for the entrance of each new voice as well as to the interplay of the melodies. The tonality will be diatonic modal, diatonic major or minor, or even to be without a feeling of key center.

In homophonic music one hears a single line of tones with a chordal style (may be embellished) accompaniment. The tonality will be diatonic major or minor, modal, whole tone, or to even be devoid of a feeling of key center. In the case of the chromatic examples, listen for the movement of the melodic line by half steps, which is usually limited to a small group of notes. The tonality will be modal, major, minor, or whole tone.

In listening to music employing the whole-tone technique, one feels that the melodic line reposes in a continuous block of sound. Another distinguishing feature may be the parallel motion or "side-slipping" of the chords. In the whole-tone technique the melodic line tends to fuse with the substructure, making the music sound more obscure or vague. The feeling of key center is practically obliterated and dissonance becomes an outstanding feature.

Remember to listen melodically! Please study the following examples abstractly—as music—before announcing the titles.

Composer	Title
Monophonic Music	
	Gregorian Chant Before the Year 1000 (in L'Anthologie Sonore, a collection of records in 6 volumes published under the direction of Dr. Curt Sachs), Vol. IV, AS-34

Composer	Title	Movement
Monophonic Music—(*Cont.*)		
	Gregorian Chant, recorded by the Monk's Choir of St. Pierre de Solesmes Abbey (12 records)	
Bach	Mass in B Minor	Christe Eleison
Vaughan Williams	Mass in G Minor	Kyrie
Polyphonic (or Contrapuntal) Music		
	Organum duplum (in L'Anthologie Sonore), Vol. VII, AS-65	
	Organum triplum (in L'Anthologie Sonore), Vcl. VII, AS-65	
	Plainsong with Organum (in Columbia History of Music by Ear and Eye), Vol. I, C-5710	
	Plainsong with Counterpoint (in Columbia History of Music by Ear and Eye), Vol. I, C-5710	
Debussy	La Cathédrale Engloutie (example of use of organum)	
Debussy	La Fille aux Cheveux de Lin (example of use of organum)	
Kodály	Epitaph for Piano (modified form of organum)	
Ruggles	Organum for Orchestra	
	Sumer is icumen in (in Columbia History of Music Set), Vol. I, C-5710	
	Conductus (in L'Anthologie Sonore), Vol. VIII, AS-71	
	Music in the Time of Saint Louis—Conductus (in L'Anthologie Sonore), Vol. X, AS-99	
	Polyphony at the Court of Cyprus—Conductus (in L'Anthologie Sonore), Vol. XIII, AS-126	
Dufay	Motet for Four Voices (in L'Anthologie Sonore), Vol. XIII, AS-121	
Lassus	Douce Mémpire	Benedictus
Lassus	Super le Bergier et la bergière	Sanctus and Agnus Dei

Composer	Title	Movement
Polyphonic (or Contrapuntal) Music—(*Cont.*)		
Lassus	Missa pro Defunctis	Benedictus
Palestrina	Motet "Vulnerasti"	
	Motet du Roman de Fauvel (in L'Anthologie Sonore), Vol. X, AS-91	
	Secular madrigals "La cruda mia nimica," "Alla riva del Tebro" (in L'Anthologie Sonore), Vol. V, AS-47	
Palestrina	Magnificat	
Palestrina	Missa Brevis	
Palestrina	Missa Iste Confessor	
Palestrina	Missa Papae Marcelli	
Gesualdo	Moro Lasso	
Gesualdo	Resti di darmi noia	
Monteverdi	Chiome d'oro	
Monteverdi	Ecco mormorar l'onde	
Monteverdi	Hor ch'el ciel e la terra	
Monteverdi	Lasciatiemi morire	
Vecchi	L'Amfiparnasso (madrigal opera)	
Byrd	This Sweet and Merry Month	
Byrd	Though Amaryllis Dance in Green	
Dowland	Say, Love, if ever thou didst find	
Dowland	Weep no more, sad fountains	
Gibbons	What is our life	
Gibbons	The Silver Swan	
Morley	Shoot, False Love, I Care Not	
Morley	Fire, Fire, My Heart!	
Weelkes	As Vesta was from Latmos Hill Descending	
Wilbye	Lady when I Behold	
Wilbye	Stay Corydon, thou Swain	
Bach	Concerto in D Minor for Two Violins	Second
Bach	Great Fugue in G Minor	
Bach	Little Fugue in G Minor	
Bach	Mass in B Minor	Choruses
Bach	Well-Tempered Clavier, Book I	Fugue in E-Flat Minor
Handel	The Messiah	No. 4: And the Glory of the Lord No. 30: Behold the Lamb of God
Mozart	Mass in G, No. 12, K. 232	Choruses
Mozart	Symphony No. 41 in C, K. 551	Fourth

Composer	Title	Movement
Polyphonic (or Contrapuntal) Music—(*Cont.*)		
Beethoven	Grosse Fugue in B-Flat, Op. 133	
Brahms	A German Requiem, Op. 45	Choruses
Franck	Prelude, Chorale, and Fugue	Fugue
Verdi	Falstaff	Act III: Scene 1
Verdi	Rigoletto	Act III: Bella figlia dell'amore
Wagner	Die Meistersinger	Prelude
Vaughan Williams	Mass in G Minor	Choruses
Copland	Passacaglia	
Griffes	Sonata for Piano	
Harris	Symphony No. 3	Section IV: Fugue
Hindemith	Mathis der Mahler	
Holst	The Planets, Op. 32	Mars
Honegger	Pacific 231	
Křenek	Eleven Short Piano Pieces	Walking on a Stormy Day
Křenek	Sonata for Viola and Piano	
Milhaud	String Quartet No. 14	
Milhaud	String Quartet No. 15	
Russo	Fugue for Jazz Orchestra	
Schoenberg	Six Little Piano Pieces, Op. 19	No. 5
Schoenberg	Suite for String Orchestra	
Schoenberg	Three Little Piano Pieces, Op. 11	
Schuman, W.	Symphony No. 3	Passacaglia
Scriabin	Prelude in B Minor, Op. 11, No. 6	
Thomson	Suite for Orchestra, Louisiana Story	Fourth: Fugue
Weinberger	Schwanda, Opera	Fugue
Homophonic Music—Diatonic		
Cesti	Il Pomo d'Oro	Arias
Monteverdi	Incoronazione di Popea	Arias
Monteverdi	Orfeo (complete)	Arias
Pergolesi	La Serva Padrona (complete)	Arias
Peri	Euridice	Arias
Purcell	Dido and Aeneas (complete)	Arias
Lully	Au clair de la lune	Arias
Lully	Alceste	Arias
Bach	Mass in B Minor	Laudamus Te
Handel	Atalanta	Care Selve
Handel	The Messiah (complete)	Arias
Handel	Xerxes	Largo: Ombra mai fu
Gluck	Alceste (complete)	Arias
Haydn	My Mother Bids Me Bind My Hair	

Composer	Title	Movement
Homophonic Music—Diatonic—(*Cont.*)		
Haydn	She Never Told Her Love	
Haydn	The Creation (complete)	Arias
Hopkinson	My Days Have Been so Wondrous Free	
Mozart	Alleluja	
Mozart	Das Veilchen, K. 476	
Mozart	Don Giovanni, K. 527 (complete)	Arias
Mozart	Le Nozze di Figaro, K. 492 (complete)	Arias
Beethoven	Symphony No. 9 in D Minor, Op. 125	
Brahms	Alto Rhapsody, Op. 3	Arias
Brahms	Marienlieder, Op. 22	
Delibes	Lakme	Indian Bell Song
Grieg	Peer Gynt, Op. 23	Act IV: Solvejg's Song
Leoncavallo	I Pagliacci (complete)	Arias
Mahler	Das Lied von der Erde	No. 1: Das Trinklied vom Jammer der Erde
Mendelssohn	Elijah, Op. 70 (complete)	Arias
Moussorgsky	Boris Godounov (complete)	Arias
Puccini	La Bohème (complete)	Arias
Puccini	Madame Butterfly (complete)	Arias
Rossini	Il Barbieri di Siviglia (complete)	Arias
Rossini	William Tell (complete)	Arias
Saint-Saëns	Samson and Delilah, Op. 47	My Heart at Thy Sweet Voice
Schubert	Die Schöne Müllerin, Op. 25 (song cycle)	No. 2: Wohin?
Schubert	Schwanengesang (Lieder)	No. 4: Ständchen
Schumann, R.	Dichterliebe, Op. 48	
Schumann, R.	Frauenliebe und Leben, Op. 42	
Strauss, J.	Fledermaus (complete)	Arias
Strauss, R.	Songs, Op. 10	No. 8: Allerseelen
Strauss, R.	Songs, Op. 27	No. 4: Morgen
Strauss, R.	Rosenkavalier, Op. 59	Arias
Verdi	Aïda (complete)	Arias
Verdi	La Traviata (complete)	Arias
Verdi	Rigoletto (complete)	Arias
Wagner	Die Meistersinger (complete)	Arias
Wagner	Lohengrin (complete)	Arias
Barber	Essay for Orchestra, Op. 12	Second theme
Beach	Ah! Love But a Day	
Britten	Serenade for Tenor, Op. 31	No. 3: Elegy
Burleigh	Deep River	
Burleigh	Go Down, Moses	

Composer	Title	Movement
Homophonic Music—Diatonic—(*Cont.*)		
Cadman	Four American Indian Songs, Op. 45	
Campbell-Tipton	A Spirit Flower	
Carpenter	Gitanjali (song cycle)	
Charles	Let My Song Fill Your Heart	
Coward	Bittersweet	I'll See You Again
Folk Songs	Leadbelly's Legacy, Vols. 1, 2, 3	
Gershwin	Porgy and Bess (complete)	Arias
Gilbert and Sullivan	The Mikado (complete)	Arias
Hageman	Do Not Go, My Love	
Hanson	Centennial Ode	Arias
Hanson	Merry Mount	Arias
Herbert	Naughty Marietta (complete)	Arias
Herbert	Sweethearts (complete)	Arias
Kern	Show Boat	
Lehar	The Merry Widow (complete)	Arias
MacGimsey	Shadrack	
Menotti	The Consul	Arias
Menotti	The Medium	Arias
Menotti	The Telephone	Arias
Ravel	Sonatine	First
Respighi	Gregorian Concerto	Second
Rodgers and Hammerstein	Oklahoma!	Arias
Rodgers and Hammerstein	South Pacific	Arias
Romberg	Student Prince (complete)	Arias
———	Spirituals for Solo Voice	
Straus, O.	The Chocolate Soldier (complete)	Arias
Stravinsky	Symphony of Psalms	
Vaughan Williams	Symphony No. 3 (Pastoral)	Third
Villa-Lobos	Bachianas Brasileras No. 5	
Homophonic Music—Chromatic		
Bach	Chromatic Fantasia and Fugue	
Haydn	String Quartet in C, Op. 76, No. 3	Second: Third Variation
Mozart	Quartet in C, No. 10, K. 465 (Dissonant)	Introduction
Mozart	Quartet No. 16 in E-Flat, K. 462	Third
Mozart	Symphony No. 38 in D, K. 504 (Prague)	Second
Mozart	Symphony No. 41 in C, K. 551	Third
Berlioz	Fantastic Symphony, Op. 14	Third: Second theme
Bizet	Carmen (complete)	Habañera
Bizet	L'Arlésienne Suite, No. 1	Le Carillon

Composer	Title	Movement
Homophonic Music—Chromatic—(*Cont.*)		
Chopin	Etudes, Op. 10	No. 10: A-flat
Franck	Symphony in D Minor	First
Liszt	Die Lorelei	
Liszt	Les Préludes, Symphonic Poem No. 3	Part II
Rimsky-Korsakov	Le Coq d'Or	Act II: Hymn to the Sun
Rimsky-Korsakov	Sadko	Scene IV: Song of India
Rimsky-Korsakov	Scheherazade, Op. 35	Second: Second theme
Rimsky-Korsakov	Tsar Sultan	Flight of the Bumblebee
Schubert	Trio in B-Flat (1817)	Second
Schumann, R.	Carnaval, Op. 9	Valse Noble
Schumann, R.	Hebrew Melodies, Op. 95	No. 2: An den Mond
Schumann, R.	Mit Myrthen und Rosen, Op. 24	No. 9
Schumann, R.	Symphony No. 2 in C, Op. 61	First: Second theme
Strauss, R.	Till Eulenspiegel's Merry Pranks, Op. 28	Part II
Wagner	Tristan and Isolde (complete)	Act I: Prelude Act III: Prelude
Wolf, H.	Dereinst, dereinst, Gedanke mein	
Wolf, H.	Wie glänst der helle Mond	
Barber	Knoxville, Summer of 1915, Op. 24	
Britten	Peter Grimes, Four Sea Interludes, Op. 39a	Fourth Interlude: Second theme
Debussy	L'Après-Midi d'un Faune	First theme
Delius	Walk to the Paradise Garden	First theme
Griffes	Sorrow of Mydath, Op. 9, No. 5	
Griffes	Symphony in Yellow	
Griffes	The White Peacock, Op. 7, No. 1	
Hindemith	Ludus Tonalis	First theme
Křenek	Johnny spielt auf, Op. 45 (complete)	Swannee River Song
MacDowell	Concerto No. 1 in A Minor, Op. 15	Third: First theme
Ravel	Daphnis et Chloe No. 2	Fifth theme
Ravel	Shéhérazade	Opening theme Accompaniment
Schoenberg	Gurrelieder, Op. 35	Lied der Waldtaube
Scott	Lotus Land, Op. 49	
Scriabin	Prelude, Op. 74, No. 5	
Villa-Lobos	Nozani-ná (folk song)	No. 12: Realejo

Composer	Title	Movement
Homophonic Music—Whole Tone		
Bartók	Ten Easy Pieces	No. 9
Debussy	Ariettes Oubliées	Bois Soir
Debussy	Cinq Poèmes de Baudelaire II	Harmonie du Soir
Debussy	Estampes	Pagodes
Debussy	Etudes	
Debussy	Preludes, Book I	No. 2: Voiles
Debussy	Images, Series I	Reflets dans l'eau
Debussy	Iberia from Images No. 2	Second: Les Parfums de la Nuit
Debussy	La Damoiselle Élue (cantata)	Arias
Debussy	La Mer	
Debussy	L'Après-Midi d'un Faune	
Debussy	Nocturnes	Nuages
Debussy	Pelléas et Mélisande (complete)	Arias
Loeffler	Pagan Poem, Op. 14	
Ravel	Gaspard de la Nuit	No. 1: Ondine No. 2: Le Gibet
Rimsky-Korsakov	Sadko (complete)	Procession of the Marvels
Homophonic Music—Pentatonic		
Debussy	La Fille aux Cheveaux de Lin	
Debussy	Nocturnes	Nuages: Third theme
Ravel	Le Pastour	
Ravel	Ma Mère l'Oye	
Stravinsky	Le Chant du Rossignol	Second

UNIT V—THE VERTICAL ASPECTS OF MUSIC: HARMONY

In Unit IV you were asked to listen primarily to one or more lines of music. In this Unit on Harmony, your listening becomes somewhat more complex. Though the whole is greater than its parts, you will want to be able to identify the parts. First, you will need to be able to concentrate on one or more lines so that you will know whether the texture of the music is basically monophonic, polyphonic, or homophonic. Second, if the texture is homophonic or polyphonic, the harmonic structure will vary with each style; if homophonic there is a principal melodic line supported by a chordal accompaniment which is called vertical harmony (or block style); if polyphonic, the music will move by two or more independent melodic lines (listening to a different voice each time) which form harmonies at the point where they coincide. This type of texture we have learned is called horizontal. In other words, we are expected to learn to listen both vertically and horizontally. To express it differently, the way you listen to Palestrina and composers of that period will differ from the way you will listen to the music of Haydn, Mozart, Beethoven, etc. Third, having decided on the harmonic texture, repeated listening will help you with interval recognition, simple and complex chords, nonharmonic tones, kinds of melody (diatonic, whole tone, or chromatic), tonality (adherence to a key center or not), and modulations (those which are unexpected and distant will be the easiest to hear). These parts of the whole are demonstrated in the compositions which follow to help make you *aware* of their presence and function in music. The parts may be more easily recognized by sight than sound, in which case the music should be examined. For easier listening, begin with the chorales and piano compositions. At first you may be able to tell only whether the composition is monophonic, homophonic, or polyphonic. Think of the harmonic structure in terms of relaxation and tension. To do this, is to hear harmonically.

The monophonic, polyphonic, and homophonic records listed in Unit IV will not be given again, but can and should be used in the present Unit. While the records listed in Unit IV were predominantly vocal, the ones given in this Unit will be primarily instrumental examples.

Composer	Title	Movement
Intervals		
	Examples of Organum (see p. 278)	
Bellini	La Sonnambula (thirds, sixths)	D'un Pensiero e d'un Accento
Bizet	Carmen (augmented seconds)	Act I: Prelude
Brahms	Hungarian Dance No. 5 in F♯ Minor (thirds, sixths)	
Brahms	Waltz in A-Flat, Op. 39 (thirds, sixths)	
Chopin	Mazurka in C No. 9, Op. 7 (fifths)	
Dvořák	Waltz, Op. 54 (fifths)	No. 3
Elgar	"Enigma" Variations, Op. 36 (thirds, sevenths)	Ninth variation
Liszt	Hungarian Rhapsody No. 5 in E Minor (thirds, sixths)	
Rimsky-Korsakov	Le Coq d'Or (augmented seconds)	Act II: Hymn to the Sun
Rimsky-Korsakov	Scheherazade, Op. 35 (seconds)	Fourth
Schubert	Hark, Hark, the Lark (diminished fifths)	
Strauss, J.	The Blue Danube, Op. 317 (thirds, sixths)	
Strauss, R.	Ein Heldenleben, Op. 40 (sevenths, ninths)	First theme
Tschaikowsky	Marche Slave, Op. 31 (augmented seconds)	Opening measures
———	Chopsticks (seconds, sevenths)	

COMPOSER	TITLE	MOVEMENT
Intervals—(*Cont.*)		
Debussy	La Cathédrale engloutie (fourths, fifths)	
Friml	Rose Marie (thirds, sixths)	Indian Love Call
Gershwin	Rhapsody in Blue (diminished octave, fifths)	First theme
Guion	Turkey in the Straw (fifths)	
Simple Triads		
Bourgeois	Old Hundredth	
Bach	Lobt Gott, ihr Christen, allzugleich (chorale)	
Haydn	Symphony No. 88 in G	Fourth
Mozart	Symphony No. 40 in G Minor, K. 550	First: First theme
Beethoven	Symphony No. 3 in E-Flat, Op. 44 (Eroica)	First: First theme
Beethoven	Symphony No. 5 in C Minor, Op. 67	Finale
Schubert	Wohin? (Whither?) Op. 25, No. 2	
Brahms	Songs, Op. 94	No. 4: Sapphische Ode
Brahms	Songs, Op. 99	No. 4: Wiegenlied
Dvořák	Symphony No. 5 in E Minor, Op. 95.	First: Second theme
Foster	Old Folks at Home	
Humperdinck	Hänsel and Gretel	Act II: Evening Prayer
Offenbach	Les Contes d'Hoffmann	Act III: Barcarolle
Tschaikowsky	1812 Overture, Op. 49	Beginning
Wagner	Parsifal	"Grail" motive
Berlin	Alexander's Ragtime Band	
Queen Lilinokalani	Aloha Oe	
Negro convict song	Water Boy	
Negro spiritual	Deep River	
Russian Folk Song	Song of the Volga Boatman	
A Spanish Air	Juanita	
Cowboy Song	Home on the Range	
Diminished Triad		
Bach	Aus meines Herzens Grunde (chorale)	Second phrase
Mozart	Don Giovanni, K. 527	Act III: Statue Scene
Barnby	Sweet and Low (diminished seventh)	
Gounod	Roméo et Juliette	Act III: Scene 2
Wagner	Tristan und Isolde	Act II: King Mark Scene

Composer	Title	Movement
Diminished Triad—(*Cont.*)		
Woodbury	Stars of the Summer Night (diminished seventh)	
Augmented Triads		
Puccini	Madame Butterfly	Act I: Entrance of Cio-Cio-San
Wagner	Die Walküre	Act II: Scene 1: Call of the Walküre
Dukas	L'Apprenti Sorcier	Bringing broomstick to life
Debussy	Pelléas et Mélisande	
Debussy	Reflêts dans l'eau (Also see whole tone, p. 295.)	
Stravinsky	L'Oiseau de Feu	Infernal Dance of King Kastchei
Seventh Chords		
Old Dutch	Prayer of Thanksgiving	Ending
Bach	Chorales	
	O Herre Gott, dein göttlich Wort	First phrase
Bach	Gott lob, es geht nun mehr zu Ende	First phrase
Bach	Herzliebster Jesu, was hast du	Fourth phrase
Bach	Ein' feste Burg ist unser Gott	Third phrase
Bach	Erbarm' dich mein, O Herre Gott	Second phrase
Bach	Singen wir aus Herzens Grund	Third phrase
Bach	Allein zu dir, Herr Jesu Christ	Third phrase
Bach	O Ewigkeit, du Donnerwort	Second phrase
Brahms	Symphony No. 1 in C Minor, Op. 68	First
Chopin	Mazurka No. 21, Op. 30	No. 4
Chopin	Prelude in F, Op. 28	No. 23: Closing measures
Dvořák	Songs My Mother Taught Me	Opening
Herbert	Naughty Marietta	I'm Falling in Love with Someone
Strauss, J.	The Blue Danube	
Verdi	La Traviata	Act I: Ah! fors e lui
Wagner	Die Walküre	Act I: Love motive
Gershwin	Rhapsody in Blue	Last three measures
Ninth Chords		
Franck	Sonata for Violin and Piano	Opening section
Franck	Symphony in D Minor (V^9)	Third

Composer	Title	Movement
Ninth Chords—(*Cont.*)		
Puccini	La Bohème (V^9)	Act I: Mimi's narrative
Debussy	Preludes, Book I	No. 12: Minstrels
Griffes	The White Peacock, Op. 7	No. 1: Fourth measure
Ravel	Jeux d'eau	
Ravel	Pavane pour une Infante Défunte	
Eleventh Chords		
Grainger	Mock Morris	
Ravel	Le Tombeau de Couperin	Forlane: First theme
Scriabin	Sonata for Piano, Op. 8, No. 66	
Thirteenth Chords		
Goossens	Nature Poem, No. 3	
Debussy	Reflêts dans l'eau	
Modulation		
de Lisle	Marseillaise Hymn	Begin twelfth measure
Bach	Ach Gott und Herr, wie gross und schwer	Fourth phrase
Mozart	Fantasia, K. 397 (common chord)	
Mozart	Symphony No. 40 in G Minor, K. 550	First
Beethoven	Sonata, Op. 14, No. 1 (No. 6)	
Brahms	Waltz No. 15 in A-Flat, Op. 39	
Brahms	Symphony No. 1 in C Minor, Op. 68	Finale
Chopin	Mazurka, Op. 68, No. 4 (Posthumous) (Chromatic)	
Franck	Symphony in D Minor	Second and Third
Liszt	Liebestraum, No. 3	
Meyerbeer	Le Prophète	Coronation March
Rubinstein	Melody in F, Op. 3	No. 1
Schubert	Symphony No. 8 in B Minor (Unfinished)	Second
Schumann, R.	Abendlied, Op. 85	No. 12
Sullivan	Patience	Willow, Willow, Waly
Verdi	Aïda	Act II: Scene 2: Grand March
Wagner	Parsifal	Prelude: Faith motive

Composer	Title	Movement
Modulation—(*Cont.*)		
Wagner	Tannhäuser	Pilgrims' Chorus
Wagner	Tristan und Isolde	Act I: Tristan's entrance
		Act III: Scene 3: Liebestod
Borrowed and Altered Chords		
Bach	Lebensfürst, Herr Jesu Christ	Third phrase
Bach	Puer Natus in Bethlehem	Third phrase
Bizet	L'Arlésienne Suite, No. 1	Le Carillon
Chopin	Prelude, Op. 28	No. 20
Elgar	Enigma Variations, Op. 36	End of eighth variation
		Beginning of ninth variation
Franck	Symphony in D Minor	First
Gounod	Roméo et Juliette	Act IV: Opening
Rachmaninoff	Prelude, Op. 3	No. 2: First theme
Schumann, R.	Die beiden Grenadiere, Op. 49	No. 1: Begin measure 26
Passing-Tones		
Old Elizabethan Air	The Three Ravens	
Bach	Ach Gott, vom Himmel sieh' darein	Second
Bach	An Wasserflüssen Babylon	Sixth phrase
Bach	Mach's mit mir, Gott	
Bach	O wir Armen Sünder	Fifth phrase
Tschaikowsky	Symphony No. 5 in E Minor, Op. 64	Second: First theme
Wagner	Tristan und Isolde	Act III: Prelude
Suspensions		
Bach	Haut' ist, O Mensch, ein grosser	Third phrase
Bach	Wie schön leuchtet der Morgenstern	Third phrase
Tschaikowsky	Concerto No. 1 in B-Flat Minor, Op. 23	First
Tschaikowsky	Symphony No. 6 in B Minor, Op. 74 (Pathétique)	Fourth
Appoggiatura (unprepared suspension)		
Bach	Jesu, nun sei gepreiset	Last phrase
Chopin	Etude in F Major, Op. 25	
Herbert	A Kiss in the Dark	
Ravel	Miroirs	Oiseaux tristes

Composer	Title	Movement
Neighboring Tone		
Bach	Herr Gott, dich loben alle wir	Fourth phrase
Échappée—Chords		
Bach	Ach Gott, wie manches Herzeleid	Second
Debussy	Preludes, Book II	No. 6: General Lavine—Eccentric, Closing section
Debussy	Reflêts dans l'eau	
Stravinsky	L'Oiseau de Feu	Closing
Anticipations		
Morley	Now is the Month of Maying	Seventh measure
Bach	Werde munter, mein Gemüte	Second phrase
Pedal Point		
Bach	Well-Tempered Clavier, Vol. I	Prelude XXII, Fuga XX: Coda
Bach	Well-Tempered Clavier, Vol. II	Prelude I
Brahms	Symphony No. 1 in C Minor, Op. 68	First: Opening
Sullivan	The Gondoliers	When a Merry Maiden Marries
Tschaikowsky	Symphony No. 6 in B Minor, Op. 74 (Pathétique)	First
Casella	Five Pieces for String Quartet	Preludio Valse Ridicule
Whole Tone (see p. 283 f.)		
Modal Music		
Dvořák	Symphony No. 5 in E Minor, Op. 95 (Aeolian)	Finale
Moussorgsky	Boris Godounov (Phrygian)	Act I: Scene 2: Varlaam's Song
Pierné	Cydalise (Lydian)	Entrance of the Little Fauns: First theme B
Pierné	Cydalise (Hypolydian)	Dance Lesson
Debussy	Hommage à Rameau (Hypoaeolian)	Opening
Debussy	The Children's Corner (Aeolian)	Jimbo's Lullaby
Ravel	Sonatine (Hypoaeolian)	First: Opening
Vaughan Williams	Symphony No. 3, Pastoral (Mixolydian)	Third
Pentatonic		
Old Gaelic Air	Since My Loved One Has Gone	
Debussy	Estampes	Pagodes

UNIT VI—NEW TONAL CONCEPTS

The records for this Unit are examples of a harmonic structure characterized by an absence of a tonal center and increasing dissonance. At first, one may feel frustrated with this music but repeated listening will prove rewarding.

Twelve-tone music is based on counterpoint and requires one to listen to horizontal lines and therefore harkens back to the linear conception of music of the sixteenth century—repetition by means of canonic imitation, augmentation, diminution, inversion, and retrogression. In defining the difference between the type of polyphony employed prior to 1900 and that after 1900, it may be said that, in the first instance, the melodic lines may be said to "fuse," whereas, with the latter, there is no "fusion"; it is "every line for itself"—the melodic lines are separate entities, hence, their dissonant qualities.

In listening to the music of Schoenberg and other composers, the following quotation seems to be very sane advice:

. . . the best thing to do is to throw aside all preconceptions with regard to this twelve-tone music of Schoenberg's and to listen to it exactly as one would listen to any other music, whether by Palestrina, Bach, or Wagner. It is not even a matter of great import if one does not discern the tone-row on the first hearing, any more than it is necessary to be uninterruptedly conscious of the theme of a fugue. However, knowledge of the tone-row of each composition is important to the analyst and also to the performer. (Schoenberg was to learn, with the first performance of his one-act opera *Von Heute auf Morgen* [*From Today Till Tomorrow*] that the singers found it much easier to memorize their parts when they had familiarized themselves with the tone-row.) And in the future it may well be that the musical ear will assimilate the tone-row as readily as it now extracts the scale of C major from a composition in that key. (NewlinBMS 262)

In listening to polytonality, remember that the harmonic texture is again contrapuntal. In this style tonalities are superimposed upon each other. If two keys are superimposed, the music is *bitonal*, if three or more, it is polytonal. However, one key is generally allowed to predominate near the close of the composition and one feels as though he has been moving toward a tonal center.

Pan-diatonicism presents the problem of listening to a contrapuntal texture which combines the simpler diatonic keys. If the listener can fix his attention on one part, he will feel at home in the tonalities employed in traditional harmony. The objective, however, is to hear the parts as a whole, as a harmonic entity, so that the total sound may be fixed in the listener's mind.

In listening to the examples listed, one may observe the following concepts: (1) the movement away from consonance toward extreme dissonance, thus negating traditional harmony and increasing tension; (2) the use of the tone row to destroy a central tonality; (3) the creation of planes or levels of harmony by combining two or more keys; (4) the eclipse of melody by harmony; (5) the return to classical devices and forms; (6) that contemporary music is, generally speaking, non-thematic; and (7) its forms and structures are cumulative and additive and, for the most part, reject repetition.

It may also be interesting for you to know how the contemporary American composer Aaron Copland rates the music of some of the composers you are about to hear. Take heart, dear listener, for, by the looks of his list, Mr. Copland himself may have felt somewhat frustrated at first in listening to "music since 1900." (*The New York Times*, Dec. 25, 1949):

Very easy: Shostakovitch and Khatchaturian, Francis Poulenc, Erik Satie, early Schoenberg and Stravinsky, Vaughan Williams, Virgil Thomson.

Quite approachable: Prokofieff, Roy Harris, Villa-Lobos, Ernest Bloch, William Walton.

Fairly difficult: late Stravinsky, Béla Bartók, Chávez, Milhaud, William Schuman, Honegger, Britten, Hindemith, Walter Piston.

Very tough: middle and late Schoenberg, Alban Berg, Anton Webern, Varèse, Křenek, Charles Ives, Roger Sessions.

Composer	Title	Movement
Fourth Chord		
Milhaud	Saudades do Brazil	IX: Sumare
Schoenberg	Chamber Symphony No. 2	
Schoenberg	Erwartung, Op. 17	
Scott	Lotus Land, Op. 47	
Scriabin	Le Poèm de l'extase, Op. 54	
Scriabin	Masque No. 1, Op. 63	Deux Poèmes
Scriabin	Prelude No. 2, Op. 37	Opening
Scriabin	Prometheus: The Poem of Fire, Op. 60	
Scriabin	Quasi Valse, Op. 47	
Shostakovitch	Symphony No. 5, Op. 47	First: Beginning
Atonal		
Bartók	Allegro Barbaro (12 tone)	
Bartók	Concerto for Violin and Orchestra	Third
Berg	Der Wein (12 tone)	
Berg	Lulu (opera—12 tone)	
Berg	Lyric Suite for String Quartet, Op. 3 (12 tone)	
Berg	Kammer-Konzert (12 tone)	
Casella	Five Pieces for String Quartet	Nocturne
Debussy	Preludes, Book I	No. 12: Minstrels
Dubensky	Atonal Fugue	

Electronic music is but an additional facet of the listener's musical experience. The unfamiliarity of the sound source and the complexity of the form of each composition—which grows out of itself—make listening frustrating in the extreme when one tries to equate it with prior listening habits. Musical meaning results from recognition and expectation that a given sound event will lead to a probable result. In contemporary music, and especially electronic music, this does not necessarily obtain. The young will have less difficulty in identifying with the new since they have fewer preconditioned listening habits.

In listening to electronic music, one may observe the following concepts: (1) the music is *sound-* rather than *theme*-oriented; (2) pitch is manipulated; (3) an absence of rhythmic pulse; (4) there is a control of the duration of sound—stop-watch timed; (5) new timbres through synthesis—mixture; (6) the concept of density—sound is spatial; (7) the control of attack and decay—the envelope; (8) a seeming lack of form; and (9) music which is totally serialized, serial-derived, or aleatoric may seem equally random to the extent that the listener will be unable to hear which principle is operating.

If one is to listen to and understand electronic music, it is essential that he provide himself with a glossary of terms, for its vocabulary is largely that of the electronics engineer and is worlds apart from conventional musical language. (MEJ contains a limited glossary of terms. See Appendices II and III.)

Composer	Title	Movement
Atonal—(*Cont.*)		
Henze	Double Concerto for Oboe, Harp, and Strings	
Hindemith	Ludus Tonalis (12 tone)	
Hindemith	Mathis der Maler (modal, 12 tone)	
Hindemith	Tanzstück, Op. 37, No. 4	
Honegger	Le Roi David	
Honegger	Pacific 231 (12 tone)	
Honegger	Symphonie Liturgique	Dies Irae
Křenek	Twelve Little Piano Pieces (12 tone)	Dancing Toys
Piston	The Incredible Flutist (from diatonic to 12 tone)	
Riegger	Third Symphony (modified 12 tone)	
Ruggles	Man and Mountains	
Ruggles	Sun-Trader	
Schoenberg	Concerto for Piano and Orchestra, Op. 42 (12 tone)	
Schoenberg	Concerto for Violin and Orchestra (12 tone)	

Composer	Title	Movement
Atonal—(*Cont.*)		
Schoenberg	Das Buch der hängenden Garten, Op. 15	
Schoenberg	Drei Klavierstücke, Op. 11	
Schoenberg	Ewartung, Op. 17 (12 tone)	
Schoenberg	Five Orchestral Pieces, Op. 16 (12 tone)	
Schoenberg	Piano Suite, Op. 25	
Schoenberg	Quintet for Flute, Oboe, Clarinet, Bassoon, Horn (12 tone)	
Schoenberg	Sechs kleine Klavierstücke, Op. 19	No. 5
Schoenberg	Serenade, Op. 24 (12 tone)	Fourth
Schoenberg	Variations for Orchestra, Op. 31 (12 tone)	
Schoenberg	Violin Concerto, Op. 36 (12 tone)	
Sessions	String Trio	
Strauss, R.	Electra (also polytonal)	
Thomson	Louisiana Story (12 tone)	Fugue
Varèse	Arcana, Symphonic Poem	
Polytonality		
Mozart	Musikalischer Spass, K. 522 (Musical Joke)	
Barber	Concerto for Violin and Orchestra	
Bartók	Bagatelle	
Casella	Eleven Pieces for Children	Preludio
Casella	Sonatina for Piano	Finale
Debussy	Preludes, Book II	Brouillards
Griffes	Roman Sketches	Clouds
Harris	Concerto for Piano, Clarinet, and String Quartet	Fantasia
Harris	Sonata, Op. 1	First and Second
Honegger	Symphonie Liturgique	De profundis clamavi
Honegger	Pastorale d'Été	Closing measures
Křenek	Piano Pieces, Op. 39, No. 1	
Milhaud	Concerto for Piano and Orchestra	Très vif
Milhaud	Saudades do Brazil	VII: Corcovado VIII: Tijuca IV: Sumare
Milhaud	Second Orchestral Suite	Finale
Milhaud	Sonate for Piano	Second: near middle
Prokofieff	Sarcasmes	
Ravel	Valses Nobles et Sentimentales	
Strauss, R.	Also sprach Zarathustra	The ending

Composer	Title	Movement
Polytonality—(*Cont.*)		
Stravinsky	L'Histoire du Soldat	
Stravinsky	Petrouchka	Chez Petrouchka Dance of the Nurses The Barrel Organ
Stravinsky	Le Sacre du Printemps	Augeries of Spring Sacrificial Dance
Vaughan Williams	Symphony No. 3, Pastoral	First
Pan-Diatonic		
Auric	Les Fâcheaux	
Berkeley	Overture	
Carter	Minotaur	
Casella	Sonata for Cello, Piano	
Harris	Little Suite for Piano	
Malipiero	Concerto for Violin	First
Poulenc	Mouvements Perpétuels	No. 1: Beginning
Rieti	Concerto for Wind Quintet and Orchestra	
Schuman, W.	Symphony No. 4	First
Strauss, R.	An Alpine Symphony, Op. 64	Night
Stravinsky	Petrouchka	Mardi Gras
Stravinsky	Suite for Two Pianos	Var. 4
Wellesz	Short Suite for Seven Instruments	
Comparative Style of Ten Different Composers		
Ballantine	Variations on Mary Had a Little Lamb	
Microtonal		
Eaton	Microtonal Fantasy	
Hába	Fantasy for Violin in ¼-Tones, Op. 9a	
Ives	Three Quartertone Piano Pieces	
Partch	King Oedipus	
Scientism in Music		
Aitken	Neosis	
Arel	Stereo Electronic Music No. 1 (1964)	
Arel	Music for a Sacred Service (1961)	
Arel	Fragment (1960)	
Avni	Vocalise (1964)	
Babbitt	Composition for Synthesizer (1964)	
Babbitt	Ensembles for Synthesizer (1964)	

Composer	Title	Movement
Scientism in Music—(*Cont.*)		
(Bach-Carlos)	Switched-On Bach (Moog Synthesizer 1969)	
Badings	Genese (1958)	
Badings	Evolutions—Ballet Suite (1958)	
Badings	Capriccio for Violin and 2 Sound Tracks	
Berio	Momenti (1960)	
Berio	Omaggio à Joyce (1959)	
Berio	Visage (1961)	
Boucourechliev	Texte I (1958)	
Bress	Fantasy	
Brown	Four Systems (Four Amplified Cymbals)	
Brün	Futility	
Bussotti	Coeur pour batteur—Positively Yes	
Cage	Cartridge Music (1960)	
Cage	Variations II (1960)	
Cage	Variations V (1965)	
Cage	Fontana Mix (for Magnetic Tape alone)	
Cage and Hiller	HPSCHD (Harpsichord)—Mixed Media	
Carlos	Dialogues for Piano and 2 Loud-speakers (1963)	
Carlos	Variations for Flute and Electronic Sound (1964)	
(Collection)	Nonesuch Guide to Electronic Music	
Davidovsky	Electronic Study No. 1	
Davidovsky	Study No. 2	
Dockstader	Drone (1962)	
Dockstader	Electronic Pieces (1960)	
Dockstader	Luna Park (1961)	
Dockstader	Apocalypse (1961)	
Dockstader	Traveling Music (1960)	
Dockstader	Water Music (1963)	
Dockstader	Quartermass (1964)	
Dufrène and Baronnet	Ŭ 47 (1960)	
Eimert	Sélection I (1959)	
El-Dabh	Leiyla and the Poet (1962)	
El-Dabh	Symphonies in Sonic Vibration	
Feldman	King of Denmark	
Ferrari	Visage IV (1959)	
Gaburo	Lemon Drops (1965)	
Gaburo	For Harry (1966)	
Gassman	Electronics: Music to the Ballet (1961)	

Composer	Title	Movement
Scientism in Music—(*Cont.*)		
Grauer	Inferno	
Hambraeus	Constellations and Interferences: Constellations II for Organ Sounds (1959)	
Hambraeus	Interferences for the Organ (1961–2)	
Henry	Investigations: Entité (1959)	
Henry	Variations for a Door and a Sigh	
Hiller and Baker	Computer Cantata (1963)	
Hiller and Isaacson	Illiac Suite for String Quartet (1957)	
Hiller	Machine Music for Piano, Percussion and Tape (1964)	
Ivey	Pinball (1965)	
Kagel	Transition I (1958–60)	
Kagel	Transition II for Piano	
LeCaine	Percussion and 2 Tapes (1958–9)	
Lewin-Richter	Study No. 1 (1963)	
Ligeti	Artikulation (1958)	
Luening	Gargoyles (1962)	
Luening	Concerted Piece for Electronic Sounds and Orchestra	
Luening and Ussachevsky	Tape Music—An Historic Concert	
Maderna	Continuo (1958)	
Marks and Lebzelter	Rock and Other Four Letter Words	
Maxfield	Night Music (1960)	
Mimaroglu	Agony (Visual Study 4 after Arshile Gorky) (1965)	
Mimaroglu	Piano Music for Performer and Composer	
Mimaroglu	Tombeau d'Edgar Poe (1964)	
Mimaroglu	Intermezzo (1964)	
Mimaroglu	Six Preludes for Magnetic Tape	
Mimaroglu	Bowery Bum (1964)	
Oliveros	I of IV (1966)	
Pfeiffer	Electronomusic—9 Images (1965)	
Pousseur	Scambi (or Exchanges) (1958)	
Pousseur	Trois Visages de Liège (1961)	
Powell	Events, M. (1963)	
Powell	Improvisation (1963)	
Powell	Second Electronic Setting (1962)	
Powell	Two Prayer Settings	
Raaijmakers	Contrasts (1959)	
Reich	Come Out (1966)	

Composer	Title	Movement
Scientism in Music—(*Cont.*)		
Reichert and Dockstader	Omniphony I	
Robb	Collage (1964)	
Rudin	Tragoedia	
Sala	Five Impressions on Tape	
Stockhausen	Mikrophonie I for Tamtam, 2 Microphones, 2 Filters and Potentiometers (1964)	
Stockhausen	Microphonie II, for Choir, Hammond Organ and Ring Modulators (1965)	
Stockhausen	No. 9 Zyklus for One Percussionist	
Stockhausen	Gesang der Jünglinge (1955–6)	
Stockhausen	Kontakte (1959–60)	
Subotnick	Silver Apples of the Moon	
Subotnick	Wild Bull	
Ussachevsky	Composition	
Ussachevsky	Creation—Prologue (1962)	
Ussachevsky	Of Wood and Brass	
Ussachevsky	Wireless Fantasy	
Ussachevsky	Sonic Contours	
Ussachevsky	Underwater Waltz	
Ussachevsky	Metamorphosis (1957)	
Ussachevsky	Linear Contrasts (1958)	
Ussachevsky	Improvisation No. 4711 (1958)	
Ussachevsky	Piece for Tape Recorder (1955)	
Varèse	Poème électronique (1958)	
Varèse	Déserts (1954)	
Varèse	Ionisation (1931)	
Whittenberg	Electronic Study II with Contrabass (1962)	
Xenakis	Atrées (1958–62)	
Xenakis	Métastaseis (1953–4)	
Xenakis	Pithoprakta (1955–6)	
Xenakis	Eonta (1963–4)	
Xenakis	Diamorphosis (1957)—Electronic Tape	
Xenakis	Concert PH (1958)—Electronic Tape	
Xenakis	Analogiques A and B (1959)—Electronic Tape	
Xenakis	Orient-Occident (1960)—Electronic Tape	
Xenakis	Bohor (1962)—Electronic Tape	

UNIT VII—THE ACOUSTICAL ASPECTS OF MUSIC: TONE COLOR

One of the many pleasures in listening to music is in the identification of the many tone colors which are used singly and in combination. The old saying that "practice makes perfect" is only too true when applied to learning the tone colors of the various voices and instruments.

Obviously, the best way to learn the various tone colors is (1) to listen to each voice or each instrument individually—the records which follow have been chosen primarily with this in mind; (2 when you are sure you can identify the tone colors separately, then try hearing a specific tone color in combination with several other tone colors, (3) listen to an entire piece of music, identifying the tone colors as they come into prominence; and (4) associate the specific instrument with the music which it plays—this not only helps with recognition of the tone color, but will indicate the kind of music for which the instrument or voice is best suited. Whole compositions have become renowned just because a composer has used a specific tone color in a certain passage.

Since the following list is rather formidable, much time and effort can be saved by concentrating on those tone colors which may be vague or unfamiliar to the listener.

In the case of the vocal tone colors listed, it is left to the instructor or listener to choose specific titles to illustrate them.

Coloratura Soprano

Anna Maria Alberghetti
Eva De Luca
Patrice Munsel
Beverly Sills
Roberta Peters
Lily Pons

Lyric Soprano

Licia Albanese
Ellabelle Davis
Dorothy Kirsten
Dorothy Maynor
Eleanor Steber
Frances Yeend

Dramatic Soprano

Kirsten Flagstad
Margaret Harshaw
Zinka Milanov
Regina Resnik
Helen Traubel
Astrid Varnay

Mezzo Soprano

Herta Glaz
Mildred Miller
Gladys Swarthout
Risë Stevens
Blanche Thebom
Jennie Tourel

Contralto

Marian Anderson
Jean Madeira
Elena Nikolaidi
Claramae Turner

Lyric Tenor

Kurt Baum
Jussi Bjoerling
Richard Crooks
Charles Kullman
Mario Lanza
James Melton
Jan Peerce
Richard Tucker

Dramatic Tenor

Lauritz Melchior
Set Svanholm
Ramon Vinay

Baritone

Walter Cassel
Donald Dickson
Mack Harrell
Robert Merrill
Martial Singher
Lawrence Tibbett
William Warfield
Leonard Warren

Bass Baritone

Jerome Hines
Hans Hotter
George London
Ezio Pinza
Cesare Siepi

Basso Buffo

Salvatore Baccoloni

Composer	Title	Movement
For comparative tone color of all instruments:		
Britten	Young Persons' Guide to the Orchestra	
	Symphony Orchestra Series, 4 vols. (Decca)	
Piccolo		
Berlioz	Damnation of Faust, Op. 24	Minuet
Pierné	Cydalise, Ballet	Entry of the Little Fauns
Rimsky-Korsakov	Scheherazade, Op. 35	Second
Sousa	Stars and Stripes Forever	
Tschaikowsky	Nutcracker Suite, Op. 71a	Chinese Dance
Tschaikowsky	Symphony No. 4 in F Minor, Op. 36	Scherzo
Copland	Appalachian Spring, Ballet	
Schoenberg	Pierrot Lunaire, Op. 21	Dandy
Stravinsky	Petrouchka, Ballet	Carnival
Flute		
Bach	Sonatas for Flute, Harpsichord	
Bach	Suite No. 2 in B Minor	
Bach	Suite No. 4 in D Major	
Handel	Water Music	
Haydn	Sonata in G for Flute, Piano	
Mozart	Concerto No. 1 in G Major, K. 313	

Composer	Title	Movement
Flute—(*Cont.*)		
Beethoven	Octet in E-Flat Major, Op. 103	
Barber	Capricorn Concerto for Flute, Oboe, Trumpet	
Debussy	Sonata No. 2 for Flute, Viola, Harp	
Gould	Spirituals for Orchestra	
Griffes	Poem for Flute and Orchestra	
Hindemith	Sonata for Flute, Piano	
Milhaud	Sonata for Flute, Oboe, Clarinet, Piano (1918)	
Piston	The Incredible Flutist	
Ravel	Schéhérazade	La Flûte Enchantée
Henze	Double Concerto for Oboe, Harp, and Strings	
Oboe		
Bach	Brandenburg Concerto No. 1 in F Major	Adagio
Handel	Sonatas for Flute, Oboe, Continuo	
Cimarosa	Concerto for Oboe, Strings	
Haydn	Concerto in C for Oboe	
Mozart	Concerto in C for Oboe, Strings, K. 314	
Rimsky-Korsakov	Scheherazade, Op. 35	Second
Strauss, R.	Concerto for Oboe	
Loeffler	Two Rhapsodies for Oboe, Viola, Piano	
Milhaud	Pastorale for Oboe, Clarinet, Bassoon	
Piston	Suite for Oboe, Piano	
English Horn		
Berlioz	Fantastic Symphony, Op. 14	Third
Donizetti	Concertino in G for English Horn	
Dvořák	Symphony No. 5, The New World	Second
Franck	Symphony in D Minor	Second
Ippolitoff-Ivanoff	Caucasian Sketches	In the Village
Rimsky-Korsakov	Spanish Caprice	Second
Rossini	William Tell	Pastorale
Wagner	Tristan und Isolde	Act III: Shepherd's tune
Copland	The Quiet City	
Honegger	Concerto da Camera for Flute, English Horn	
Vaughan Williams	London Symphony	Second

Composer	Title	Movement
E-Flat Clarinet		
Strauss, R.	Ein Heldenleben, Op. 40	
Strauss, R.	Till Eulenspiegel	Scaffold Scene
Ravel	Daphnis and Chloe, Suite No. 2	
Stravinsky	Le Sacre du Printemps	
Clarinet		
Mozart	Concerto for Clarinet, K. 622	
Spohr	Clarinet Concerto	
Brahms	Quintet for Clarinet in B Minor, Op. 115	
Glinka	Trio Pathétique for Clarinet, Piano, Bassoon	
Weber	Concerto for Clarinet in F Minor, Op. 73	
Bartók	Contrasts for Violin, Clarinet, Piano	
Copland	Concerto for Clarinet, String Orchestra	
Gershwin	Rhapsody in Blue	
Hindemith	Sonata for Clarinet, Piano (1939)	
Ives	Largo for Violin, Piano, Clarinet	
Sowerby	Sonata for Clarinet, Piano	
Bass Clarinet		
Tschaikowsky	Nutcracker Suite, Op. 71a	Dance of the Sugar Plum Fairy
Wagner	Götterdämmerung	Rhine Journey
Wagner	Lohengrin	Act II: This Woman is Wondrous
Wagner	Tristan und Isolde	Act II: King Mark Scene
Wagner	Tristan und Isolde	Act III: Scene 3: Commencement of Liebestod
Wagner	Die Walküre	Wotan's Anger
Schoenberg	Serenade for Septet, Baritone Voice, Op. 24	
Stravinsky	Petrouchka, Ballet	Death of Petrouchka
E-Flat Saxophone		
Bizet	L'Arlesienne Suite No. 1	Prelude
Glazounov	Concerto for Saxophone (1936)	
Carpenter	Skyscrapers	
Creston	Sonata for Saxophone, Piano, Op. 19	

Composer	Title	Movement
E-Flat Saxophone—(*Cont.*)		
Debussy	Rhapsody for Saxophone, Orchestra	
Ibert	Concertino da Camera for Saxophone	
Janssen	New Year's Eve in New York	
Webern	Quartet for Saxophone	
Bassoon		
Vivaldi	Concerto in B-Flat Major for Bassoon	
Mozart	Concerto in B-Flat Major for Bassoon, K. 191	
Dukas	L'Apprenti Sorcier	
Grieg	Peer Gynt Suite No. 1	In the Hall of the Mountain King
Strauss, R.	Duet Concertino (Clarinet, Bassoon)	
Hindemith	Sonata for Bassoon	
Ravel	Mother Goose Suite (double bassoon)	Beauty and the Beast
Stravinsky	L'Oiseau de Feu	Lullaby
Stravinsky	Le Sacre du Printemps	Beginning
Taylor	Through the Looking Glass	Jabberwocky
Horn in F		
Haydn	Concerto No. 1 in D Major for Horn	
Haydn	Concerto No. 2 in D Major for Horn	
Mozart	Concerto in E-Flat for Horn, Orchestra	
Brahms	Trio in E-Flat for Piano, Violin, Horn, Op. 40	
Mendelssohn	Midsummer Night's Dream, Op. 61	Nocturne
Rimsky-Korsakov	Scheherazade, Op. 35	Second
Strauss, R.	Concerto in E-Flat Major for Horn, Op. 11	
Wagner	Götterdämmerung	Rhine Journey
Wagner	Die Meistersinger	Act III: Prelude
Wagner	Das Rheingold	Valhalla: Final Scene
Chávez	Concerto for 4 Horns, Orchestra	
Debussy	Iberia	Second
Stravinsky	L'Oiseau de Feu	Last
Trumpet		
Bach	Brandenburg Concerto No. 2	Allegro

Composer	Title	Movement
Trumpet—(*Cont.*)		
Handel	Royal Fireworks Music	
Haydn	Concerto in E-Flat Major for Trumpet	
Sibelius	En Saga, Op. 9	
Strauss, R.	Ein Heldenleben	
Verdi	Aïda	Triumphal March
Copland	The Quiet City	
Debussy	Nocturnes	Fêtes
Honegger	Symphony No. 2 for Strings, Trumpets	
Jolivet	Concerto for Trumpet, Piano, Strings	
Bernstein	The Age of Anxiety	Part II: The Epilogue
Trombone		
Haydn	Divertimenti Nos. 82, 6	
Beethoven	Symphony No. 5 in C Minor, Op. 67	Fourth
Chabrier	España	
Rimsky-Korsakov	Russian Easter Overture	
Tschaikowsky	Symphony No. 6 in B Minor, Op. 74 (Pathétique)	Fourth
Wagner	Das Rheingold	Scene II
Wagner	Tannhäuser	Overture
Harris	Symphony No. 3	
Hindemith	Sonata for Trombone	
Poulenc	Trio for Trumpet, Trombone, Horn	
Stravinsky	Octet for Wind Instruments	
Tuba		
Berlioz	Fantastic Symphony, Op. 14	Last
Sibelius	Finlandia	
Wagner	Götterdämmerung	Funeral Music
Wagner	Siegfried	Prelude
Stravinsky	Petrouchka	Peasant and Bear
Percussion:		
Timpani		
Handel	Royal Fireworks Music	
Beethoven	Symphony No. 9 in D Minor, Op. 125	Second
Lalo	Symphonie Espagnole	
Strauss, R.	Burleska	
Bartók	Sonata for Two Pianos, Percussion	
Loeffler	A Pagan Poem, Op. 14	
Gould	Latin-American Symphonette	

Composer	Title	Movement
Percussion—(*Cont.*)		
Martin	Concerto for Winds, Percussion, Strings	
Scriabin	Poem of Fire, Op. 60	
Thomson	Five Portraits	Percussion Piece
Glockenspiel		
Tschaikowsky	Nutcracker Suite, Op. 71a	Chinese Dance
Wagner	Die Meistersinger	Dance of Apprentices
Weinberger	Schwanda	Polka and Fugue
Bernstein	The Age of Anxiety	Part II: The Masque
Ravel	Daphnis et Chloé, Suite No. 2	
Xylophone		
Bernstein	The Age of Anxiety	Part II: The Masque
Surinach	Ritmo Jondo	
Taylor	Through the Looking Glass	
Thomson	Five Portraits	Percussion Piece
Chimes–Bells		
Sibelius	Symphony No. 4 in A Minor, Op. 63	Fourth
Tschaikowsky	1812 Overture, Op. 49	
Mahler	Symphony No. 2 in C Minor	
Cowell	Symphony No. 4	
Vibraphone		
Gould	Latin-American Symphonette	
Gould	Spirituals for Orchestra	
Celesta		
Tschaikowsky	Nutcracker Suite, Op. 71a	Dance of the Sugar Plum Fairy
Bartók	Music for String Instruments, Percussion, Celesta	
Drums, Cymbals, etc.		
Tschaikowsky	1812 Overture, Op. 49	
Strauss, R.	Till Eulenspiegel, Op. 28 (snare drum)	
Strauss, R.	Don Quixote (wind machine)	
Wagner	Lohengrin (cymbals)	Act III: Prelude
Bartók	Concerto for Orchestra (snare drum)	
Copland	Rodeo (bass drum)	
Gershwin	Rhapsody in Blue (cymbals)	
Organ		
Bach	Fantasia and Fugue in G Minor	
Handel	Concerti for Organ, Op. 4	
Franck	Fantasia in C	
Guilmant	Sonata No. 1 in D Minor	
Weinberger	Schwanda, the Bagpiper	Polka and Fugue

COMPOSER	TITLE	MOVEMENT
Organ—(*Cont.*)		
Widor	Symphony No. 6 in G Minor for Organ, Op. 42	
Hindemith	Sonata for Organ	
Holst	The Planets	
Poulenc	Concerto in G Minor for Organ, Strings, Timpani	
Sowerby	Symphony in G Major for Organ	
Thomson	Variations on Sunday School Tunes	
Piano		
Bach	Concerto No. 2 in C Major for Three Pianos	
Beethoven	Concerto No. 5 in E-Flat Major, Op. 73	
Grieg	Concerto in A Minor for Piano, Op. 16	
Tschaikowsky	Concerto No. 1 in B-Flat Minor, Op. 23	
Bartók	Music for Strings, Percussion, Celesta	
Bernstein	Age of Anxiety	
Bernstein	Seven Anniversaries	
De Falla	El Amor Brujo	
Gershwin	An American in Paris	
Gould	Latin-American Symphonette	
Ives	Piano Sonata No. 2 (Concord)	
MacDowell	Concerto No. 2 in D Minor, Op. 23	
Riegger	New Dance	
Sessions	Sonata No. 2 for Piano	
Varèse	Ionization	
Harp		
Glière	Concerto for Harp, Orchestra	
Rimsky-Korsakov	Scheherazade	
Saint-Saëns	Concert Piece for Harp, Orchestra, Op. 154	
Strauss, R.	Don Juan, Op. 20	
Strauss, R.	Ein Heldenleben, Op. 40	
Barber	The School for Scandal	Overture
Bax	Quintet for Harp, Strings (1919)	
Hanson	Symphony No. 1 (Nordic)	
Hanson	Symphony No. 2 (Romantic)	
Henze	Double Concerto for Oboe, Harp, and Strings	
Holst	The Planets	
Ravel	Introduction and Allegro for Harp, Strings	

Composer	Title	Movement
Harp—(*Cont.*)		
Ravel	Ma Mère l'Oye	
Salzedo	Eight Dances for Harp	
Violin		
Bach	Concerto in D Minor for Two Violins	
Handel	Sonata No. 4 in D Major for Violin, Piano	
Mozart	Concerto No. 4 in D Major for Violin, K. 218	
Beethoven	Sonata No. 9 in A Major, Op. 47 (Kreutzer)	
Brahms	Concerto in D Major for Violin, Op. 77	
Chausson	Poème for Violin, Orchestra, Op. 25	
Mendelssohn	Concerto in E Minor for Violin, Op. 64	
Bartók	Divertimento for Strings	
Berg	Concerto for Violin, Piano, 13 Wind Instruments	
Ives	Sonata No. 2 for Violin, Piano	
Piston	Sonata for Violin, Piano	
Viola		
Bach	Suite No. 2 for Viola Unaccompanied	
Handel	Concerti for Viola, Orchestra	
Mozart	Duo in G for Violin, Viola, K. 423	
Stamitz	Concerto for Viola in D Major	
Brahms	Songs for Alto, Viola, Piano, Op. 91	
Bartók	Concerto for Viola and Orchestra	
Bloch	Five Pieces for Viola, Piano	
Debussy	Sonata No. 2 for Flute, Viola, Piano	
Kohs	Chamber Concerto for Viola, String Nonet	
Martinu	Three Madrigals for Violin, Viola	
Cello		
Couperin	Pièces en Concerto for 'Cello, Orchestra	
Mozart	Quartet in C Major, K. 465 (Dissonant)	
Beethoven	Concerto in C for Violin, 'Cello, Piano, Op. 56	

Composer	Title	Movement
Cello—(*Cont.*)		
Brahms	Concerto in A Minor for Violin, 'Cello, Op. 102	
Lalo	Concerto for 'Cello, Orchestra	
Fauré	Elegie for 'Cello, Orchestra, Op. 24	
Kabalevsky	Concerto for 'Cello	
Khachaturian	Concerto for 'Cello, Orchestra	
Phillips	Sonata for 'Cello, Piano	
Double Bass		
Berlioz	Fantastic Symphony, Op. 14	Fifth
Bottesini	Grand Duo Concertante for Violin, Double Bass	
Dragonetti	Concerto for Double Bass	
Saint-Saëns	Carnival of Animals	L'Elephant
Berg	Concerto for Violin, Orchestra	First
Copland	Rodeo	First
Milhaud	Quintet No. 2	
Poulenc	Concerto for Two Pianos, Orchestra	
Thomson	Louisiana Story	
Villa-Lobos	Chôros No. 10	

PART III–SYNTHESIS OF MUSICAL ELEMENTS

UNIT VIII–JUXTAPOSITION OF MUSICAL ELEMENTS

In listening to the records listed here, the listener's problem becomes more complex. Not only must he decide whether the music is (1) basically rhythmic, melodic, or harmonic, (2) horizontal—contrapuntal—polyphonic, or vertical—block style—homophonic; (3) polyharmonic, or polyrhythmic; or (4) a combination of any of the preceding; but, in addition, he must determine in what manner these elements have been juxtaposed, and observe the juxtaposition of color.

If desired, additional material can be obtained by referring to any of the record lists in Appendix V. In fact, the more a given composition can be used for illustration, the greater the cumulative effect and value of that piece of music.

The following records illustrate one or more phases of juxtaposition. Test, now, the musical resources which you have gained through the musical experiences you have had with the music and study material of this and the other Units.

Composer	Title	Movement
Bach	Well-Tempered Clavier, Books I, II	Preludes, Fugues
Beethoven	Symphony No. 3 in E-Flat, Op. 55	First
Beethoven	Symphony No. 7 in A Major, Op. 92	Second
Brahms	Symphony No. 1 in C Minor, Op. 68 (juxtaposed themes)	Fourth
Chopin	Etudes, Op. 10, No. 8 in F Major (juxtaposed themes)	
Franck	Symphony in D Minor	Second
Moussorgsky	The Nursery (song cycle)	No. 6: The Hobby Horse
Rachmaninoff	Prelude in C♯ Minor, Op. 3, No. 2	
Rimsky-Korsakov	Scheherazade, Op. 35	First
Saint-Saëns	Danse Macabre, Op. 40	
Saint-Saëns	Phaeton, Op. 39	
Strauss, J.	Tales from the Vienna Woods	
Strauss, R.	Death and Transfiguration, Op. 24	Exposition
Tschaikowsky	Eugene Onégin, Op. 24	Act II: No. 13: Waltz
Tschaikowsky	Symphony No. 5 in E Minor, Op. 64	Second
Copland	El Salón México	
Debussy	Preludes, Book I	Danseuse de Delphes
Griffes	Roman Sketches	Clouds
Harris	Sonata for Violin, Piano	First
Schoenberg	Sechs kleine Klavierstücke, Op. 16	
Scriabin	Prelude, Op. 31, No. 4	

UNIT IX—THE ARCHITECTURAL ASPECTS OF MUSIC: FORM

The following examples are intended to show the use of the motive as a device in musical construction. First, listen to the whole composition. Replay, this time observing its organic growth through the manipulation of the motive by means of repetition, sequence, augmentation, diminution, and/or its embellishment. To hear these details, repeated listening is required. Perhaps it will be necessary to replay and compare small sections with each other though the whole method is again recommended.

In the short pieces listed next, the motive can be heard simply, briefly, and clearly, uncluttered by irrelevant matters. A brief additional list of recordings is appended if the listener wishes to try his hand with the motive in a somewhat more complex setting. Humming or singing the motive as it is introduced will help the listener to follow its repetitions.

Composer	Title	Movement
Beethoven	Bagatelles, Op. 33	Nos. 1, 2, 3, 6, 7
Chopin	Preludes, Op. 28	Nos. 1, 5, 7, 9, 12, 15, 20
Mendelssohn	Songs without Words	
	Op. 19, No. 6 in G Minor	No. 6: Venetian Boat Song No. 1
	Op. 53, No. 23 in A Major	No. 5: Folk Song
	Op. 62, No. 25 in G Major	No. 1: May Breezes
	Op. 67, No. 34 in C Major	No. 4: Spinning Song
	Op. 102, No. 45 in C Major	No. 3: Tarantella
	Op. 102, No. 47 in A Major	No. 5: The Joyous Peasant
Schumann	Album for the Young, Op. 68	Nos. 6, 8, 17, 29, 34
Schumann	Scenes from Childhood, Op. 15	Nos. 1, 2, 6, 12
Songs		
Sequence		
Böhm	Calm as the Night, Op. 26, No. 27	
Calkin	I Heard the Bells on Christmas Day	
Crouch	Kathleen Mavourneen	
Schubert	Schwanengesang (14 lieder)	No. 4: Ständchen (Serenade)
Spirituals	Steal Away	
	My Lord, What a Mourning	
Supplementary List		
Motive		
Haydn	Symphony No. 94 in G Major	First
Mozart	Symphony No. 40 in G Minor, K. 550	First
Beethoven	Quartet in F Major, Op. 135	Fourth—Intro.
Beethoven	Symphony No. 5 in C Minor, Op. 67	First
Brahms	Symphony No. 4 in E Minor, Op. 98	First
Dukas	L'Apprenti Sorcier	
Franck	Symphony in D Minor	Third theme
Liszt	Les Préludes, Symphonic Poem No. 3	
Rimsky-Korsakov	Scheherazade, Op. 35	Second
Sibelius	Symphony No. 2 in D Major, Op. 43	First
Tschaikowsky	Symphony No. 6 in B Minor, Op. 74	First

Simple Part Forms

The recordings listed below are examples of the simple part forms. The list comprises the two-part, three-part, and five-part forms. The plan for study should be that already shown, using the steps which seem pertinent in each case.

Play the composition as a whole. Then replay, observing the continued growth of the music by the addition of the principle of variety—contrast. Notice, also, the interplay—organic growth—of unity and variety. Replay as many times as necessary, listening for such details as: the phrase, period, cadences, irregular phrases, double period, phrase groups, and the resultant part forms—two-, three-, and five-part forms. The uninitiated listener will find that it is much more difficult to pick out the details than it is to hear the interplay of unity and variety. Repeated listening and forbearance will prove rewarding.

Composer	Title	Movement
Two-Part Form		
Haydn	Quartet Op. 3, No. 5 in F Major	Serenade
Mozart	Don Giovanni, K. 527	Minuet
Brahms	Waltz, Op. 39, No. 3	
Brahms	Waltz, Op. 39, No. 9	
Chopin	Prelude, Op. 28, No. 22	
Schubert	Ellen's Zweiter Gesang, Op. 52, No. 2	No. 6: Ave Maria
Schubert	Die Forelle (The Trout), Op. 32	
Schubert	Der Tod und das Mädchen (Death and the Maiden), Op. 7, No. 3	
Schubert	Schwanengesang	No. 4: Ständchen (Serenade)
Three-Part Form		
Brahms	Nightingale, Op. 97, No. 1	
Brahms	Waltz in A-Flat Major, Op. 39, No. 15	
Chopin	Mazurka in E-Flat Major, Op. 6, No. 4	
Chopin	Nocturne in E-Flat, Op. 9, No. 2	
Chopin	Waltz in D-Flat Major, Op. 64, No. 15	
Grieg	Le Papillon (The Butterfly), Op. 43, No. 11	
Mendelssohn	Songs without Words	
	Op. 62, No. 25	No. 1: May Breezes
	Op. 62, No. 30	No. 6: Spring Song

COMPOSER	TITLE	MOVEMENT
Three-Part Form—(*Cont.*)		
Rachmaninoff	Prelude in C♯ Minor, Op. 3, No. 2	
Saint-Saëns	The Carnival of Animals	The Swan
Schubert	Moment Musical, Op. 94, No. 5, in F Minor	
Schumann	Romance, Op. 28, No. 2, in F♯ Major	
Debussy	Preludes, Book I	No. 3: The Wind on the Plain
Debussy	Preludes, Book I	No. 8: The Maid with the Flaxen Hair
Gardiner	From the Canebrake, Op. 5, No. 1	
MacDowell	To a Water Lily, Op. 51, No. 6	
MacDowell	To a Wild Rose, Op. 51, No. 1	
Five-Part Form		
Beethoven	Sonata, Op. 13, No. 8, in C Minor	Adagio Cantabile
Chopin	Mazurka, Op. 56, No. 2, No. 33 in B Major	
Chopin	Nocturne, Op. 27, No. 2 in D-Flat Major	
Chopin	Prelude, Op. 28, No. 17, in A-Flat Major	
Gounod	Faust	Act IV: Soldiers' Chorus
Mendelssohn	Songs without Words, Op. 67, No. 4	No. 34: Spinning Song
Tschaikowsky	Nutcracker Suite, Op. 71a	Dance of the Flutes
Debussy	The Children's Corner Suite	Serenade of the Doll
Prokofieff	The Love for Three Oranges, Op. 33	March

Larger Forms

The recordings in the list that follows represent examples of the larger part forms. The listening suggestions given for the motive, and the several part forms should be carried forward now to the larger part forms. Listen for the large divisions of the form first, leaving the details for repeated listening, the whole being greater than its parts.

It will be observed that the Song Form with Trio—a larger A–B–A form—sounds like two distinct pieces. Listen for the first melody at its recurrence after the deviating section—B, the Trio. In a contrasting style and tempo, the Trio is generally in the tonic or subdominant key or contrasting mode. If any transitional material is present, it will occur between the Trio and the return of the principal song. It is an exception if any transitional material appears between the Principal Song and the Trio. If there are two Trios, A is heard after each trio.

In listening to the Rondo forms, it again is well to listen first for the large divisions and the inevitable recurrence of the principal theme which, though shortened or modified, is always in the tonic key. Grasping the themes as a whole will help stabilize your listening, much as a person stabilizes his body while holding on to a strap hanger in a bus thus giving himself a certain sense of security and confidence.

Observe the statement of the theme and the variations of it in listening to the Variation form. Of all of the larger forms, the theme and variation is the most easily perceived, due to the simplicity in the statement of the theme and the likeness of the form of the variation to the theme itself—especially is this true in the classical variation. Variety is solely dependent on rhythmic, melodic, harmonic, or coloristic variation of the theme. The listener will find the small variation form is the easiest to grasp since the variations are uncluttered with nonessentials. Starting with Beethoven, the large variation form is the more complex, due to the fact that there is likely to be a variety of keys, thematic manipulation, and the use of two themes. One is impressed first by the content of these large variation forms, their structure last. Their complexity is best shown by contrasting examples of the small variation with the larger form. The listener will find it very rewarding if first he recognizes these more complex compositions as great works of art, leaving the details for repeated listening. The more complex the works, the greater is the need for a feeling of security, so, the listener will do well to sing or hum the theme as it is first introduced, thus making it easier for him to identify the variations as they are presented.

Unit IV of this Appendix lists examples of polyphonic music. The listener would do well to select some of the choral examples from this list for rehearing before going on to the more complex examples of the Fugue. The listener will find that words will help to particularize the melodic line. Start with two-voiced rounds and canons and follow them with the somewhat more complex choral examples of polyphony, such as the madrigal and the motet. In listening to any polyphonic music, priority must be given to the most important melodic line as it occurs in whatever voice. At first you may be able to hear only the beginning of the melodic line as a motive, but through repeated listening, the entire melody will be grasped as a unit in a more or less unbroken line as it threads its way through the musical fabric. Polyphonic music is not for casual listening. Active attention is required in order to follow two or more simultaneous lines and the interplay of unity and variety.

In the beginning, the listener should content himself with the following in listening to the Sonata-Allegro Form: (1) the point where the Exposition ends and the Recapitulation begins—thus, the deviating middle section is marked off and the broad A–B–A form will be outlined; and (2) recognizing the several themes which should be grasped as a whole. As suggested before, humming or singing the principal theme will help not only to recognize its subsequent appearances, but also to fix the subordinate theme and its return, the theme or themes used in the development section, and finally the recognition of the smaller deviations. Repeated listening will provide the additional details of structure and form, e.g., phrase, period, cadences, etc.

Composer	Title	Movement
Song Form with Trio		
Haydn	Symphony No. 6 in G Major, B.H. No. 94 (Surprise)	Third
Mozart	Sonata No. 11 in A Major, K. 331	Menuetto
Beethoven	Symphony No. 5, Op. 67, in C Minor	Third
Brahms	Hungarian Dance in D-Flat Major, No. 6	
Chopin	Polonaise in A Major, Op. 40, No. 1 (Military)	
Mendelssohn	Midsummer Night's Dream, Op. 61 (two trios)	Wedding March
Molloy	The Kerry Dance	
Sousa	Stars and Stripes Forever	
Debussy	The Children's Corner Suite	Golliwog's Cake Walk
Dett	In the Bottoms Suite	Juba Dance
First Rondo		
Mozart	Sonata No. 9, K. 284	Rondeau en Polonaise
Mozart	Sonata No. 11 in A Major, K. 331	Turkish March
Beethoven	Sonata, Op. 2, No. 1	Adagio
Beethoven	Sonata, Op. 2, No. 2	Largo
Beethoven	Sonata, Op. 2, No. 3	Adagio
Beethoven	Sonata No. 3 in E-Flat Major, Op. 92	Second
Chopin	Nocturne, Op. 55, No. 1	
Chopin	Nocturne, Op. 55, No. 2	
Chopin	Nocturne, Op. 62, No. 1	
Chopin	Nocturne, Op. 62, No. 2	
Mendelssohn	Midsummer Night's Dream, Op. 61, No. 7	Nocturne
Schumann, R.	Symphony No. 1, Op. 38, in B-Flat Major	Larghetto

Composer	Title	Movement
Second Rondo		
Haydn	Trio No. 5 in E-Flat	Gypsy Rondo
Mozart	Eine kleine Nachtmusik, K. 525	Second
Mozart	Rondo in A Minor, K. 511	
Beethoven	Sonata, Op. 49, No. 2	
Beethoven	Symphony No. 3 in E-Flat, Op. 55	Marche Funèbre
Franck	Symphony in D Minor	Second
Schubert	Sonata, Op. 53	Rondo
Third Rondo		
Mozart	Eine kleine Nachtmusik, K. 525	Fourth
Beethoven	Sonata, Op. 2, No. 2, in A Major	Fourth
Beethoven	Sonata No. 3 in E-Flat, Op. 12	Third
Beethoven	Sonata No. 8 in C Minor, Op. 13 (Pathétique)	
Beethoven	Symphony No. 4 in B-Flat, Op. 60	Adagio
Beethoven	Symphony No. 6 in F Major, Op. 88	Finale
Brahms	Sonata No. 2 in A Major, Op. 100	Finale
Mendelssohn	Midsummer Night's Dream, Op. 61 (Rondo-Sonata Form)	Scherzo
Variation		
Bach	Goldberg Variations	
Handel	Suite No. 5 in E Major	Fourth: "Harmonious Blacksmith"
Haydn	Symphony No. 6 in G Major, B.H. No. 94	Second
Beethoven	Sonata, Op. 47 (Kreutzer)	Second
Beethoven	Symphony No. 3 in E-Flat, Op. 55	Fourth
Beethoven	Symphony No. 5 in C Minor, Op. 67	Second
Franck	Variations Symphoniques	
Mendelssohn	Variations Sérieuses	
Schubert	Quartet No. 14 in D Minor	
Dohnányi	Variations on a Nursery Theme	
Elgar	Enigma Variations, Op. 36	
Kodály	"Peacock" Variations	
Ravel	Bolero	
Thomson	Variations on Sunday School Tunes	

Composer	Title	Movement
Fugue or Fugal Treatment		
Bach	"Little" Fugue in G Minor (organ)	
Bach	Fantasy and Fugue "Great" in G Minor (organ) No. 12	Fugue
Bach	Passacaglia and Fugue in C Minor (organ) (Triple Fugue)	Fugue
Bach	Toccata and Fugue in D Minor (organ)	Fugue
Bach	Well-Tempered Clavier	Book I: Fugues 1, 11 Book II: Fugue 1
Handel	The Messiah	No. 4: And the Glory No. 7: And He shall purify No. 25: And with His stripes
Haydn	The Creation	No. 28: Achieved is the Glorious Work
Mozart	Adagio and Fugue in C Minor, K. 546	Fugue
Mozart	Requiem	No. 2: Kyrie Eleison No. 9: Domine, Jesu Christe
Mozart	Symphony No. 41 in C Major, K. 551	Finale
Beethoven	Quartet No. 8 in C Major, (Rasoumovsky No. 3)	Finale
Berlioz	Fantastic Symphony, Op. 14	Fifth: Fugue
Smetana	The Bartered Bride	Overture
Wagner	Die Meistersinger	Act I: Church Scene Act III: Prelude
Weinberger	Schwanda	Fugue
Bloch	Concerto Grosso for Piano and String Orchestra	Finale
Bloch	String Quartet No. 2	Fourth: Fuga
Stravinsky	Octet for Wind Instruments	
Taylor	Through the Looking Glass	
Sonata-Allegro		
Haydn	String Quartet in C Major, Op. 76, No. 3	First
Haydn	Symphony No. 6 in G Major, B.H. 94	First, Fourth
Mozart	Symphony No. 41 in C Major, K. 551	First

COMPOSER	TITLE	MOVEMENT
Sonata-Allegro—(*Cont.*)		
Beethoven	Sonata No. 9 in A Major, Op. 47 (Kreutzer)	First
Beethoven	Sonata No. 10 in G Major, Op. 14	First
Beethoven	Symphony No. 5 in C Minor, Op. 67	First, Fourth
Franck	Symphony in D Minor	First
Grieg	Sonata No. 2 in G Major, Op. 13	First
Mendelssohn	Midsummer Night's Dream, Op. 21	Overture
Mendelssohn	Quartet No. 14 in D Minor	First
Schubert	Symphony No. 8 in B Minor (Unfinished)	First
Schumann, R.	Symphony No. 1 in B-Flat Major, Op. 38	First
Wagner	Eine Faust Overture	
Barber	The School for Scandal (Overture)	
Bartók	Divertimento for Strings	First

UNIT X—THE FINAL OUTCOME: STYLE

The achievement of a distinctive style is the goal of every artist; the recognition of a specific style is the goal of the listener. What qualities in a piece of music make it sound the way it does? The foregoing Units have supplied (1) a body of facts which were intended to help the listener to answer this ultimate question, and (2) a quantity of music literature from the several periods of music history which were not only illustrative of those facts but were, at the same time, examples of the style in its many ramifications. In learning style recognition through listening, the following steps are suggested: (1) classify each composition as to texture —monophonic, homophonic, or polyphonic; (2) classify each work as to a specific period—Renaissance, Baroque, Classic, etc.; finally, (3) by repeated listening, pin down your style recognition to a specific composer. Every period and consequently every composer employs certain devices and even clichés, e.g., the *leitmotif* of Wagner, or the sequences of Tschaikowsky. Learn to recognize them. They are guideposts of style. Repeated listening is indicated. Refer to the charts on p. 217 ff. frequently. When the styles of the works and the composers in the following list have been assimilated, compare the styles of various countries; the style of an opera compared to another opera by the same composer; the style of two composers; chamber music with symphonic music; instrumental style with vocal style and/or keyboard style, etc.

Composer	Title
Palestrina	Missa Papae Marcelli
Bach	Mass in B Minor
Haydn	Symphony No. 6 in G Major, B.H. 94
Mozart	Symphony No. 40 in G Minor, K. 550
Beethoven	Symphony No. 9 in D Minor, Op. 125
Schubert	Die Winterreise
Wagner	Die Walküre
Franck	Symphony in D Minor
Tschaikowsky	Symphony No. 6 in B Minor, Op. 74
Brahms	Symphony No. 4 in E Minor, Op. 98
Debussy	Pelléas et Mélisande
Debussy	Preludes, Books I, II
Scriabin	Poem of Extasy, Op. 54
Scriabin	Poem of Fire, Op. 60
Schoenberg	Piano Pieces, Op. 11 and 19
Schoenberg	Pierrot Lunaire, Op. 21
Schoenberg	Second String Quartet (with voice)
Stravinsky	Le Sacre du Printemps
Stravinsky	Octet for Wind Instruments
Hindemith	Das Marienleben (song cycle)
Hindemith	Mathis der Maler

Index